Political Genealogy After Foucault

Savage Identities

Michael Clifford

ROUTLEDGE
New York and London

Published in 2001 by
Routledge
29 West 35th Street
New York, NY 10001

Published in Great Britain in 2001 by
Routledge
11 New Fetter Lane
London EC4P 4EE

Copyright © 2001 by Routledge
Routledge is an imprint of the Taylor & Francis Group

Printed in the United States of America on acid-free paper.
Design and typography: Jack Donner

Library of Congress Cataloging-in-Publication Data

Clifford, Michael, 1957–
    Political genealogy after Foucault : savage identities / by Michael Clifford.
        p. cm.
    Includes bibliographical references and index.
    ISBN 0-415-92915-6 – ISBN 0-415-92916-4 (pbk.)
        1. Political sociology. 2. Political science. 3. Liberty. 4. Foucault,
    Michel–Contributions in political science. I. Title.

JA76.C54 2001
306.2–dc21
                                                                00-044632

Advance Praise for *Political Genealogy After Foucault*

"A lucid, stimulating, and persuasive account of the emergence of the modern political subject."

—Rey Chow, Brown University

"In a fresh and imaginative encounter with Foucault, Michael Clifford restages the central concept of 'genealogy' to explore the mythos of American social life. Tracking the ideological forces of rugged individualism in the spirit of Davy Crockett, Ernest Hemingway, Clint Eastwood, Clifford provides us with a rich genealogy of political subjectivity—the Savage Noble. This hybrid figure, both courageous and civil, white and native, will make a fine and fresh contribution to the urgent debates around cultural difference and political identification."

—Homi K. Bhabha, University of Chicago

"Clifford's book is an original work of genealogy that provides a critique of modern political identity as well as an expression of an alternative kind of political identity. It is accessible to people in many disciplines, well grounded in historical scholarship, and exceptionally well conceived. He combines first rate interpretations of Foucault's work with a compelling, constructive account of political identity in the 'new' world. It is a book to enjoy as well to learn from."

—Charles E. Scott, Penn State University

"Clifford's most important contribution may be his bold appropriation of the late Foucault's notion of 'technologies of the self,' whereby we fashion ourselves as ethical subjects. Re-reading J. S. Mill's *On Liberty* as a 'manual for living/subjectivation,' Clifford enables us to experience our own self-fashioning as political selves identifying with Mill's ideals of individualism. Most controversially, Clifford maintains that freedom is an issue of identity rather than power, and that through genealogy we can liberate ourselves from forms of subjection, 'always being able to become other than what we are.' Clifford offers a sophisticated political optimism that is welcome in these deflationary times."

—Patricia Mann, author of *Micro-Politics: Agency in a Postfeminist Era*

For Marissa and Melanie

Contents

Preface

One of the more interesting oddities in the whole history of Western philosophy is the case of the great British utilitarian and social philosopher Jeremy Bentham. When Bentham died in 1832, his body was bequeathed to the University of London. However, that did not mean that his cadaver was used to help advance the study of medicine. Rather, when his flesh had finally decomposed, his skeleton was dressed in his own clothing, except for his skull, which was removed and replaced with a wax head fashioned to look exactly like the original Bentham. This figure—I'm not certain if one may still refer to this figure as Jeremy Bentham—was then seated in one of Bentham's favorite chairs, and placed in a tall, wooden box along with his wide-brimmed yellow hat, meerschaum pipe, and eyeglasses. To this day the box sits in a hallway at the University of London, usually open for students to look in and see Bentham as they pass through the halls on their way to classes.

I have long thought that Bentham—the dead man in his box more so than the live one—would make an appropriate symbol for modern political subjectivity, not so much in its ideological aspects, but rather in the sense that political identity is largely a fabrication, a construct, that as political subjects we are trapped in a corrugated "box" or enclosure of sorts, identified through being rendered visible—identity itself a function of a certain kind of public display.

In a way, then, the dead but unburied Jeremy Bentham is the inspiration behind this book, which conducts a genealogical critique of modern political identity. Relying upon the work of Michel Foucault, I will trace the emergence of the private, autonomous *individual*—of what might be called the "Savage Noble."

The Savage Noble represents a reversal of the immortal terms conventionally identified with Jean-Jacques Rousseau, whose "noble savage" still plays in the background of Western consciousness. Indeed, Rousseau's pre-civilized figure of man animates that dark region known as "wilderness" against which the European imagination would define "civilization" itself. In the tradition of political philosophy to which Rousseau belongs, the noble savage inhabits the political hinterland known as the state of nature. A convention associated with Thomas Hobbes says that modern political identity is born from a social contract whereby the savage leaves the state of nature and becomes the political citizen of civil society. Yet something savage—something base, primitive, natural, pure—persists in this transformation. Rousseau lamented the corruption of the noble savage that necessitated civil laws and a sovereign power. Yet what he couldn't anticipate was that in the "New World" wilderness a form of political identity was taking shape that made the savage the foundation of a new kind of nobility. In the guises of frontier spirit and rugged individualism, icons of this new nobility have been those with the courage to plunge back into the wilderness and to tame it. What these icons represent is the enduring romance of individuality and personal autonomy—both now the measures of "nobility" in the New World. Yet with every step westward through the New World, the Old World of Europe followed to fill in the space opened up by the advance. Europe brought to American shores a form of power— "disciplinary" power—that would seize the body in its every aspect and transform it into a form of political subjectivity that quietly makes a mockery of autonomous individuality. This power is silent, quotidian, ubiquitous, and irresistible—moreover, it uses the political identity of the savage noble, of free individuality, as an ideological veil to conceal its machinations.

To appreciate fully the emergence and formation of modern political identity, the work of Michel Foucault offers a rich and potent methodology for cultural critique that has yet to be fully exploited. Here I bring the main movements of Foucault's work together to show that political subjects emerge within an axial interplay of discursive practices, power relations, and the self-appropriation of cultural values. This understanding is applied critically to traditional notions of political subjectivity, focusing especially on the concept of the private, autonomous individual found in traditional political philosophy from Hobbes to Rousseau to Robert Nozick. Ultimately, my purpose is to trace out the origins of this idea; the transformations it has undergone; how it has affected our understanding of rights, freedom, and power; and how, finally, we might eventually move beyond it.

The scope of a project such as this is broad, so below I have sketched out, in no particular order, what I consider to be the main features of this book:

- A genealogical critique of our history as political subjects that helps us to better understand the origins and character of our present political identities, including those identities that animate the "political spectrum," namely, liberals and conservatives. This examination identifies their common genealogical origins, challenges the necessity of their oppositional character, and points toward the possibility of a form of political identity that might avoid this dichotomous and antagonistic structure.
- The development of Political Genealogy as a theoretical model and its contribution to the emergent fields of postnationalism, postcolonialism, multiculturalism, Queer Theory, and certain strands of feminism.
- A new understanding of political freedom that avoids the fractious and philosophically suspect opposition between so-called positive freedom and negative freedom.
- A new interpretation and application of Foucault's thought that brings together twenty-five years of his work to bear on the most intriguing and persistent problems in political philosophy. Much of this interpretation is based upon research conducted at Le Centre Michel Foucault in Paris.

The present work has, I believe, two main contributions of scholarly value. First, in bringing together the three main movements of Foucault's thought on discourse, power relations, and ethics, it develops a methodology for cultural and philosophical critique—which I call political genealogy—that goes beyond the narrow juridical orientation of most conventional political theory. Previous studies of Foucault have been largely interpretative/critical (such as Jon Simons's *Foucault and the Political* or Barry Andrew, Thomas Osborne, and Nikolas Rose's *Foucault and Political Reason*), or have tended to focus on one area over another, preferring to emphasize, say, power or ethics over discourse (see, for example, Thomas L. Dumm's *Michel Foucault and the Politics of Freedom* or David Halperin's *Saint Foucault: Toward a Gay Hagiography*). In fact, there seems to be a working consensus (perhaps fostered by Hubert L. Dreyfus and Paul Rabinow's early study, *Michel Foucault: Beyond Structuralism and Hermeneutics*) that Foucault abandoned, or at least distanced himself from, his early work on discourse. In this study, I recover much of that early work to show it to be an essential feature of Foucault's overall genealogical project, as is his work on power and ethics. Moreover, I do so by emphasizing aspects of Foucault's work that have been largely neglected by previous commentators (especially those who have co-opted Foucault to political theory); namely, his thought on "enunciative modalities" and counter-memory. These ideas serve as the linchpin to what I consider to be

the second main contribution of this study: an understanding of the formation of American political identity, of what I herein call, with proper defer-
ence to Rousseau, the Savage Noble. With regard to the latter, this book is
not so much *about* Foucault as it is a study of our identities as modern
political subjects *through* Foucault. In that sense, Foucault's work serves as
a lens through which we may see who and what we are as political subjects
more clearly. However, much of what I have done here is not explicitly
found in Foucault, though in most instances I use his work as a point of
departure and as a framework for understanding.

Of course, Foucault has much to say about modern political identity,
much of which has not been rendered entirely perspicuous by previous
commentators. Moreover, there is much relating to modern political identity that is latent but undeveloped in Foucault's thought. I attempt to
develop that thought here. But I think that Foucault's ongoing value lies
not only in what he has said explicitly or even in insinuation and latency,
but also in the development of a comprehensive methodology for cultural
critique. The components of this methodology were laid down, but never
properly conjoined, by Foucault in his separate work on discourse, power
relations, and ethics. His work in these areas extends over the entirety of
his professional life and defines his contribution as a philosopher, historian,
social theorist, and cultural critic. Yet, for all of that he was never able to
bring the components of his work together, though he spoke often of doing
so toward the end of his life. Nor have the plethora of commentators who
have arisen after Foucault's death offered an adequate vision into what
such a comprehensive methodology would look like. I try to rectify that in
this work, but this is as much an exercise in application as it is in interpretation.

Aristotle, who more or less invented the field, considered political theory
to be a subbranch of ethics. Yet even an encyclopedic mind such as Aristotle's would perhaps be intimidated by the enormous, variegated field that
political theory has become, a true leviathan in every sense of the word.
There is probably no area of intellectual or scientific inquiry with more disciplinary slippage or more proprietary disagreement over the appropriate
issues, problems, concepts, figures, approaches, and methodologies than
contemporary political theory. Thus, it is with a healthy trepidation that
one advances a study such as this. Because the field is so vast, I have been
forced to narrow my purview to a tradition some three hundred years old,
and to do so by focusing on a few exemplary texts. It does not help matters
that Foucault himself thought that the sort of study that this book represents was necessary because he considered conventional political theory to

be largely a failure.[1] In any event, despite appearances at times to the contrary, while I offer here a critique through Foucault of traditional political philosophy, it is certainly not to be taken as an indictment of that tradition. Rather, I have emphasized a certain kind of strategic approach to political concerns that has yet to be fully exploited. We may never want to completely replace the juridical approach of traditional political philosophy; no doubt as political subjects we will always face the issues of rights, freedom, power, and obligation. Yet a genealogy of political identity can be made to inform that approach, although much of what has been considered important or even canonical may be irrecoverably lost or transformed. So much the worse for political theory, perhaps. So much the better for real political subjects. Perhaps.

Many people contributed to the realization of this project. First, I would like to thank those who read all or part of the manuscript in its various instantiations, and who offered helpful comments toward its revision, including John Compton, Jean Bethke Elshtain, Michael Hodges, John McCumber, Barry Smart, and especially Charles Scott. I am grateful to François Ewald and Le Centre Michel Foucault in Paris for allowing me to have access to the Foucault collections, and to the staff of La Bibliotheque du Saulchoir for their gracious assistance once I was there. I would be remiss if I did not also recognize Frank Mininni, with whom I first read Foucault. A special thanks goes to Melanie Eckford-Prossor for her patience, support, editorial prowess, and critical ear.

Finally, a warm thanks to the custodial staff at the University of London who were kind enough to unlock and open the large cabinet that Jeremy Bentham calls home.

A portion of chapter 4 was originally published as "The Cultivation of Individuality: Foucault Reading Mill," in *A Partir De Michel Foucault*, special issue of *Daimon: Revista de Filosofia* 11 (July–December 1995), 27–38, commemorating the 10th anniversary of Foucault's death. A portion of chapter 5 was originally delivered at the International Conference on Persons, Oxford University, Mansfield College, Oxford, England, September 11–14, 1991, and later published as "Corrugated Subjects: Foucault's Three Axes of Personhood," *Personalist Forum* 8, no. 1 (spring 1992 Supplement), 31–41.

1

Introduction

From Noble Savage to Savage Noble

My native country, thee,
Land of the noble free,
Thy name I love;
I love thy rocks and rills,
Thy woods and templed hills;
My heart with rapture thrills
Like that above.

—Samuel Francis Smith, "America" (1831)

In 1755, Jean-Jacques Rousseau published his *Discourse on the Origin and Foundation of Inequality among Mankind*, whose purpose, in part, was to offer us a "history" of the origins of the modern political subject. It is in this work that Rousseau elaborates on his thoughts on the "Noble Savage," the iconic figure that served as the focal point of the fateful distinction between "wilderness" and "civilization" through which the European imagination defined the new world.[1]

Rousseau sought to retrieve something from the noble savage that had been lost with man's "advancement" into civilized society. Thomas Hobbes had attacked the avarice and hostility that men displayed against their fellows in the state of nature, which compelled them to quit the state of nature and to join together under a civil government. Rousseau adamantly challenged this view. In fact, by asserting the nobility and purity of what he called "original man," Rousseau sought to reverse the mechanistic and pessimistic view of political identity advanced by Hobbes. "But above all things let us beware of concluding with Hobbes, that man, as having no idea of goodness, must be naturally bad," says Rousseau. "This author, to argue from his own principles, should say that the state of nature being that in which the care of our own preservation interferes least with the preservation of others, was consequently the most favorable to peace, and the most suitable to mankind; whereas he advances the very reverse. . . ."[2] Above all, perhaps, Rousseau wished to recover what he referred to as the "natural pity" of the savage, which he assumed had been the basis of man's happiness and virtue prior to man's transmutation into the avaricious, disingenuous, and "degenerate" being he had become in modern society. From "the force of natural pity," contends Rousseau, "flow all the social virtues. . . . In fact, what is generosity, what democracy, what humanity, but pity applied to the weak, to the guilty, or to the human species in general?" It is just this natural pity that is adulterated and repressed by our becoming "sociable."[3] Rousseau sought to reverse not only Hobbes's pessimistic estimation of natural man, but also to reverse the trend toward degeneration in civilized man by recovering something of the nobility of the innocent savage.

Of course, not everyone on the Continent shared Rousseau's admiration of the noble savage. In fact, the image came under attack by many of France's leading *philosophes*, including Voltaire, who likened the life of Rousseau's savage to that of the orangutan. And it didn't help that Europe's preeminent natural historian of the time, George Louis Leclerc, Comte de Buffon, applied his own theory of degeneracy to the real "savages" of the New World, the indigenous peoples whom Rousseau admired and whom he considered vestigial reminders of what European man no doubt had been in a long-forgotten past. Yet contrary to Rousseau's estimation, Buffon declared that "the savage is feeble," not noble in body, mind, or character, a description that gave an appearance of scientific legitimacy to prejudices and stereotypes that had been forming at least since the early 1600s.[4] Compared to European man, asserted Buffon, the New World savage was "less strong in body . . . less sensitive, and yet more timid and cowardly." Buffon even undermined the notion of natural pity Rousseau had assumed to be the very basis of the savage's virtue; he described the New World natives as "cold and languid" and said that they "have no love for their fellow man."

Nevertheless, Rousseau's faith in the noble savage was vindicated to a large extent by Thomas Jefferson. In fact, Jefferson vigorously challenged Buffon's contentions, and offered his own account of the American savage that largely reconfirmed all those noble traits that Rousseau had attributed to him, saying that "in contradiction to [Buffon's] representation, [the New World savage] is brave . . . he meets death with more deliberation and endures tortures with a firmness unknown almost to religious enthusiasm with us; . . . he is affectionate to his children, careful of them, and indulgent in the extreme; . . . his friendships are strong and faithful to the uttermost

extremity; . . . his sensibility is keen, even the warriors weeping most bit-
terly on the loss of their children, though in general they endeavour to
appear superior to human events; . . . his vivacity and activity of mind is
equal to ours in the same situation; hence his eagerness for hunting, and
for games of chance."5

Jefferson's description of the New World natives was later bolstered by
the publication of John Heckewelder's *Account of the History, Manners,
and Customs of the Indian Nations, Who Once Inhabited Pennsylvania
and the Neighboring States* in 1819, long considered to be "one of the
most authoritative early sources on Native Americans."6 Based on intimate
experience, including living fifteen years with the Moravian Christian Indians and as government advisor in negotiations with the Iroquois, Heckewelder painted a picture of Native Americans that would challenge the
prevailing attitudes dramatically, asserting "Those brutes, those savages,
from whom, according to some men, no faith is to be expected, and with
whom no faith is be kept . . . are susceptible of the noblest and finest feelings of genuine friendship."7

However idealized they may have been, however at odds with actual
practice (especially Jefferson's), comments like those from Jefferson and
Heckewelder are to be viewed as more than simple defenses of a mistreated
and misunderstood group of people. Beyond that, they reflect a growing
impatience with the whole European disdain for the New World. Europe
itself was increasingly viewed as feckless and feculent. The American
wilderness, as well as those hearty natives who inhabited it, on the other
hand, were increasingly valorized and romanticized on both sides of the
Atlantic. This shift in perspective was no doubt fueled by positive reports
of encounters with Native Americans by such explorers as Meriwether
Lewis and especially William Clark, who, as secretary of Indian Affairs
under Thomas Jefferson, often spoke on behalf of those whom he called
"civilized savages."

By the 1830s a reversal of perspectives had taken place, confirmed in
part by the popularity of such literature as the "Leatherstocking" tales of
James Fenimore Cooper, in which native Americans played a prominent
and often heroic role.8 Yet it wasn't just that Rousseau's noble savage had
been revitalized. In the New World a form of political identity was taking
shape that incorporated the savage, made it the basis of a new kind of
nobility, one no longer defined by blood, heritage, power, or position, but a
willingness to grapple with nature itself. As Cooper mentions in *The Last
of the Mohicans*, "The hardy colonist, and the trained European who
fought at his side, frequently expended months in struggling against the

rapids of the streams, or in effecting the rugged passes of the mountains, in quest of an opportunity to exhibit their courage in a more martial conflict. *But emulating the patience and self-denial of the practised native warriors,* they learned to overcome every difficulty."[9] In this passage, Cooper is not simply expressing an appreciation for certain qualities that are (stereotypically) attributed to Native Americans. In fact, according to Richard Slotkin, the narratives of Cooper, Henry Wadsworth Longfellow, Herman Melville, and others reflect a dramatic change from the literature of the early Puritans, who characterized the native population as "devils" to be either converted or exterminated. The Puritans assumed a clear cultural divide between the colonists and Indians, but later we see the formation of a cultural figure who begins to take on those very traits that the Puritans so passionately feared and despised.[10] Thus, the "emulation" of the Native American that Cooper describes in *The Last of the Mohicans* intimates an assimilation that is tantamount to a transmutation of Western identity itself, a form of identity characterized in part by a reconceptualization of personal virtue, of what it is to be noble.

Historically, we have recognized this "new" form of nobility in the guises of frontier spirit and rugged individualism. In fact, "the frontier is *productive* of individualism," according to Frederick Jackson Turner. Turner describes a process through which the European colonist is, in effect, "transformed" into an American: "The wilderness masters the colonist. It finds him a European in dress, industries, tools, modes of travel, and thought. It takes him from the railroad car and puts him in the birch canoe. It strips off the garments of civilization and arrays him in the hunting shirt and the moccasin. It puts him in the log cabin of the Cherokee and Iroquois and runs an Indian palisade around him. Before long he has gone on to planting Indian corn and plowing with a sharp stick; he shouts the war cry and takes the scalp in orthodox Indian fashion. In short, at the frontier the environment is at first too strong for the man. He must accept the conditions which it furnishes, or perish, and so he fits himself into the Indian clearings and follows the Indian trails. Little by little he transforms the wilderness, but the outcome is not the old Europe. . . . The fact is, that here is a new product that is American."[11]

The process of transformation that Turner describes occurs through an encounter, or engagement, with the wilderness, the success of which depends on the assimilation of traits and skills that are decidedly "Indian" in character. This encounter gives rise to a "product" that is perhaps best described as a new form of Euro-American nobility. Icons of this new nobility have been those with the courage to take on what Cooper calls "the toils and dangers of the wilderness" and to tame it. Besides Natty Bumppo there is a long line of such icons, which include figures both historical and fictional, and sometimes both in the same figure. We have already mentioned Meriwether Lewis and William Clark, who preceded Bumppo historically but who have survived well after him in the American imagination; we should add Davy Crockett, Daniel Boone, Andrew Jackson, John Chapman (aka Johnny Appleseed), Paul Bunyan, Henry David Thoreau, James Butler Hickok, William Frederick Cody, the American Cowboy generally, Theodore Roosevelt, Ernest Hemingway, John Wayne, Clint Eastwood, Hawkeye, John Rambo, Mountain Jack, and the Lone Ranger.[12] These icons represent the enduring romance of individuality and personal autonomy—both now the measures of "nobility" in the New World. In fact, it wasn't so much the noble savage that came to be revered, to be the central figure of a new American mythos, but rather a "hybrid" of sorts, a new form of identity that married the courage and robustness of the native American savage with the reason, culture, and civility of the white, European male—a form of identity that might be called the Savage Noble.[13]

This book conducts a genealogical critique of modern political identity. Methodologically, I rely on the work of Michel Foucault to trace out the transmutation of Rousseau's Noble Savage into what I have called the Savage Noble. Specifically, I wish to reveal the mechanisms through which this form of political identity has been both constituted and subjugated. It is important to note, however, that for the purposes of my project the term *savage noble* is largely a trope for a form of political subjectivity—namely, autonomous individualism—that informs the texts of traditional political philosophy and animates modern politics. It is this form of political subjectivity, and the specific types of political identity to which it gives rise (and not so much the popular figures of the American mythos) that will be my primary object of concern.

By *individual* I mean the traditional notion of the political subject as "a titular control of personal rights subjected to the laws of nature and society."[14] Individuality is without doubt the principle and privileged register of political subjectivity in modern political philosophy, and of our own self-conception as political subjects.[15] However, this juridical, rights-based notion of the political subject is a relatively recent development. It can be traced back to the seventeenth and eighteenth centuries, and it is only since the nineteenth century that "individualism" has been separated from the problem of absolute monarchy and conceived as a political philosophy on its own terms.[16] Since that time the notion of the individual has become so entrenched in our culture that it is seldom even put into question. Of course, it goes without saying that the individual has received a great deal of attention in traditional political discourse, but it is usually in terms of a juridical project to define the rights, freedoms, power, and obligations of the political subject. In this study, by contrast, I will suspend the "givenness" of the individual, in order to see what happens to the necessity of such juridical projects. I want to show how this individual is not merely a symbolic representation of political subjectivity, but a fabrication by an anonymous technology that turns individuality into an instrument of domination and subjection.

Why undertake such a study? A genealogical critique of our history as political subjects cannot only help us to better understand the origins and character of our present political identities, but in so doing may cause us to reevaluate the way we presently understand the tasks of political philosophy. In particular, genealogical critique forces us to rethink the notions of political freedom and political power, and to examine the source and necessity of our ideological oppositions, which is the source of so much political conflict. This examination roots out the common genealogical origins of our various political positions, challenges the necessity of their oppositional character, and points toward the possibility of forms of political identity that might avoid (or at least alter in a way less polarizing and hence paralyzing) the fractious and agonistic structure peculiar to modern politics—not in the name of some utopian political brotherhood or sisterhood, but through artful experimentations with identity itself.

Outline of a Political Genealogy

Following Foucault, the guiding methodological question of this study is not, "What is the political subject?" but rather, "How are political subjects formed?" The first question is metaphysical; that is, it inquires into the essence of political subjectivity. The second question, on the other hand, is *genealogical*; it inquires into the contingent historical, discursive and non-discursive conditions of the emergence of political subjects. Genealogical critique, in fact, challenges the metaphysics of essence, which posits a substantive, given subject. As Foucault explains, "One has to dispense with the constituent subject, to get rid of the subject itself, that is to say, to arrive at an analysis which can account for the constitution of the subject within a historical framework. And this is what I call genealogy."[17] Genealogical critique is not only "different" from metaphysical inquiries, it puts into play a *difference* (a suppressed event, a marginalized practice, a forgotten desire) that undermines the necessity of certain metaphysical postulates such as those supporting traditional understandings of the human subject. In other words, genealogy "disturbs what was previously considered immobile; it fragments what was thought unified; it shows the heterogeneity of what was imagined consistent with itself."[18] For centuries we have been enamored of the idea of a human subject as a self-identical being animated by spirit, consciousness, or will. This notion of a self-identical subject has been imported into the discourses of traditional political philosophy, which take this subject for granted in its projects to define rights and freedoms or to lay down principles of political justice.

"There is a history of the subject just as there is a history of reason," says Foucault.[19] The effect of much of his genealogical work has been to reveal a subject whose origins, it might be said, are humble, quotidian, "gray." But there is another "history" to account for, the origins of the Western political subject, on which the juridical projects of the liberal tradition are (implicitly or explicitly) based. I am referring to the ostensible political subject of traditional political philosophy and ideology. A genealogical critique can render the historical emergence of modern political subjectivity intelligible by attending to the smallest discursive and nondiscursive gestures. For example, in Machiavelli's *The Prince*, we might note that a simple gesture of capitalization distinguishes the Sovereign from his subjects. In this discourse, all of the attention is focused on the Prince, while political subjects are drawn as rather nebulous figures, a populous mass distributed more or less randomly across the Sovereign's principality. The Prince attends to political subjects as potential nuisances; his patience for them displays itself rather narrowly, alternating between a reluctant benevolence and a fearful wrath. But no particular identity can be attributed to political subjects at this point. They are shadowy, ill-defined figures who carry knives and pay taxes. By some point in the seventeenth century, however, this situation is reversed. The spotlight then begins to shine most brightly on the political subject. Or rather, the Sovereign now becomes an illustrious beacon illuminating political subjects and defining their rights and obligations. Yet because Sovereignty is now recognized as the source of light (drawn from the "eternal lamp of Reason"), the Prince becomes a hazy, indefinite figure, his outline almost obliterated by Reason's luminous intensity. This makes the Prince all the more imposing. At the same time, political subjects come distinctly into view, taking concrete forms before our eyes. In this *enlightenment* of the political subject, we see the emergence of a discursive practice dedicated to sketching political figures down to the finest detail. It becomes important to know political subjects in truth, from their physical makeup to how, and to what extent, they can partake of Reason itself. The political discourse that predominates in this period tells the story of the subject's brutish origins in the state of nature, and of his entrance into civil society. It finds a place for the subject in the political hierarchy of the body politic, taking care to impress upon the subject the privilege of this position and the allegiance he owes to the head of this body by virtue of being a part of it.

By the eighteenth century, however, we see the rise of a political discourse in which the political subject has developed a marked resentment against the authority of the crown. Eventually, this resentment is played out in the theater of revolution, and the political subject captures the freedom of self-determination that was always his rational destiny.[20] The struggles of the revolutionary subject will pave the way for the emergence of the private autonomous individual.

Thus, the conventionally accepted "history" of the modern political subject is the story of heroic exploits, of downtrodden individuals rising against a Sovereign oppressor in the fulfillment of their proper liberty. This romance of revolution, and the concern with autonomy and self-government that attends it, still very much animates contemporary political discourse belonging to the liberal tradition, even in the rigorous analytical projects of John Rawls and Robert Nozick. Genealogy, on the other hand, listens to this story with a certain calculated detachment that permits its reconstitution as historical fiction. Genealogy cuts through this fiction by exposing it as an instrument of subjection to arbitrary political and ideological constraints. The romantic, ideological history of freedom perpetuated by the discourses of traditional political philosophy in fact arrests resistance and permits a governmental integration. This history conceals, through the imposition of an ideological veil, a vast, anonymous technology of political subjects.

"There are two meanings to the word *subject*," says Foucault, "subject to someone else by control and dependence, and tied to his own identity by a conscience or self-knowledge."[21] Both of these meanings are operative in the conceptions of the political subject found in the liberal tradition. But both meanings can be challenged by genealogical critique, not by showing them to be false, but by showing them to be *unnecessary*.[22] Genealogical critique should be distinguished from other philosophical critiques of the liberal tradition. In particular, this is not a Marxist critique.[23] It is not so much the ideology of the liberal tradition that is being challenged, nor does this critique assume an "alienated" subjectivity that can be somehow restored. But this is also not a communitarian critique, which historicizes the political subject of liberal theory but otherwise largely retains the same metaphysical baggage.[24] Rather, genealogical critique confronts the problem of how political subjects are constituted as surface *effects* of an anonymous interplay, how this interplay attaches an identity and an ideology to subjects, how it commits them to certain practices and modes of being that have the most serious consequences in the political world.

Since Foucault's death in 1984, there has been much debate over whether and in what way his disparate analyses of epistemes, technologies of power, and sexuality could be organized into a single coherent philosophy.[25] Foucault would be skeptical of such projects. He would resist the imposition of limits involved in attempting to define "a coherent position" attached to his name. "I don't feel that it is necessary to know exactly what I am," he once said.[26] If there is any value in his work, Foucault would prefer that it be in its use and applications, in its effects and openings, rather than in the artificial and empty solace of a consistent position. Thus, instead of trying to offer the "definitive" reading of the "true" Michel Foucault, my primary interest here is methodological. That is, my intent is to retrieve those aspects of Foucault's thought that would allow one to trace out genealogically the emergence of the modern political subject.[27] This genealogy will have three areas, or "domains" of analysis. As Foucault explains, "Three domains of genealogy are possible. First, an historical ontology of ourselves in relation to truth through which we constitute ourselves as subjects of knowledge; second, an historical ontology of ourselves through which we constitute ourselves as subjects acting on others; third, an historical ontology in relation to ethics through which we constitute ourselves as moral agents."[28] These three domains of genealogy correspond to the three main movements of Foucault's work: the archaeology of discursive practices, the genealogy of power relations, and his last work on the history of sexuality in that he is conducting an "ethics" of self-formation. All three of these movements can fall under the heading of genealogy in the sense that they are historical critiques which put into play a difference that has the effect of calling into question transcendental structures and received values. In fact, Foucault came to see these "domains" as three axes of the same inquiry, although he was never able to bring them together in a concentrated project. We will see that the modern political subject emerges in a matrix of experience structured by the axial interplay of discourse, power, and subjectivation.

Following Foucault, then, the present study is structured by the following questions: "How are we constituted as subjects of our own knowledge? How are we constituted as subjects who exercise or submit to power relations?

How are we constituted as moral subjects of our own actions?"[29] To understand the emergence of the political subject these three questions belong
together. However, in order to recognize political identity as a convergence
of formative elements, an interplay of determining but contingent factors,
it will be necessary to take each question in turn, with the understanding
that eventually they will be brought together to illustrate the complex matrix
of the political subject's emergence. Since each question corresponds to a
different movement of Foucault's thought, I will devote a chapter to each
movement, developing it as it is related to political subjectivity. This will be
the focus of Part 1, "The Three Domains of Genealogy," consisting of separate chapters on discourse, power relations, and modes of subjectivation,
respectively.

Specifically, I consider first what might be called the "discourse of threat"
peculiar to traditional political philosophy. This discourse extends itself
beyond the realm of theory to various institutional structures and installs
itself ideologically across the entire political landscape. This discourse at
once isolates us to a private autonomy and permits a governmental integration of subjects within the body politic. This integration is made possible, in part, through traditional appeals to "rights"—human rights, natural
rights, civil rights, inalienable rights. To appreciate how this integration is
accomplished, we have to examine an aspect of Foucault's thought the
importance of which has not been commonly recognized or acknowledged
in previous commentaries on Foucault. I am referring to what Foucault calls
"Enunciative modalities."[30] With regard to modern political subjects, we
shall see that one of the most important of these modalities is the "site" of
their emergence. There are two general sites of that emergence, each corresponding to what I call the practical and ideological registers of modern
political identity. With regard to the ideological register, the conceptual and
geographical space of the *nation* serves as the site of the emergence and formation of that modern political identity I call the Savage Noble. With regard
to the practical register, I will show how modern political identity is forged
in the "disciplinary" sites of the school, the hospital, military barracks, and
the prison, and how, moreover, the ideological register of savage nobility
(i.e., autonomous individuality) is superimposed on this form of disciplinary
subjectivity as a veil and an instrument of subjugation.

Foucault introduces the concept of enunciative modalities in *The Archaeology of Knowledge*, where they are part of his larger examination of discourse. Yet the significance of enunciative modalities extends beyond that
of discourse and, in fact, serves as a linchpin between his work on power
and ethics as well. With regard to power, my main concern is with demon-

strating the emergence of the private, autonomous individual, with the way that form of political subjectivity is an effect of a set of power relations peculiar to what Foucault calls "disciplinary" society. Individualism is obviously coextensive with Liberalism and its contractual view of power. In contrast, disciplinary power operates through subtle coercions and petty manipulations; it seizes the body and subjects it to a complex series of practices and procedures in order to produce a form of political subjectivity that is docile, manageable, *safe*. Part of the success of disciplinary power is due to its ability to use traditional notions of power (as something that can be possessed and contracted away) and of autonomous individuality as an ideological veil to conceal the fact that it is producing an entirely different form of identity, one for whom traditional notions of power and freedom are rhetorically familiar but practically alien. As James Bernauer points out, however, the modern notion of individuality is not merely *used* by disciplinary power to conceal itself; that notion of individuality is to a very large extent *produced* by disciplinary power.[31] Later, I will show how these two indices of individuality—ideological and disciplinary—are brought together within the political rationality of what Foucault calls "Governmentality," and how they are played out on the enunciative site of the nation. Nevertheless, the disciplinary individual is not the same as the private, autonomous individual—the Savage Noble—of the liberal tradition. There are important conceptual and practical differences between the two that should not be elided. Indeed, to the extent that much contemporary political theory and philosophy still appeals to traditional notions of individuality and power, it is important to demonstrate how Foucault's work challenges some of the basic assumptions of traditional political philosophy.

With regard to Foucault's last work on ethics, enunciative modalities can help us to define and delineate those spaces, or sites, in which individuals fashion their own identity as political subjects. Drawing upon Foucault's later work on the history of sexuality, in which he attempts to elaborate the various processes of "subjectivation," or self-formation, I select out those aspects of his work that can help us to understand the self-formation of the political subject. More specifically, Foucault reads various texts, such as Plato's *Republic* and Epictetus's *Discourses*, not as philosophical treatises in the traditional sense, but as "manuals of living" that outline the practices and regimes through which one may turn oneself into an ethical subject. Using this as a model of analysis, I trace out such a "technology of self" in the texts of traditional political philosophy. The focus of my analysis is John Stuart Mill's *On Liberty*. If we read *On Liberty* as a manual of subjectivation rather than as the juridical project to identify a principle designed to set limits on the exercise of power, we see Mill offering detailed guidelines about how to "cultivate" our own individuality. One crucial feature of the form of political subjectivity that Mill elaborates relates to *tolerance*. In fact, going beyond Mill, it seems to me that the quality of tolerance can help us to make sense of the different forms of modern (Western) political identity, and of how they are expected to relate to each other in order to act "ethically." I appeal to tolerance to map out the ideological oppositions—left and right, liberal and conservative, fascist and anarchist—that constitute the political spectrum. Toleration is considered by Mill and Rawls to be one of the principle virtues of autonomous individuality (and hence of savage nobility). However, this virtue accrues to a form of abstract political identity that requires us to be oblivious (e.g, color-blind; the idea that "all men are created equal") to the very real differences between us. Yet if we examine the sites wherein we have seen the formation of that identity we have known as the noble savage—the native American Indian—we see how *both* toleration and the lack thereof have served as instruments of power. In fact, the political spectrum is a kind of prism through which the white light of European male reason is refracted along an abstract ideological line that leaves little room for recognition of genuine cultural difference.

In part 2 of this book, "Against Identity," I show how these three movements of Foucault's thought belong together and how, as such, this forces us to rethink the problems of power, political freedom, and the tasks of political philosophy. Specifically, I discuss the axial interplay of discourse, power relations, and modes of self-formation, this time with an emphasis on their interplay and complicity. My aim is to demonstrate how the political subject is fabricated within a complex "matrix of experience" structured and defined by this axial interplay. This matrix houses the "political technology" through which individuals are "constructed." At the heart of this matrix is the concept of *conduire*, or conduct, which weaves together the multifarious modes of *self*-government—understood in a very literal sense, as referring to a form of "self" attenuation and effectuation—with the rationality and instrumentality of governmentality, in such a manner as to constitute the form of selfhood animating modern political identity.

The problem of freedom is perhaps the most important issue in any philosophical consideration of political subjectivity. In contrast to the juridical, rights-based conceptions of freedom peculiar to the liberal tradition, Foucault offers us an understanding of freedom that is quite different, an understanding that is in part effected by rethinking, through genealogy, the formation of political subjectivity. Genealogy can be understood as the "discipline" that exposes the entrenched forms of valuation and structuralized practices that determine what we are. In so doing, genealogy creates distance—that is, spaces of freedom—from those forms. In this sense, Foucault's own work is, potentially at least, a vehicle of such freedom. That is, there is a liberational aspect to Foucault's work which consists in "delimiting," or transgressing, the historically contingent limitations imposed upon us by the interplay of discursive practices, power relations, and modes of subjectivation. I shall want to show that this liberational aspect lies in what Foucault has called "counter-memory." Freedom through counter-memory presents itself as a strategic option to the ideological and philosophically suspect notions of positive and negative freedom offered to us from the liberal tradition.

I have already mentioned how the notion of savage nobility, or free individuality, represents a reversal of the terms immortalized by Rousseau. In a very important sense this whole project represents yet a second reversal of Rousseau, that pertaining to the difference between a hypothetical political history such as Rousseau's and genealogy as it is understood by Foucault. This is in part accounted for by the difference between *Ursprung*, or "origin," and *Entstehung*, or "emergence," as Friedrich Nietzsche understood and employed the terms.[32] Rousseau's history, like Hobbes's, is meant to have the juridical function of justifying a certain kind of political relation between subjects and sovereign power. To accomplish this, Rousseau's *Discourse on the Origin of Inequality* adopts the approach of what Nietzsche calls a "Monumental" history: the project of such a history is to convince us "that the great which once existed was at least *possible* once and may well again be possible sometime," if only we learn to recover and venerate that which is "exemplary and worthy of imitation" from the past.[33] The *Ursprung* that Rousseau would like to recover is the condition of "original man," the noble savage.[34] Not that Rousseau would have us abolish society and "retire to the woods," but it is by recovering their lost historical origins that so-called civilized men will learn again to "respect the sacred bonds of those societies to which they belong; they will love their fellows, and will serve them to the utmost of their power."[35]

Genealogy, on the other hand, appeals to a notion of origin—*Entstehung*—that subverts the very ground upon which a monumental project such as Rousseau's would stand. This is what Foucault refers to as the "parodic" use of genealogy, whereby the "alternate identities" that the monumental historian would like to recover for us are exposed as "ephemeral props that point to our own unreality."[36]

What, however, is the "ground" upon which genealogy stands? What is the basis of its own intelligibility and accountability? In the final chapter, I consider a number of possible objections to Foucault's thought, and to a project such as this one based upon that thought. In fact, the objections that are typically raised against Foucault are so common and so similar—coming from a range of critics including Michael Walzer, Richard Rorty, Jürgen Habermas, Nancy Fraser, and Alasdair MacIntyre—that I have given the dilemma upon which these criticisms are based a name: the Foucault Conundrum. This conundrum has to do, first, with the critical observation that Foucault's description of our subjection is so thorough that it is not clear how we can speak of freedom in any meaningful sense, since we always find ourselves constrained to a set of power relations. Second, genealogy historicizes both rationality and morality such that it tends to undermine any appeal to normative standards, so it is not clear how Foucault, or for that matter any political theory built on genealogy, can say that we *ought* to try to free ourselves. As such, it is typically argued, Foucault's thought leads to a kind of moral inertia. I attempt to resolve this conundrum in part by turning to Jeremy Bentham (not the live Bentham, but the Bentham presently housed in a mahogany box at the University of London) and to the notion of political identity that he represents symbolically and that is traced out by genealogical critique.

I conclude the book with a discussion of the implications of Foucault's thought for future political theory. I think we can already see the direction toward which theory will move in a number of related politicotheoretical projects that have emerged in recent years and that have been influenced, directly or indirectly, positively or negatively, by an, if not explicitly Foucauldian, then at least broadly "postmodern" sensibility toward the political. These include the politics of difference peculiar to certain feminist projects (versions of which can be found in Luce Irigaray, Judith Butler, Honi Fern Haber, and Jana Sawicki); the politics of recognition found in the projects of multiculturalism (Charles Taylor, Jürgen Habermas, Cornel West, Nancy Fraser, and Fazal Rizvi, among others); and the politics of alterity informing certain postcolonial theories (for example, in Homi Bhabha and Gayatri Spivak).[37] Ultimately my aim in this book is not so much to establish an ethics or a politics based on Foucault's philosophy, but rather to articulate the outlines of a methodology, political genealogy, the application of which would affect the very way we conceive of the projects of an ethics or politics. This methodology, which consists in studying discourse, power relations, and modes of self-formation in their axial interplay, can help us to better understand the emergence of political subjects and, in so doing, provoke us to rethink the tasks of political theory.

My focus here is on the savage noble, on free individuality, but the methodology on which I have been elaborating could be used to study the emergence of other, non-Western, modes of political subjectivity. Moreover, political genealogy can be used, I think, to inform those projects of feminism, multiculturalism, and postcolonial theory that already push the boundaries of conventional political thought.

Regarding the possibility of a "new" political philosophy, Foucault once observed, "We need to cut off the King's head; in political theory that still has to be done."[38] Yet Foucault's analysis of disciplinary society and governmentality shows how anachronistic political theories are that are still bound to the problem of sovereignty. At the same time, these theories maintain an apparent viability precisely because they play a vital role, that of concealment and the integration of subjects, for the mechanisms of the disciplinary technology of power. Thus, saying that political theory needs to "cut off the King's head" cannot be understood as the traditional rights-based project to place sovereignty in the hands of political subjects.[39] Rather, the project should be to "wipe the slate clean," in the sense of constructing a political philosophy that refuses to be enamored of sovereignty, that recognizes it as an instrument of subjection. This would require transgressing a time-honored tradition, not in the sense of producing a "better" or more "profound" political philosophy, but of escaping the limits of a tradition that structures and determines our thought, an escape that would consist simply in *thinking otherwise*—and of seeing what might emerge from this difference.

To recast Nietzsche, the *King* is dead. Yet we continue to display his ominous figure within our theoretical and institutional structures as a symbol of our liberation from particular powers and petty tyrannies. We pay homage to the King every time we assert our rights and autonomy, all the while refusing or unable to hear behind us the low hum of a vast machinery that fabricates us as individuals. Foucault's work lifts the veil of nostalgia and allows us, for the first time perhaps, to be repelled by the sight of the King's decaying flesh. The King is dead. The question now is, are we ready for it? Are we strong enough yet to affirm our freedom from right and sovereignty, and to create new possibilities, new emergences, for ourselves as political subjects? Is it possible that our political identities could at last manifest themselves in some ways other than those prescribed for us by the narrow Western dichotomy between Noble Savages and Savage Nobles?

part 1

The Three Domains
of Genealogy

2

The Subject of Political Discourse

Are you determined to misunderstand discursive practices, in their own existence, and . . . to maintain . . . a history of the mind, of rational knowledge,
ideas, and opinion? What is that fear which makes you reply in terms of consciousness when someone talks to you about a practice, its conditions, its rules,
and its historical transformations?

—Michel Foucault, *The Archaeology of Knowledge*

One of the most unquestioned assumptions about modern politics is that it
has to do primarily with, as Hannah Arendt has observed, "the struggle for
power."[1] Foucault echoes this characterization: "'Politics' has been conceived as a continuation, if not exactly and directly of war, at least of the
military model as a fundamental means of preventing civil disorder."[2] But
this has not always been the case. Both Aristotle and St. Augustine conceived of politics in very different terms. For Aristotle, perhaps the central
task of political rationality was to determine how to instill virtue (understood broadly in terms of *Pan Metron Ariston*, the Apollonian emphasis on
moderation and the control of desire) in the state: "A State is good in virtue
of the goodness of the citizens who have a share in the government. In our
state all the citizens have a share in the government. We have therefore to
consider how a man can become a good man" (*Politics*, VII, 13, 1132a).
This view, in fact, assumes a general continuity between governing oneself,
governing one's household, and governing a city, with first and determinative emphasis given to governing oneself. For St. Augustine, on the other
hand, these terms are in some sense reversed, with the nature of politics
determined by the nature of the city to which one (figuratively) belongs: an
earthly city of men, or a heavenly City of God. The task of secular politics
is largely to secure the "well-ordered concord" of the former until it can be
usurped by the full and complete realization of "eternal peace" in the latter
at the Last Judgment. "And thus we may say of peace [*both* temporal and

eternal] . . . that it is the end of our good," says Augustine (*The City of God*, Book XIX, c. 11–14). Thus, politics, rather than being conceived as intrinsically fractious, is viewed as a curative to "the collapse into division and disharmony" that necessitated it in the first place.[3] The question we might ask, then, is, how did the modern, agonistic view of the political originate? Can it be traced back to a discourse that bases the juridical limits of power and political obligation on the hypothetical threat of the State of Nature?

In this chapter, I trace out the discursive origins of such an assumption by focusing on Thomas Hobbes's *Leviathan*. I am keen to draw out from Hobbes a conception of political subjectivity peculiar to the entire liberal tradition. This analysis will have two methodological tracks: one track will focus on actual discursive practice, identifying the ostensible concepts, objects, and themes that characterize the discourse of traditional political philosophy as found in Hobbes. The other track analyzes, using Foucauldian terminology, the underlying "discursive regularities" of a given historical "discursive formation." Such regularities structure and determine the content of an ostensible discursive practice. This latter methodological path appeals to Foucault's work in *The Archaeology of Knowledge*. Hubert L. Dreyfus and Paul Rabinow have suggested that Foucault abandoned this work, and his "archaeological" analysis of discourse, primarily because of the way that project came to be aligned with structuralism.[4] This is partially true; however, much of the elements of Foucault's archaeology can be recast as genealogy in the sense that these elements become provisional instruments of a critical inquiry that sheds light on given historically contingent events, without pretense that they refer to foundational or universal structures that govern the formation of human thought and/or practice.[5] In fact, the privilege of thought and practice as abiding in and issuing from a self-identical human subject is undercut when it is demonstrated through archaeology/genealogy that subjectivity is an *effect*, not the cause, of a given discursive formation.

In what follows, I will trace out the conceptual outline of the form of political subjectivity found in the texts of seventeenth- and eighteenth-century political philosophy. By focusing on Hobbes and the discursive practice he is typically credited with inaugurating, I identify what I call the "discourse of threat," which animates modern political subjectivity and the contentious domain of modern politics in which that subjectivity has life. This discourse represents the genetic source of concepts and ideas that will eventually issue in the emergence of that form of political identity that I have called the Savage Noble.

The Discourse of Threat: Hobbes and the Social Contract Tradition

Broadly speaking, Foucault's work, from *Madness and Civilization* to his last work on the history of sexuality, is concerned with *limits*: the ways in which the world has been enclosed by language, thought, and practice so as to constitute a domain of knowledge and truth. The effect of Foucault's work has been to transgress such limits by exposing the historical contingency and nonessentiality of their formation. Foucault's archaeology/genealogy undermines the privilege of any particular domain and compromises its claims on truth and rationality by showing it to be one possible ordering of the world among many, carrying its own internal (yet ultimately arbitrary) rules for its organization as a field of inquiry, a discipline, a practice, or a weltanschauung. In short, Foucault's work suggests that truth, rationality, and knowledge only have meaning—and power—within the organized epistemological domains in which they appear. More narrowly, Foucault is concerned with the limits that circumscribe human beings so as to transform them into *subjects*: medical subjects, sexual subjects, incarcerated subjects, and so on. "My objective," says Foucault, "has been to create a history of the different modes by which, in our culture, human beings are made subjects."[6] Just as there have been a variety of different epistemological formations, there have been a variety of different forms of subjectivity; and in fact the specificity of any particular subject is tied to the broader epistemological domain in which it emerges. In each case, one of the principal factors (along with, as we shall see, power relations and the self-appropriation of values and practices) in the formation of human subjects is discourse. The possibilities for subjectival delimitation is a function of what particular discourses allow us to think, believe, and say regarding who and what we are. Rather than being the cause or originator of discourse, subjects are the effects of a given discursive formation, of a dominant epistemological order.[7] Subjectivity in whatever form it appears is thus always discourse specific: how we view ourselves is determined by what concepts emerge in a given historical field of discursive regularities.

Political subjectivity is perhaps the most elusive of forms of subjectivity because of its relation to politics in general. Modern political subjects traverse a tenuous space bound at one end by peaceful coexistence, and at the other by war and civil disorder. Where subjects are political is precisely where the exercise of power becomes an issue. The political subject is, in a sense, absent until moments of encounter and confrontation put her political status into question, to which she responds in a political way (which may range from paying taxes to voting to taking up arms). The delimitation of political power, which in Western culture is a delimitation of rights, freedoms, obligations, and force, is definitive of modern political subjectivity. In this section, I want to show how this conception of political subjectivity is rooted in the discursive regularities of the Enlightenment, and how, more important, these regularities give rise to a "discourse of threat" that animates modern political subjects.

A genealogy of modern political identity might begin with the sixteenth century. At the time, the theory of Natural Law was beginning to dissolve the centuries-old medieval theocratic view of the state. With works such as Jean Bodin's *de Republica* in 1577, the modern concept of sovereignty and civil society began to take shape. As Otto Gierke explains, "The State was no longer derived from the divinely ordained harmony of the universal whole."[8] Disputes about the basis of sovereign authority and the rights of subjects were increasingly decided with reference to the dictates of Natural Law. This emphasis on Natural Law set the stage for seventeenth-century English individualism, which constituted, in turn, the roots of modern Liberal Theory.

One could easily (if bluntly, by glossing over a range of other concerns) characterize the political thought of the seventeenth and eighteenth centuries, including that of Hobbes, John Locke, Robert Filmer, Baruch Spinoza, Samuel Pufendorf, James Harrington, Algernon Sidney, the third Earl of Shaftesbury, Bernard Mandeville, Frances Hutcheson, Henry Bolingbroke, David Hume, John Balguy, and Adam Smith as a discourse of threat. One of the principal concerns of political theory in this era is the idea of social contract, but social contract makes little sense without the idea of a state of nature, a primitive state of constant danger without law or the hope of restitution, which necessitates the contract. It is the threat posed by the state of nature that compels men to erect civil society through social contract; and, more important, it is the threat of a return to the state of nature that compels men (now political subjects) to respect the contract, to live in accordance with the laws of the land. Where political subjects fail to respect the contract the threat of sovereign power looms over them to punish them. Likewise, where sovereignty exceeds the boundaries of just authority, this poses the threat of civil unrest, the usurpation of the sovereign, the collapse of the state, the return to the state of nature. Civil society is a kind of balancing act of mutually opposed and offsetting threats that maintain its stability and equilibrium—at one end is the threat of the state of nature that makes civil society necessary, and at the other the threat of a state of nature that would mark civil society's demise. Nowhere is this threat articulated more clearly than in Jean-Jacques Rousseau, who says that, when despotism takes over and the rule of law breaks down, "everything returns to the sole law of the strongest, and of course to a *new state of nature* different from that with which we began, inasmuch as the first was the state of nature in its purity, and this one the consequence of excessive corruption."[9]

Of course, one the earliest formulations of the contractual idea that "the state is a human contrivance, in which men agree not to harm others so long as others abstain from harming them," is found in Epicureanism.[10] In the modern era prior to Hobbes, important variants of this idea and others (including the self-interested appeal to the laws of nature and the rejection of the theory of Divine Right) can be found in Johannes Althusius, Hugo Grotius, and Richard Hooker.[11] Nevertheless, it is helpful, even if "misleading,"[12] to locate the origin of modern liberal discourse or, more precisely, what I have called the discourse of threat, in Hobbes's *Leviathan*.

Hobbes's delimitation of the political subject dominated Western thought for the next three hundred years.[13] Specifically, and not to put too fine a point on it, *Leviathan* defines political subjects in terms of their relationship to a sovereign power:

And in him consisteth the Essence of the Common-wealth; which (to define it,) is One Person, of whose Acts a great Multitude, by mutuall Covenants one with another, have made themselves every one the Author, to the end he may use the strength and means of them all, as he shall think expedient, for their Peace and Common Defence.

And he that carryeth this Person, is called SOVERAIGNE, and said to have Soveraigne Power, *and every one besides, his SUBJECT.*[14]

This definition of the political subject is very close to the original Latin, *subjectus*, meaning "to place under." Clearly Hobbes conceives the political subject as a person under the authority or control of another and to which the person owes allegiance.[15]

According to the most common readings of the *Leviathan*, Hobbes bases his concept of the political subject on a particular conception of man that conforms in many ways to the prevalent historical views regarding physical nature. The first chapter of *Leviathan* is entitled "Of Sense" and from this then novel point of departure Hobbes derives a political theory that receives its legitimacy from an understanding of the nature of man. Hobbes views man materialistically as a kind of machine almost totally motivated by external stimuli and internal appetites.[16] Of man's most pressing desire, Hobbes contends, "I put for a general inclination of all mankind a perpetual and restless Desire of Power after Power, that ceaseth only in Death" (I, 11, 161). Because men are motivated by the desire for power, prior to the formation of civil society men lived in a constant state of insecurity that Hobbes calls the "State of Nature." In this state of nature, human beings constantly struggle against each other for survival. There is no industry, no culture, no law—just perpetual competition, fear, violence, and death.

The *Leviathan* presents a view of the formation of civil society that sees human beings as driven to agreement precisely because of the insecurity that exists in the state of nature. In the absence of any governmental protection, men are always at risk from the hostility and avariciousness of their fellow men. The only way out of the state of nature is by way of a social contract in which all men agree to relinquish their rights and freedoms.[17] The creation of civil society and the establishment of sovereign authority, under the terms of mutual consent, is meant to protect men from the state of nature, to preserve the peace, and to foster social progress (particularly economic advancement).

However we characterize them, Hobbes's concerns will be definitive of subsequent political philosophy.[18] For example, John Locke's *Two Treatises of Government* (1689/90) repeat almost exactly the same discursive gestures as the *Leviathan*.[19] Like Hobbes, Locke appeals to the idea of a state of nature to explain the formation of civil society. Locke shares Hobbes's view that human beings are motivated by appetite and aversion, and although unsavory inclinations and desires could be overruled by reason, the corruption of some individuals in the state of nature put everyone's property and well-being in jeopardy. This made it necessary, again through social contract, to establish civil government. Like Hobbes, Locke believed that certain things were lacking in the state of nature, particularly a known law, impartial judges to settle disputes, and a uniform power of execution, all of which call for the erection of a commonwealth. "God hath certainly appointed Government to restrain the partiality and violence of Men," says Locke. "I easily grant, that *Civil Government* is the proper Remedy for the Inconveniences of the State of Nature . . ." (Locke, 316). However, the power and authority of government, far from being absolute, is vested in the freely given consent of the governed and may never extend beyond the common good. Where it does, individuals have the right to take back their consent and the powers that go with it (see Locke, bk. II, ch. viii and ch. ix).

Unlike Hobbes, Locke takes pains to distinguish between a "state of nature" and a "state of war," two ideas that he feels have been "confounded" together by earlier theorists. Where men live together in reason, without a common authority, they live in a state of nature. The state of war, on the other hand, is "a State of Enmity, Malice, Violence, and Mutual Destruction." It is the danger of a state of war in the state of nature which compels men to form a commonwealth. "To avoid this State of War . . . is one great *reason of Men's putting themselves in Society*, and quitting the state of nature" (Locke, 323). Yet the state of war may occur whether or not a common authority has been established; that is, it may occur in either the state of nature *or* in civil society. Men have certain basic rights and freedoms in the state of nature that are not relinquished with the creation of civil government. The end of law in civil society, in fact, is "to preserve and enlarge freedom" (Locke, 348). Individuals have the right to resist anything that threatens this freedom, whether it be a simple thief or an absolute sovereign. In such cases it is lawful "to kill him if I can."

It makes little or no difference that the state of nature is largely a hypothetical concept in social contract theory, that it is only a methodological device for justifying a particular conception of sovereignty.[20] On the contrary, the Hobbesian contract has the real consequence of justifying sovereign exercise of authority. Moreover, it obligates political subjects to submit to that authority, not because they really agreed to do so according to an actual historical contract, but by virtue of being a citizen of the state. Not to do so—not to honor this hypothetical contract which obligates subjects to sovereign authority—is to *risk something like* a return to a state of nature, or a state of war, which presumably no rational, self-interested citizen would desire. It is the *threat* of such a "return" that matters, not that any such state ever did exist.

In fact, because the social contract is (historically, though not juridically) hypothetical, political theorists deal with already constituted political subjects, abstract individuals whose relation to sovereignty is already established. The principal task of political theory, then, will be to determine the limits of mutual power and obligation. The relation of political subjects to each other and to sovereignty is, thus, always a juridical one based on the delimitation of rights, freedoms, and mutual expectations, and the establishing of laws and powers to see that such delimitations are respected. The important differences in political philosophies since Hobbes have been differences in understanding such delimitations: how much power should be vested in sovereignty, what rights and freedoms should be respected in subjects, what political subjects can justifiably expect from government regarding the distribution of goods and services, and so on. Every delimitation, no matter what its specific characteristics, carries the expectation, at once juridical and moral, to respect it—that is, a kind of contractual obligation attends it. At the limits of such delimitations is the threat of their violation.

In social contract theory, in which much contemporary political theory has its roots, this threat is the threat of the state of nature. The ideology of contract theory would have us think (even if only hypothetically) that this threat precedes the contract and makes it necessary, when in fact *the contract precedes threat* and makes it definitive of the relationship between political subjects and the body politic. As Hobbes has said, before the contract there is no injustice; but even more, before the contract there is no *threat* (of injustice). The notion of contract is necessary to give meaning to the notion of threat (in a political context). The contract represents a delimitation of politico-moral expectations; as such, the contract is necessary to define threat, to say what would constitute a violation of that delimitation. In this sense, social contract does not end the state of nature; it perpetuates it—it carries the state of nature forward as a perpetual threat.

By reference to the always looming danger of the state of nature, social contract can gain acquiescence and observance; it can compel obligation to itself as a juridical-ethical standard of political conduct. In this way it can justify retribution against those who do not respect the contract (i.e., the delimitation of politico-moral expectations), against those who constitute a threat to the welfare of the commonwealth.

Conventional intellectual history tells us that Hobbes was influenced by Galileo and that he wanted to bring the same deductive rigor of geometry to political theory. The laws of nature allowed him to do the latter; they serve as axioms from which he can deduce principles of political obligation.[21] According to Hobbes, the laws of nature are "immutable and eternal"; they are "dictates of reason ... delivered in the word of God" (*Leviathan*, I, 15, 216–17). Man is compelled to follow the laws of nature because one of his greatest passions is the fear of death; in everything man is a victim of his passions. Yet somehow man knows the laws of nature through reason. Here we have this curious juxtaposition, so typical of the seventeenth and eighteenth centuries, of a mechanistic materialism which interprets the world entirely according to the principles of the physical sciences, the view that all things may be explained in accordance with the laws that govern matter and motion; and, on the other hand, the view that man somehow participates in a reason that issues ultimately from God, and which no doubt transcends the finite world, but which nevertheless has a worldly manifestation, even suzerainty, through the eternal laws of nature.

Like so much of the political discourse of the seventeenth and eighteenth centuries we see in *Leviathan* an appeal to a particular conception of man, an arbitrary metaphysics that places man somewhere on a continuum between animality and rationality. Where man is placed on this scale determines the limits of the rights and freedoms he will enjoy in civil society. It likewise determines, and is in fact meant as a justification of, the limits of sovereign authority. It is, apparently, the *Leviathan's* metaphysics of man that necessitates an all-powerful sovereign. At first glance, the mechanistic materialism that begins the *Leviathan* appears to determine everything that follows. By painting a picture of man as this hostile, malicious creature at the mercy of his passions and appetites, Hobbes is faced with the problem of explaining how civil society could ever be established in the first place. Enter the laws of nature, as a kind of deus ex machina, delivered from the mouth of God Himself, which tell these nasty little creatures that, in order to survive, they need to enter into a social contract wherein each one will relinquish his rights to an absolute sovereign. The power of sovereign authority must be absolute, it must extend over each and every individual and over the affairs of the entire commonwealth, in order to prevent a return to the state of nature.

Hobbes's dark, utilitarian description of man perhaps can be (and has been) attributed to an aversion to the civil strife he witnessed in his own country. The political climate at the time of *Leviathan*'s emergence was volatile. Struggle in parliament, civil war, constitutional revolution—all of this seemed to bring about "a new belief in the value and the rights of the individual."[22] It was in this environment, in 1651, that the *Leviathan* was born; but it is somewhat ironic that this work, which congealed and gave expression to the emerging individualism of the time, which was a seminal work in refining political theory into a science, and which would dictate the concerns and structure the inquiry of the political discourse which followed it, was perhaps the most pessimistic in its estimation of man and the most authoritarian in what it granted to sovereignty.

Instead of attributing this to biographical and historical influences, I would like to suggest that the political and metaphysical orientation of the *Leviathan* stems from its participation in discursive regularities already in place before its emergence. Though as a text it does arguably organize those regularities into a political discourse which will be exceptional in its influence, it is nonetheless an effect of the underlying epistemic configuration of the Enlightenment, just as were the increasing influence of the physical sciences and the emergence of rationalism. In this sense, Hobbes bears much the same discursive relation to political theory as Carolus Linnaeus does to natural history and Galileo does to the scientific description of heavenly bodies. In the next section I discuss the discursive regularities that underlie, and give rise to, the kind of political order—referring both to theories about the nature of man and the sort of political organization man thereby requires—that appears on the ostensible level of "Enlightenment-era political discourse.

Discursive Regimes and the Order of the Political

The dichotomous separation of the physical and rational is well documented in the history of philosophy and has its best known expression in Cartesian dualism. However, Foucault has argued that this separation yet tenuous affinity of mind and body, reason and passion, is a surface effect of a particular discursive configuration. In *The Order of Things*, Foucault insists that different ways of ordering the world have been dominant in different periods in history. Each order can be understood as a nexus of exclusion. That is, the epistemic formations peculiar to a particular historical period allow certain things to be thought, believed, and said within that formation, and certain other things to be excluded, so as to constitute a relatively autonomous domain: a domain of discourse. The concepts that are allowed to hold sway in each domain, the dominant epistemic themes, the strategies for appropriating and disseminating knowledge, the theoretical choices of science and philosophy are all determined within, and at the same time constitute, the discursive order. Each order is a kind of delimitation that appropriates and organizes differences under the identity of the same configuration or discursive practice. By focusing on difference rather than identity, and by casting the nexus of exclusion/inclusion of a given epistemological order genealogically side by side with those of other orders, Foucault is able to show the elements of a discursive formation to be historically contingent and nonessential modes of evaluation, of *giving meaning* to the world.

Foucault defines discourse as "a group of statements in so far as they belong to the same discursive formation . . . it is made up of a limited number of statements for which a group of conditions of existence can be defined."[23] This rather austere definition is notable above all for its lack of reference to a speaking subject. This begins as a methodological device of archaeology/genealogy that allows Foucault to explore "discourse not from the point of view of the individuals who are speaking . . . but from the point of view of the rules that come into play in the very existence of such discourse."[24] By setting aside the speaking subject, and with it the privilege of transcendental consciousness, Foucault highlights the autonomy of discourse. He sees that discourse is made up of a body of statements. Rather than interpreting such statements as the utterances of subjects, he examines them in their specificity and particularity. Statements are characterized by their continuity of reference with regard to the objects, concepts, and themes that make up the content and identity of (any particular) discourse. It is the *sameness* of statements, their commonality of form, articulation, emergence, and reference, that constitutes the identity of any particular discursive formation.

Within any particular discursive formation, the emergence of statements conforms to the same rules or conditions of existence. These rules or conditions are not transcendental principles in the Kantian sense. "The fact of [a statement's] belonging to a discursive formation and the laws that govern it are one and the same thing" (*AK*, 116). Statements do not belong—are not accepted—within any particular discourse unless they share a sameness with respect to the domain of truth which that discourse is meant to articulate. The acceptability of statements (and it is acceptability which determines the emergence of statements) conforms to "a law of coexistence," that is, a law defined by the mere fact of dispersion of similar statements, the regularity of which "is defined by the discursive formation itself." The rules for the formation of statements, the rules governing the "discursive practice" of their formation, are contingent upon and peculiar to the historical discursive formation in which statements are formed. To define the conditions of existence is to define the sameness of (the formation of) the statements that characterize any given discursive practice.

The sameness of statements also plays a limiting function. Discourse is "made up of a *limited number* of statements" precisely because of the sameness that all statements must share within discourse. The formation of statements conforms to what Foucault calls "a law of rarity."[25] Rarity refers to the simple fact that, within discourse, "everything is never said" (*AK*, 115). In fact, everything *cannot* be said because every discursive formation is a "limited system" of statements that excludes, on the basis of the continuity of the formation itself, *other* possibilities of what may be said (thought, written down, put into practice). The internal continuity of discourse, the sameness of the statements that constitute it, is at the same time a discontinuity with respect to other discourses, and to everything that might, but does not, take the form of a statement. Thus, every discursive formation constitutes a limit that "separates [statements] from what is not said . . . that allows them to emerge to the exclusion of all others" (*AK*, 119).

The rarity of statements is also their principle of reproduction, repeatability, and transformation. "Because statements are rare, they are collected in unifying totalities, and the meanings to be found in them are multiplied" (*AK*, 120). Those statements that are permitted within the discursive formation are precisely those that conform to the discursive regularities of the formation itself.

Thus, statements are rare. They are of limited number, and this also serves to limit what may join their fold. Yet exclusion is not a repression, says Foucault. There is no subtext, no vast suppressed realm of the unsaid hidden beneath that which is said. Rather, discourse is "a distribution of gaps, voids, absences, limits, divisions" (*AK*, 119). These gaps, voids, and absences, which flank discourse on all sides, are just that; they do not hide "a silent, common text" from which statements proceed, a text that is covered over by their emergence. These gaps—the gaps of pure difference—are opened by the pure dispersion and organization of statements within a discursive formation. The void is a testimony to the power of discourse to constitute a domain of knowledge through excluding other possible statements, that is, through appropriating differences through the exclusion of pure difference.[26] Discourse, thus, has a sovereignty over what may pass as truth. Truth (in the form of true statements) is that which falls within the limits of the domain. Error, falsity, nonsense have meaning only as a transgression of those limits, and are given meaning from within the system itself.

Statements are not to be identified with sentences, propositions, or speech acts, although they may take any of those forms.[27] Statements may be written or spoken, but they are not defined by being either. Statements are events. Or more precisely, statements are "a function that cuts across a domain of structures and possible unities, and which reveals them, with concrete contents, in time and space" (*AK*, 87). Statements emerge in time and space as "heterogeneous regions" whose discontinuity undermines the notions of a progressive history or transcendental rationality. Instead, "we have in the density of discursive practices, systems that establish statements as events (with their own conditions and domain of appearance)" (*AK*,128). Discourse is a rupture in the fabric of time and space whose autonomy and discontinuity is understood purely in terms of its appearance, as an event, and not by reference to any transcendental, a priori structures.[28] Discourse is where truth *happens*, rather than where it is discovered, reflected, or revealed. Truth happens as statements bound together by their sameness, constituting a community of truth, a domain of knowledge in which, and only in which, such statements make sense. Truth is peculiar to the domain of discourse in which it emerges; and furthermore, it never extends beyond that domain. The privilege of truth, as something "out there" to be discovered, as somehow transcending the discourses that try to appropriate and reflect it—to make it speak, in other words—is undermined when it is realized that truth is coextensive with such discourses, and that discourse is a historically contingent unity of common statements. The rules for what passes as truth are internal to the discourse itself.

When one examines discourse in its specificity, which amounts to examining statements and the discursive regularities which govern their formation, the conventional (largely Cartesian) notion of a speaking, knowing subject becomes suspect. Foucault has argued that any particular conception of the subject is bound to a particular discursive order. Thus, what begins as a methodological device becomes an archaeological/genealogical discovery: that discourse "refers neither to an individual subject, nor to some kind of collective consciousness, nor to a transcendental subjectivity; but that it is . . . an anonymous field whose configuration defines the possible position of speaking subjects" (*AK*, 122). The configuration of a discursive practice opens the space on which subjects emerge.

For example, in the sixteenth century, where (and one might say "where" rather than "when" if one identifies historical periods as archeological sites, as Foucault does) discourse conforms to "the semantic web of resemblance" (*OT*, 17), man is understood as the passive interpreter of signs through which the truth of the world is randomly revealed. But in the seventeenth and eighteenth centuries, where the discursive order "distributed across space the non-quantitative identities and differences that separated and united things" (*OT*, 218), man is the rational locus of a universal science of order. "It is this [discursive] network," says Foucault, "that *made possible* the individuals we term Hobbes, Berkeley, Hume, or Condillac" (*OT*, 63, emphasis added).

The *Leviathan*, as a discourse, belongs to what Foucault calls the Classical *episteme*. Two of the governing epistemological features of this configuration are the *taxinomia* and the *mathesis*. The taxinomia refers to the attempt to order knowledge of things according to rigorous tables based on a representation of their objective differences, while the mathesis is based on the assumption that the elements of the taxinomia will always be quantifiable. As Foucault explains, "What makes the totality of the Classical *episteme* possible is primarily the relation to a knowledge of order.

When dealing with the ordering of simple natures, one has recourse to a mathesis, of which the universal method is algebra. When dealing with the ordering of complex natures (representations in general, as they are given in experience), one has to constitute a taxinomia . . ." (*OT*, 72). According to Foucault, knowledge in the classical episteme was based on the objective representation of empirical beings according to a grid of identity and difference. The mathesis and the taxinomia, which are the methods of this representation, are commensurate with a rational being (i.e., man) who is able to bring order to the objective, yet jumbled chaos of the empirical world. This produces a necessary separation of the rational and the physical. Man stands at the juncture of this separation, his body subject to the laws of physical nature, his mind, his reason, the source of rational representations of that same world. Says Foucault, "If we follow the archaeological network that provides Classical thought with its laws, we see quite clearly that human nature resides in that narrow overlap of representation which permits it to represent itself to itself . . . and that nature is nothing but the impalpable confusion within representation that makes the resemblance there perceptible before the order of the identities is yet visible" (*OT*, 71).

We can borrow key terms from Foucault's schema to cast an interesting light on the connection between Hobbes's general metaphysics and his political theory in the *Leviathan*. That is, Hobbes's conception of the political subject arises through the discursive gesture, typical of this period, of constituting a table, a taxinomia, that distinguishes Man from a plurality of other physical and natural beings. In fact, *Leviathan* is replete with tables, structural hierarchies, rankings, and orderings that distinguish— down to the finest, almost absurd detail—everything from motion to manners, from passions to powers, from modes of speech to models of government. There is even a "Table of Sciences" wherein Hobbes shows the derivation and relational significance of different forms of knowledge, from geometry to rhetoric (interestingly, optics and poetry are derived from the same epistemological line, that of "Physiques"). According to Hobbes's taxonomy, one of the distinguishing features of political man is his ability to "make covenant" with other men. In contrast, Hobbes takes time to observe, "To make Covenant with bruit Beasts, is impossible; because not understanding our speech, they understand not, nor accept of any translation of Right." Such an observation would seem unnecessary today, even strange, especially in political theory; but this is not a quaint peculiarity of a bygone intellectual era. On the contrary, Hobbes's taxonomic gesture is representative of a comprehensive structural organization that will determine, with a lawful, algebraic necessity, the elements of this configuration and their relations to each other. There is thus a method and a coherency behind Hobbes's ordering of things. He is sketching a relational schema of identities and differences that will allow for the placement of Man in an objective order. This order will permit a rational and compulsory deduction. Based on an understanding of the nature of Man, a political structure and set of requirements can be derived that is proper to men. This deduction will be absolute and irrefutable, a natural law that had only to be perceived by constituting a taxinomia of (ostensibly) disparate beings and properties. Men enter into a commonwealth by relinquishing their rights to an absolute sovereign because this is what man's nature requires, as is revealed by the taxonomy. Even more, we see here the beginnings of a conception of political identity that breaks down along lines that separate what Hobbes calls "bruit beasts"—or savages—from those "civilized" beings whose level of rationality is a direct reflection of their willingness to leave the state of nature and to form civil society through social compact.

Leviathan puts into play and concretizes a discursive practice to which virtually all later Western political thought must conform. This discursive practice is characterized above all by an overriding concern with the juridical limits of political authority and obligation. "Schematically, we can formulate the traditional question of political philosophy in the following terms," explains Foucault. "[H]ow is the discourse of truth, or quite simply, philosophy ... able to fix limits to the rights of power?"[29] Hobbes says as much in the *Leviathan*: "I will consider ... what are the *rights* and just *power* or *authority* of a sovereign." Hobbes's concerns will be definitive of subsequent political philosophy.[30] For instance, Locke's more liberal interpretation of sovereign power is coextensive with his more "generous" metaphysical estimation of man. But Locke's views are really no different than Hobbes's in terms of the discursive regime to which they conform. Locke's appeal to virtually the same ideas as Hobbes —a state of nature, social contract, laws of nature, the limits of sovereign authority and the political obligation of subjects—should be understood in terms of a conformity to entrenched discursive regularities. A discursive practice has been established in the seventeenth century to which all theory (discourse) must conform. A body of common statements consisting of the same objects, concepts, and themes emerges according to a principle of rarity that determines what will be acceptable statements in the discourse of political theory (and spilling over into moral and economic theory). These statements are repeated, become more refined, more exclusionary, until they constitute a limited system, a domain of discourse.

What emerges from the discursive practice of the seventeenth and eighteenth centuries is a political subject animated by the spirit of threat. This notion of the political subject lies at the core of liberal democratic theory. Liberal theory is founded, explicitly or implicitly, on a "contractual" model of political subjectivity whose roots can be found, as we have seen, in the beginning years of the Enlightenment.[31] This contractual model is characterized by an essential division between the individual and the State, between discrete subjects and sovereign authority. The political subject in this view is independent and abstract, and is the locus of rights, liberty, and justice. This view pervades the history of liberalism, from John Milton and the Levellers of John Lilburne, through the early contract theorists, the founding fathers, the French *philosophes*, nineteenth-century social reformers such as John Stuart Mill and T. H. Green, to the present-day political theories of John Rawls and Robert Nozick.[32] Even when political theory eschews, or at least places less emphasis on, social contract, as in forms of Kantianism and utilitarianism, there is still the emphasis on respecting the autonomy and rationality of the political subject, a binary division between sovereignty and subjects, and the concern with identifying the limits and legitimation of power and political obligation. These ideas, which Foucault would recognize as the objects of a discursive practice—autonomy, rights, sovereignty, legitimation, and obligation—presuppose threat: they are invoked in the name of an already-constituted political subject whose rights may be violated, whose freedom may be removed, whose property may be stolen or seized unjustly by a despotic sovereign, whose country may be overthrown by foreign oppressors. Even peace, the ultimate goal of the body politic, is understood as an absence of threat. Take away threat and the modern liberal political subject ceases to make sense.

This was the political discourse that was brought to American shores by the Virginia and New England colonists. We hear the appeal to social contract as the basis for civil government in what is considered to be the first truly "American" political document, the Mayflower Compact: "We whose names are underwritten," writes William Bradford, "covenant and combine ourselves togeather into a civill body politick, for our better ordering and preservation."[33] We hear the claim that political subjects have certain "rights, liberties, and privileges" in the Massachusetts Body of Liberties (1641) long before such rights were enumerated by the founding fathers in the U.S. Constitution. And, perhaps most important, we hear social contract and its attendant rights and obligations to be necessitated by the threat of the State of Nature. In 1717, using Samuel Pufendorf as his theoretical authority, John Wise invokes this notion to justify the church-based government of New England, saying, "I shall consider man in a state of natural being, as a freeborn subject under the crown of heaven, and owing homage to none but God himself. . . . [Yet] man is a creature extremely desirous of his own preservation; of himself he is plainly exposed to many wants, unable to secure his own safety and maintenance without assistance of his fellows; and he is also able of returning kindness by the furtherance of mutual good; but yet man is often found to be malicious, insolent, and easily provoked, and as powerful in effecting mischief as he is ready in designing it. Now that such a creature may be preserved, it is necessary that he . . . enter into a civil state by the law of nature."[34] However, in the New World, the hypothetical threat of the state of nature would be replaced by the very real threat of the American wilderness. Wise insisted that the man endowed by God to tame this wilderness "is a creature of very noble character." But, we cannot yet speak of modern political identity in terms of the "Savage Noble." That identity will be forged in what has been called the crucible of the American wilderness, through the European's encounter with the Noble Savage.

"The constitution of the self as an autonomous subject is rooted in the Enlightenment," asserts Foucault.[35] In the discourse of political philosophy at least since Hobbes, the political subject emerges through an act of abstraction, in the basic but fundamental separation of sovereignty and citizenry. Sovereignty and subjects are held together by a contractual link predicated on the mutual recognition of arbitrary limits imposed on the exercise of power. Yet even as this contractual relation binds the two together, it also holds them apart ontologically: political subjects are conceived as definite beings having certain rights, freedoms, powers, obligations. In their early forms, having just emerged from the State of Nature, political subjects are rather rudimentary, crude, even savage; they still require Sovereignty not just to control them, but to give them their identity. They are, at this point, very much *subjects* in the most basic sense of the word: they are subject to "the express will of the Sovereign." However, political subjects are able to maintain their ontological integrity—a separateness from the Sovereign as well as from each other—precisely through the contractual relation that binds them; for the contract implies, constitutively, the threat of its violation. This threat, carried forward from the savage world from which they came, hangs over political subjects as an emblem of their isolation and separateness, and as the seal of the necessity of their union in a commonwealth.

Later we shall see how the "maturation" of the political subject in the discourses of traditional political philosophy is characterized by increasing separateness and concretion. Political subjects come to be defined less by reference to sovereignty (although that is by no means lost), and more on their own terms as specific political beings. We see the development of notions of *personal* sovereignty and conceptions of *self*-government. In addition to the contractual obligations the political subject has to the state, there is the delimitation of a private area of concerns. Eventually we have the emergence of the private, autonomous individual—the Savage Noble. Individuality comes to be the index of political subjectivity. This is seen in the problematization of negative freedom, the carving out of spheres of personal liberty. Respecting the liberty of individuals to pursue certain private interests becomes an essential feature of contractual obligation. Problems of the exercise of power, while still conceived in juridical and binary terms, now turn on issues of interference and tolerance. The discourse of threat still animates political subjectivity, but now it bears more and more on threats to one's own personal freedom. Individuality is made problematic for the political subject; the cultivation of individuality is made a moral obligation for political subjects. In short, the individual comes to be the fundamental unit of political philosophy, of modern conceptions of political subjectivity. Political debates often disagree over the extent of privacy and autonomy an individual is entitled to, or over the proper limits of governmental interference in the lives of individuals, but the individual itself is a given—it is never thought to put this entity itself into question.

In the next chapter, I will be concerned with showing how modern political identity is the effect of the circulation of disciplinary power. This power concretizes and institutionalizes the discursive elements of Enlightenment political philosophy as they pertain to political identity, giving rise in the New World to a form of political identity, the autonomous individual, which is fundamentally split between the ideology of rights and freedoms, on the one hand, and the practical, meticulous demands of disciplinary inscriptions of the body, on the other.

3

Power and the Political Subject

> The individual is no doubt the fictitious atom of an "ideological"
> representation of society; but he is also a reality fabricated by this
> specific technology of power that I have called "discipline."
>
> —Michel Foucault, *Discipline and Punish*

There is a crucial aspect of discourse, inherent to it and not attached from outside, that Foucault would only later recognize and develop thoroughly, that is, discourse's involvement in relations of power. Foucault's concern with power relations began in earnest with his association with the Paris prison revolt of 1968.[1] Yet the problems and issues he would raise are already there in works such as *Madness and Civilization* and *The Birth of the Clinic*.[2] In *Discipline and Punish*, Foucault would move away from his archaeological investigation of discourse to an exhaustive genealogical study of power relations, and in particular, of the specific practices, techniques, and apparatuses of disciplinary power. Yet discourse is not lost or entirely set aside in this move. Discourse is linked to the circulation of such power at the juncture of what Foucault calls "power/knowledge." The effect of power relations upon the social body is dependent on the production of discourses of truth, which are commensurate with the production of a body of knowledge (*savoir*). Says Foucault, "We are subjected to the production of truth through power and we cannot exercise power except through the production of truth."[3] Among the most important of such discourses of truth are those that constitute the human sciences. In making "man" an object of reflection, the human sciences open up a whole field of political manipulation sanctioned by knowledge; that is, by the "truth," garnered through rational, scientific inquiry, of what we know about human beings, about their lives, their behavior, their needs, their desires, and so forth. From the standpoint of power relations and nondiscursive practices, such discourses are themselves in part an effect of certain practices growing out of a concern for the social body, its health and welfare, its demographic character, the ways of harnessing its productive and economic potential, of ensuring its political stability. These discourses become sanctioned politically and institutionally as mechanisms for the normalization and cohesion of the social body.

In order to avoid an equivocation on the word *political,* let us say that there are two registers for what it means to "be" a political subject: one is practical, the other ideological. The ideological register represents the political subject as the Savage Noble, that is, (minimally) as the bearer of rights and freedoms and as holding a linear relation of contractual obligation to sovereign authority. The practical register, on the other hand, refers to the intrinsic mosaic of power relations that produce disciplined and governmentalized subjects. Although the two registers are heterogenous and antagonistic, both have avenues of articulation and institutionalized modes of support in modern society. Moreover, under both registers the political subject is a fabrication: under the practical register the political subject is materially and physically produced by subjecting the body to disciplinary techniques of docility, normalization, and individualization; under the ideological register, the political subject is, as Foucault says, "a fictitious atom" consisting of metaphysical and representational abstractions. And yet, despite their heterogeneity, it is their complicity—one serving as the mask for the other—that defines "the general mechanism of power in our society."[4] Thus, if we are to understand the emergence of political subjects, at least with respect to the way power functions to produce them, it has to be by reference to these two registers, both separately and together.

In this chapter I will examine how and to what extent the Savage Noble is produced by the specific technology of power that Foucault calls "discipline." In addition, I should like to return to the discursive domain of genealogy in order to discuss what I believe can link all three domains together, namely, enunciative modalities. In particular I want to demonstrate how the notion of autonomous individualism is linked by way of these modalities to the discourse of threat we saw in Hobbes. This discourse is disseminated across the entire American political landscape, across what might be better referred to as the enunciative site of the *nation.*

You Are What You Eat: The Perils of "Indianization"

In *A Different Mirror*, Ronald Takaki points out that Shakespeare's *Tempest* was the first play performed in England, in 1611, that had the New

World as its dramatic setting. This play also introduced to the English-speaking audience its first New World character: an Indian by the name of Caliban. Caliban, it turns out, is Shakespeare's anagram of the word *cannibal,* which is itself derived from the word "Carib," a term of Spanish origin used to refer to the natives of Central America and northern South America.[5] The name Shakespeare chooses for his character is well calculated to tap into one of the deepest fears of his audience, namely, that of being eaten alive. The presumption of cannibalism was, in the European imagination, perhaps the definitive feature of American savagery. This presumption had been fostered by England's earliest explorers of the New World, who referred to the natives they encountered as "Anthropophagi, or devourers of man's flesh."[6] William Bradford would solidify this image in his graphic descriptions of the tortures performed by "the savage people" upon their enemies, the worst of which included "flaying some alive with the shells of fishes, cutting off the members and joints of others by piecemeal and broiling on the coals, eat the collops of their flesh in sight whilst they live."[7] Bradford's "reports" fed fuel to the fire for the Puritans, who already looked upon the natives as devils of the wilderness, a threat to the moral and spiritual well-being of any "civilized" man. The possibility that they might actually be eaten by these savages represented the ultimate abomination.[8]

Of course, it was these same alleged cannibals who brought food to the starving Virginia colonists during that first terrible winter. The second winter was just as harsh, except that by now there were hundreds more colonial mouths to feed. The conditions were so bad this time that there were reports of people eating not only pets and vermin to survive, but bodies dug up from local graves. And, in an irony of dizzying proportions, John Smith would write in his journals, "So great was our famine that a savage we slew and buried" was dug up by some starving colonists and "boiled and stewed with roots and herbs."[9] Of course, Puritans like Cotton Mather could blame such behavior precisely on the association of the colonists with their heathen neighbors. "We have too far degenerated into Indian vices," charged Mather. "We have [become] shamefully *Indianized* in all those abominable things."[10]

The Puritans saw their journey to the New World as a kind of spiritual mission, an "errand in the wilderness," an important goal of which was to bring the heathen natives to Christianity. To become "Indianized," then, to acquire the very traits and imperfections of those you were trying to convert, represented a failure of that mission. But, more than that, it meant a breech of the individual's covenant with God, a loss of spiritual substance, a slide into the dark abyss, the consumption of the soul by the wilderness itself. The American Indian represented the quintessential Other for the Puritan, a negative touchstone, an inverted mirror against which they could judge their own moral and spiritual worthiness, indeed through which they constructed and confirmed their own identity. Thousands of miles from their homeland, locked in struggle with a harsh yet indifferent wilderness, for the Puritans the measure of their humanity and civility came to be the degree to which they were *not* like the savages amongst whom they lived.

Yet it wasn't long before the idea of "Indianization" took on decidedly different connotations. In 1755, Michel-Guillaume-Jean de Crèvecoeur, the son of a French nobleman, emigrated to Canada, where he fought as an officer in the French colonial militia during the French and Indian War. After defeat and capture by Indian forces at Quebec in 1758, Crèvecoeur moved to New York, where he became a naturalized American citizen. He also changed his name, to J. Hector St. John, and eventually published a series of essays that would bring him fame in Europe as the "Cultivateur Américan," the American Farmer.[11] During the time of the American Revolution, Crèvecoeur/St. John found himself torn between his sympathies for Britain (where he had gone to school) and his abiding love for America, which he often referred to as "the most perfect society now existing in the world." Above all, he considered himself a man of peace and he anguished over the fact that there had to be a war at all. "I am conscious that I was happy before this unfortunate revolution," he lamented. "I feel that I am no longer so; therefore I regret the change."[12]

Having fought in a divisive, nation-threatening war himself, Crèvecoeur found it difficult to give his allegiance to either side. This, of course, endeared him to neither; he was accused of being a spy by the British and a traitor by his fellow Americans. Yet he remained in a quandary over what he should do. "To this great evil I must seek some sort of remedy adapted to remove or to palliate it; situated as I am, what steps should I take that will neither injure or insult any of the parties and at the same time save my family from that certain destruction which awaits it, if I remain here much longer?" (468). The remedy Crèvecoeur finally settled upon was the following: "I will revert to a state approaching nearer to that of nature." That is, he resolved to transport himself and his family and to live "among the Indians" (468–69).

Thus, rather than let himself be compelled to choose sides in a war he did not accept, he would immerse himself in the lives of local savages. Crèvecoeur did not consider this a temporary escape, a lying low until he could return safely to his own people; this was to be a near total cultural acquiescence and submersion. He and his family would *become* like the people they had chosen to join. "I have considered in all its future effects and tendencies," he said, "the new mode of living we must pursue." In saying this, he took time to address the concern that he and his family would become "so perfectly Indianized" that they might be lost to so-called civilized society:

> It cannot be so bad as we generally conceive it to be; there must be in their social bond something singularly captivating and far superior to anything to be boasted of among us; for thousands of Europeans are Indians, and we have no examples of even one of those aborigines having from choice become Europeans! ... Let us say what we will of them, of their inferior organs, of their want of bread, etc., they are as stout and well-made as the Europeans. Without temples, without priests, without kings, and without laws, they are in many instances superior to us; and the proofs of what I advance are that they live without care, sleep without inquietude, take life as it comes, bearing all its asperities with unparalleled patience, and die without any kind of apprehension for what they have done or for what they expect to meet with hereafter. What system of philosophy can give us so many necessary qualifications for happiness? (469–70)

Thus, unlike the Puritans, who in the century before had viewed the prospect with such horror, Crèvecoeur welcomed the "Indianization" of himself and his family.

Crèvecoeur's attitude anticipates the positive reversal of perspective toward the Native American as Noble Savage found in the writings of Thomas Jefferson, Jean-Jacques Rousseau, and James Fenimore Cooper, and in the paintings of Charles Deas and George Catlin.[13] In fact, in many ways, Crèvecoeur is the living embodiment of what I have called the Savage Noble. The earliest instantiation of this form of political identity occurs in the colonial militias, eventually giving rise to the legendary minutemen of the American Revolution. The model for the minuteman may have been distinctly American, based on the image of the Noble Savage; but the method of turning individuals into soldiers was entirely European, employing the petty procedural manipulations of disciplinary power.

In fact, for those like Thomas Hutchins and Robert Rogers, who had been involved in the "Indian wars" of the early eighteenth century and who came to appreciate the Indian's courage and skill in battle, the process of indianization was linked with "a program for training white soldiers according to the premises of Indian military discipline."[14] This new type of soldier would be, like his Indian counterpart, at one with his environment, able "to steal unperceived" upon an enemy, only to disappear again into the "trackless woods."[15] Through a regimen of harsh discipline and practice, the delicate and ineffectual colonist would be transformed into a "Euro-Indian American hero." This would be accomplished by combining the ascetic endurance and patience of the native Indian with the "intellect and sentiment" of the European white man. It turned out that this new soldier—or "ranger" as he was sometimes called—was a prelude to "the symbolic figure of Daniel Boone, [who] emerged as the myth-hero of the American frontier."[16] In the colonial ranger we see some of the earliest applications of the disciplinary inscriptions of the body through which the Savage Noble would be fabricated.

The colonial ranger represents a point of intersection between the ideological register of modern political identity and its practical register. To understand the latter requires a detailed foray into Foucault's analysis of disciplinary power relations. This analysis challenges the traditional notion of power as something that is "possessed" by some individuals and "wielded" against others; instead we should understand power as a complex web of relations that functions surreptitiously and anonymously. Power relations invest the entire social field, says Foucault. Power in that sense is "everywhere," not located in or possessed by a central governing body. This view of power has led at least one critic to charge, "The whole thing comes to look very homogeneous. Power is everywhere, and so ultimately nowhere."[17] Such a criticism is too easy, and is only possible if one forgets or ignores the complex, meticulous "micro-physical" analysis that Foucault offers of power. This analysis forces us to attend to the manifold, capillary manifestations of power, to its channels of articulation and dissemination, to where it has its real installation and institutional support, to where it has its real effects, one of which is the fabrication of the modern political subject.

Disciplinary Power: The Fabrication of Modern Identity

Disciplinary society has rather meager beginnings. It arose, in the seventeenth and eighteenth centuries, primarily in response to the nuisances of a changing Western world. While the ideologues were spouting the discourse of liberty, all around them gradual, subtle, yet profound methods of control and coercion were taking hold in the social body. Increases in population, its concentration in urban areas, the shift to a mercantile society and corresponding changes in crime and work, the industrial revolution, colonialism, epidemic disease—all this caused many problems and in response arose many subtle, tiny, seemingly insignificant techniques, mechanisms, practices, and institutions to deal with them. The complex of power relations consisting of these techniques, apparatuses, practices, and institutions Foucault calls *discipline*. Discipline began as something primarily negative, as ways to handle contagious disease, to prevent desertion in military ranks, to prevent theft and absenteeism in the factories, to deal with the increasing population in schools. Yet as disciplinary practices became entrenched and refined they began to infiltrate society as a whole and their aims became more positive—in fact, linked to the productive growth and maintenance of the entire social body.

Foucault calls discipline a "technology of power" in that it consists of certain identifiable and interconnected apparatuses, techniques, and strategies. He defines a power strategy, at least partially, as the "totality of the means put into operation to implement power effectively or to maintain it."[18] Every strategy has an object or target, and for disciplinary power this target is the *body*: at first to monitor and to punish the body, if necessary; later to turn the body into a useful, productive force. Above all, discipline acts to make the body *docile*, to produce a body that can be "manipulated, shaped, trained, which obeys, responds, becomes skillful and increases its forces. . . . A body is docile that may be subjected, used, transformed, and improved."[19] Discipline involves a whole "political technology of the body" wherein the body is invested with relations of power and domination: it is marked, trained, punished, worked, ranked, observed. The strategies of discipline directed toward the body proceed by various calculated, organized, subtle tactics, "without weapons or terror," implementing forces that bear directly, physically, materially on the body, but without recourse to violence or the dictates of ideology. Rather than appealing to the consciousness or conscience of individuals, it directly manipulates, controls, and "molds" the body through the tiniest, fussiest, most meticulous techniques applied to movements, gestures, habits, and practices, the everyday activity of the body itself. The strategy of discipline is to monitor and control the body through a direct, practical intervention concerned with the smallest details of what it does and how it lives. Discipline subjects the body, in other words, to what Foucault calls "a micro-physics of power," a power that invests bodies through a complex network of subtle mechanisms. This microphysics of power bears no resemblance to the liberal concept of power; as Foucault tells us, "The power exercised on the body is conceived not as a property, but as a strategy, that its effects of domination are attributed not to 'appropriation,' but to dispositions, manoeuvres, tactics, techniques, functionings; that one should decipher in it a network of relations, constantly in tension, in activity, rather than a privilege that one might possess . . . [or] a contract regulating a transaction or the conquest of a territory. In short, this power is . . . the overall effect of its strategic position—an effect that is manifested and sometimes entrenched by the position of those who are dominated" (*DP*, 26–27).

A micro-physics of power requires a "micro-physical" analysis in that if we were to isolate any particular objective of any particular disciplinary practice, we would find this objective, this strategy, to be very specific and tied to the concrete practices and objectives of particular social institutions: for example, to train a soldier to march correctly, to instruct a student to hold a pen in the proper manner, to separate patients in a hospital, to monitor the quality of work of factory employees. A very detailed, painstaking, micro-physical analysis allows Foucault to assert that the *general* strategy of disciplinary power is one directed toward the body as the target of its machinations. The power exercised on the body in the course of these very specific machinations and implementations is not a centrally located or appropriated power, but a network of relations—autonomous, anonymous, discontinuous—that subjects the body to a dispersed set of procedures, analyses, norms, and controls that, through the interplay of their anonymous convergence, serves both as a matrix of coercion and of individualization. Disciplinary power is above all a power of *subjection*, both in the sense of being subjugated to a set of power relations and of being turned into a subject—an identity, an *individual* with certain qualities and characteristics—as a result of this subjugation.

There are various techniques, apparatuses, and institutions through which the strategies of discipline are carried out. One of the most basic techniques regards *place*. As Foucault explains, "In the first instance, discipline proceeds from the distribution of individuals in space" (*DP*, 141). Through the technique of *enclosure*, individuals are brought under the same roof, as it were, so that disciplinary practices can be carried out more efficiently, to "derive the maximum advantages and to neutralize the inconveniences." This is done through such architectural apparatuses as schools, barracks, hospitals, and factories. Within such enclosures, whose proliferation only really began in the latter half of the eighteenth century, space is further sectioned off according to the technique of *partitioning*. Discipline proceeds by dividing space into cellular units. Each cell can serve particular functions: for example, separate hospital rooms can prevent the spread of contagious disease and allow doctors to monitor more efficiently the progress of individual patients. But partitioning in the hospital also allows for more administrative and political, and less strictly medical, functions, such as regulating the work habits of employees and keeping drugs and equipment locked away. The same kind of partitioning of space can be seen in factories, where different workers perform different tasks, and in schools, where students of different ages and abilities are assigned to different classes. The aim of partitioning, according to Foucault is "to establish presences and absences, to know where and how to locate individuals, to set up useful communications, to interrupt others, to be able to supervise the conduct of each individual, to assess it, to judge it, to calculate its qualities or merits" (*DP*, 143).

The fundamental unit of this organization and spatialization of space is the *rank*. "Discipline is an art of rank. . . . It individualizes bodies by a location that does not give them a fixed position, but distributes them and circulates them in a network of relations" (*DP*, 146). The distribution of space into cellular units not only facilitates the more efficient utilization of individuals to corresponding tasks and activities, but the arrangements themselves also serve the function of hierarchization and classification of the individuals who occupy particular places. A kind of table of rows and columns is formed, wherein the relation of cellular spaces to one another helps to determine the value and status of individuals. The rank serves to give a dimension of functional ideality to the real space marked off by architectural boundaries. We see this most evidently in schools, where *class* is the operative unit; it designates both a real architectural space that separates individuals from one another and also an evaluative designation assigned to individuals that serves to "place" them in a structural hierarchy. Disciplinary spaces "are mixed spaces: real because they govern the disposition of buildings, rooms, furniture, but also ideal, because they are projected over this arrangement of characterizations, assessments, hierarchies" (*DP*, 148). Rank allows discipline to transform "dangerous multitudes into ordered multiplicities," manageable, of course, because of simple limits on size and organization, but also *individualized* by virtue of the position they occupy in the larger tableau. The distribution and rigorous ordering of space is the most basic condition for the systematic subjection of individuals—or, more precisely, of bodies who are *turned into* identifiable individuals through a mode of subjection made possible first by the delimitation of physical space.

Delimiting space and assigning individuals to it is just the beginning of disciplinary power, however. At the most basic level, discipline is the control of activity of bodies, both individually and collectively. One technique for accomplishing this is the rigorous regulation of time: "Time penetrates the body and with it all the meticulous controls of power" (*DP*, 152). Temporal control over bodies is achieved by implementing timetables, which organize and govern the activity of individuals down to the smallest intervals. Individuals work, study, perform tasks, undergo therapy, and so on, according to definite schedules. The timetable, an apparatus borrowed from the monastery, allows discipline to "establish rhythms, impose particular occupations, regulate the cycle of repetition" (*DP*, 149). Through the regulation of time, disciplinary institutions can know where any individual should be, what she should be doing, and for how long; but more than that, the regulation of time fosters the production of *temporal norms*—expectations regarding the length of time necessary to accomplish a task, master a skill, or recuperate from an illness, against which individuals are judged and to which they are expected to conform. A soldier must disassemble and reassemble a rifle in an acceptable amount of time. Students must master appropriate educational skills within the duration of an academic year. Rank, grade, and class are all organized on institutionalized durational assessments of the activity appropriate to a given level in a hierarchy. "Thus," explains Foucault, "each individual is caught up in a temporal series which specifically defines his level or his rank" (*DP*, 159). Disciplinary time is the time of regulated, controlled, seriated, normalized activity—a time that does not merely accompany or mark the activity of individuals, but subjects them to temporal demands and expectations through which they are defined and individualized.[20]

According to Foucault, disciplinary time follows a linear model leading to a terminal state. Time is divided into graduated, successive units designed to accommodate the appropriate activities that will produce the appropriate type of individual to a particular disciplinary practice: the good soldier, the model student, the healthy patient. This requires a correlation of the activity itself to the temporal intervals in which such activity takes place. Thus, "at the heart of this seriation of time," says Foucault, is the corresponding disciplinary technique of *exercise*, "that technique by which one imposes on the body tasks that are both repetitive and different, but always graduated. By bending behavior toward a terminal state, exercise makes possible a perpetual characterization of the individual either in relation to this term, in relation to other individuals, or in relation to a type of itinerary. It thus assures, in the form of continuity and constraint, a growth, an observation, a qualification" (*DP*, 161). Exercise refers to the actual activity that takes place within specified temporal units. Historically, such exercise has been concerned with every gesture, every movement of the body, such that it will be precise, refined, perfectly appropriate to the task. It is usually repetitive and is best understood in terms of training or practice. We see this, for example, in the military drill, or in past pedagogical rituals of having students repeatedly practice certain handwriting techniques. As with time, there is also a normative aspect to exercise. It is also seriated and graduated toward a terminal state, wherein individuals are judged and ranked all along the way. Yet exercise and disciplinary time do not merely parallel one another; they are articulated onto one another so that every exercise has a specific temporal constraint, and every temporal unit is filled with a specific disciplinary exercise. Temporally regulated exercise allows discipline to produce and maintain an optimum relation between the body and its gestures, between the body and the tool it manipulates, to perform at "maximum speed and maximum efficiency" (*DP*, 154). In discipline, seriated time and graduated exercise are intrinsically united in a "temporal elaboration of the act" that dictates at once the appropriate duration and performance of any particular activity of the body.

"The chief function of disciplinary power," says Foucault, "is to 'train.'" Even though the target of disciplinary power is the individual body, with a focus on the smallest gestures, its goal is to train the individual to become a productive, contributing unit of a larger force. Discipline is not "simply an art of distributing bodies . . . but of composing forces in order to obtain an efficient machine" (*DP*, 164). Disciplinary practices are designed to produce a body that can function like a cog in the wheel of a vast machine. We can see this most evidently in the military, where the soldier is but one element in an armed force, and in industry, where the individual worker is part of a larger workforce. Discipline acts to train the soldier and the worker so that they can work in *concerted* effort with other individuals and are not just a haphazard, random arrangement of disparate units. The composition of productive forces is also the object of discipline in such institutions as education and medicine, though it is not perhaps as apparent. Disciplinary practices emerged in response to certain economic, social, and demographic changes in society. Increases in population, for example, influenced the entrenchment of disciplinary techniques in the school system. By the nineteenth century, the school had become "a machine for learning, in which each pupil, each level and each moment, if correctly combined, were permanently utilized in the general process of teaching" (*DP*, 165). Likewise, the plagues of the sixteenth and seventeenth centuries, and the general fear of contagious disease that attended the growing density of urban population, gave rise to a "political dream" of a society in which the movements of all citizens would be monitored, regulated, and controlled. This dream had its material realization, at least partially, in the disciplinary reorganization of hospitals, which became "a mechanism that pins down and partitions; it must provide a hold over this whole mobile, swarming mass . . ." (*DP*, 144). It does this, of course, by identifying and isolating individuals, their individual diseases and methods of treatment. Behind this is a political tactic, ostensibly directed toward the health and welfare of society as a whole, but in practice implemented according to a disciplinary regimentation of a broad demographic conglomerate.

The dream of a perfectly supervised society in which every individual would be accounted for, in which all activities would be regulated down to the smallest detail, gave rise to a number of disciplinary projects, says Foucault. These ranged from the great confinements in Europe to Jeremy Bentham's ideal model of perpetual surveillance: the panopticon. The panopticon was to be an annular building divided into separate cells into which individuals would be placed. A central observation tower would be able to monitor the activities of the individual at all times. While for the most part only the prison was ultimately modeled on Bentham's design, the principle of constant surveillance would become intrinsic to most modern institutions.

Perpetual surveillance is at the heart of disciplinary power. But surveillance involves much more than the crude observation afforded by a guard in a central watchtower. It consists of a complex set of simple instruments; instruments effected by, and which in turn inform and pervade, the disciplinary techniques of the distribution of space, the temporal elaboration of activity, and the composition of forces. These instruments include hierarchical observation, normalizing judgment, and the examination. These are the principle disciplinary mechanisms for the political objectification and subjection of individuals. Modern disciplinary society is a society of the *gaze*. Asserts Foucault: "The exercise of discipline presupposes a mechanism that coerces by means of observation; an apparatus in which the techniques that make it possible to see induce effects of power, and in which, conversely, the means of coercion make those on whom they are applied clearly visible" (*DP*, 170–71). Discipline achieves its effects by bringing those on whom it is exercised clearly into the view of an institutionalized and nearly perpetual gaze that subjects and coerces simply by illuminating bodies and observing them. This is accomplished in a number of different ways. Architecturally, this is achieved by altering the design and function of buildings: palaces ("built simply to be seen"), and fortresses (built to observe external space), are replaced by architecture built "to render visible those who are inside it." Hospitals, schools, factories, and prisons were constructed not just to treat, to teach, to produce, and to confine, but in such a way that these goals could be more effectively brought about in a space that afforded constant observation of those the building enclosed. The architecture itself, the way its space is partitioned and occupied, the layout of its openings and passageways, the size, shape, and function of its rooms, would "operate to transform individuals: to act on those it shelters, to provide a hold on their conduct, to carry the effects of power right to them, to make it possible to know them, to alter them" (DP, 172).

Within disciplinary institutions observation is most often carried out through a pyramidal structure of hierarchically separated relays. Modern society has seen the emergence of specialized personnel whose principle function is that of *supervision*: clerks, foremen, wardens, principals, supervisors. Supervision makes it possible to take into account "the activity of [those being observed], the way they set about their tasks, their promptness, their zeal, their behavior" (DP, 187). Yet in modern disciplinary institutions virtually all personnel—teachers, physicians, drill instructors—are a part of a hierarchy of surveillance and observation where they are relays of a disciplinary gaze: both seeing and seen, monitoring and monitored. And at the bottom of the pyramid are the workers, the students, the soldiers, the prisoners upon whom this disciplinary gaze shines most intensely, bringing into harsh relief bodies that are individualized by being seen and observed.

Supervision presupposes a set of norms by which to judge the conduct of supervised individuals. Disciplinary surveillance harbors what Foucault calls an "infra-penalty," a complex system of rewards and punishments internal to a disciplinary practice itself, operating in areas not covered by more traditional legal or juridical mechanisms. The infra-penalty concerns the slightest departures from correct behavior, the smallest aspects of activity, time consumption, speech, even sexuality: "What is specific to the disciplinary penalty is non-observance, that which does not measure up to the rule, that departs from it" (DP, 178). Sometimes the measures taken are punitive and range from "light physical punishments to minor deprivations and petty humiliations," but the disciplinary penalty is essentially *corrective*, says Foucault. It metes out punishments of exercise, "intensified, multiplied forms of training, several times repeated." An individual whose conduct falls below acceptable standards can be made to perform, repetitively and more intensely, the same tasks he would otherwise perform anyway, which has the double end of both punishment and correction.

Through such techniques discipline is able to coerce individuals to abide by certain standards of proper conduct. Discipline is the most effective neither when it is outwardly punitive or corrective in its measures, but through a process of *normalization* built into the very structure of discipline itself. Discipline is both normative, defining behavior and performance on the basis of its own internal standards of good and evil, as well as normalizing: through complex mechanisms of comparison and assessment, it establishes levels of normality to which individuals are constantly pressured to conform. The normalizing judgment of disciplinary practice differentiates and individualizes. "It measures in quantitative terms and hierarchizes in terms of value the abilities, the level, the 'nature' of individuals. It introduces, through this 'value-giving' measure, the constraint of a conformity that must be achieved" (*DP*, 183). The normalizing judgment allows for the differentiation of individuals in relation to one another based on an assessment of how such individuals conform to the normative standards of a given disciplinary practice. This assessment "fixes" the individual, both in the sense of binding the individual to a set of punishments or rewards, but also of allowing discipline to know the individual "in truth" (*DP*, 181).

The normalizing judgment brings into play all of the various techniques of disciplinary practice: of time, exercise, rank, and surveillance. Subjecting individuals to temporal constraints and demands of training allows discipline to make assessments and judge individuals in relation to others. This makes it possible to separate individuals according to their level of skill, mastery, or progress in the tasks demanded. Thus, they can be distributed according to rank or grade. Rank has the double role, says Foucault, of marking gaps and hierarchizing skills, qualities, and aptitudes, but also of punishing and rewarding (*DP*, 181). The hierarchical structure of rank permits discipline to reward by allowing individuals to advance to higher levels, and to punish by simply "reversing the process." The classification of individuals is normalizing in that it delimits rules and expectations according to the level individuals occupy. These expectations can be quantified and codified such that they constitute an established *norm*, which governs the assessment of all individuals who occupy a particular rank. The norm functions "as a minimal threshold, as an average to be respected or as an optimum towards which one must move" (*DP*, 183). In this way, the norm acts to distinguish the normal from the abnormal, to identify deviations from acceptable behavior. Moreover, the normalizing judgment situates the individual in a field of comparison and differentiation that allows disciplinary surveillance to fix its gaze even more firmly on the individual, to not only control by making visible, but to judge, to assess, to mark, to *know*.

The principal disciplinary mechanism that combines the techniques of surveillance and normalizing judgment, and which turns them into a "normalizing gaze," is the examination. The examination, which has "highly ritualized" forms in such diverse institutions as the hospital, the school, and the military, "establishes over individuals a visibility through which one differentiates them and judges them" (DP, 184). The examination brings the individual forward into the spotlight of an assessing gaze. It determines, through a structured evaluation of the individual's health, knowledge, attitude, or skill, *who* that individual is and where she belongs in an established hierarchy. But more than that, or rather through this same differentiation and assessment, the examination represents the point of convergence between power and knowledge. "The examination," says Foucault, "introduced a whole mechanism that linked to a certain type of the formation of knowledge a certain form of the exercise of power" (DP, 187). In the examination, individuals are subjected to a process of objectification, that is, turned into objects of knowledge, of scientific or pseudo-scientific inquiry. The examination not only permits the transmission of knowledge and the assessment of its appropriation by those examined; on the basis of this transmission-assessment dynamic is produced a whole body of knowledge pertaining to those who are examined, and which in turn becomes the principle of their subjection. That is, a whole corpus of data built upon the assessment of individuals permits the construction of scientific classifications and categories through which subjects are known and individualized. Through such "small techniques of notation, of registration, of constituting files, of arranging facts in columns and tables," the individual is made into a "case," an object of analysis and description. This acts as "a means of control and a method of domination" in that the "truth" based on such analysis is reinvested back into disciplinary practice and brought to bear on the individual. In fact, the examination produces a massive proliferation of documents and registration which not only makes it possible to analyze and characterize specific individuals, to give the individual "as his status his own individuality," but also this "whole apparatus of writing" permits the production of a comparative body of knowledge pertaining to groups, to populations, to the "nature of man" in general.[21] This knowledge takes the form of discourses of truth about who and what we are, and which have material implementation in disciplinary practice. In this way knowledge permits the subjection of individuals to a power which coerces by making known, predicated on the data garnered and distributed through the disciplinary technique of examination. Thus, in so many ways, "the examination is at the center of the procedures that constitute the individual as effect and object of power, as effect and object of knowledge" (*DP*, 192).

"Discipline 'makes' individuals," says Foucault. In general terms, the type of individuality that is produced by discipline has four basic characteristics: "it is cellular (by the play of spatial distributions), it is organic (by the coding of activities), it is genetic (by the accumulation of time), it is combinatory (by the composition of forces)" (*DP*, 167). The cellular, organic, genetic, combinatory individual of discipline is a product, a fabrication whose identity is the result of a material instantiation of a disciplinary strategy, a strategy that brings into play a whole network of techniques, apparatuses, and mechanisms, a whole technology of power through which individuals are spatially, temporally, and hierarchically distributed, observed, judged, and examined; subjected to real material tasks and practices; differentiated and individualized; and through which they are analyzed, registered, and known "in truth." The power of discipline is to turn disparate, random, unorganized, useless, potentially dangerous bodies into docile bodies, subjects—individuals who may be trained, used, monitored, controlled.

Yet these are only general characteristics. The real subjects produced by discipline are very specific and linked to specific practices, institutions, and bodies of knowledge, to specific strategies, tactics, procedures, and goals. Disciplinary subjects are the student, the soldier, the factory worker, the prisoner, the patient, the colonial ranger. Through various processes of hierarchization, normalization, and documentation, these subjects are even further differentiated and individualized from one another: the overachiever, the delinquent, the recidivist, the deserter, the healthy, the sick, the normal, the abnormal. Discipline produces a proliferation of different individuals, but they are all at bottom the effects of the same technology of power, the same "political anatomy of the body."

Foucault studies power where "its intention, if it has one, is completely invested in its real and effective practices." His analysis of power proceeds at the level of the multifarious ongoing processes, practices, and mechanisms that subject bodies, govern gestures, dictate behaviors. In terms of the constitution of political subjects, this represents an important departure from more traditional analyses of power. In fact, Foucault sees his approach as the "exact opposite" of Thomas Hobbes's *Leviathan* and of all political discourse wherein subjects are animated by the spirit of sovereignty.[22] Instead of the conscious exercise of power by political subjects whose existence is taken for granted, we have the anonymous circulation of power in which political subjects are effects of this circulation. By analyzing these relations of power—apart from conscious intentions, from central distributions, from the theory of right—Foucault hopes to "discover how it is that subjects are gradually, progressively, really, and materially constituted" in order to "grasp subjection in its material instance as a constitution of subjects" (*P/K*, 97).

As a network of relations, power is not—contrary to the liberal, juridical view of power—something that can be *possessed*. Properly speaking, no one *has* power; power is not something that can be found in or attributed to any one particular source of exercise or dissemination. Power is everywhere, says Foucault. "It is never localized here or there, never in anybody's hands, never appropriated as a commodity or piece of wealth" (*P/K*, 98). The idea of power as a possession is commensurate with the liberal notion of the autonomous individual. But individuals are not so much the owners of power as they are its vehicles, and its effects. As Foucault argues, "The individual is not be conceived as a sort of elementary nucleus, a primitive atom, a multiple and inert material on which power comes to fasten or against which it happens to strike, and so doing subdues or crushes individuals. In fact, it is already one of the prime effects of power that certain bodies, certain gestures, certain discourses, certain desires, come to be identified and constituted as individuals. The individual, that is, is not the *vis-a-vis* of power; it is, I believe, one of its prime effects. The individual is an effect of power, and at the same time, or precisely to the extent to which it is that effect, it is the element of its articulation. The individual which power has constituted is at the same time its vehicle" (*P/K*, 98). Individuals are always simultaneously undergoing and exercising power, says Foucault. They are mediums or channels through which power circulates, and at the same time, *as* individuals, they are effects of this circulation of power.

The private autonomous individual serves, or can serve, a very important political function in the modern state, a function tied to the state's new (i.e., beginning roughly with the Treaty of Westphalia) historical status as a nation in competition with other nations. The competition between nations takes many forms, not the least of which is war. Thus, the state has need of soldiers, to protect its interests, to serve as the instruments of its preservation and the index of its strength. The state has recourse to disciplinary mechanisms required to turn individuals into good soldiers, at least from a technical point of view. Yet is this enough to ensure that these individuals will "lay their life on the line" for the sake of the state?

The soldier is not to be understood as simply a body trained in the tactics of warfare, but rather as someone who "fights for his country." Through discourses of patriotism and nationalism, which are disseminated through institutional channels to individuals from at least the time they are able to "pledge allegiance," disciplinary power binds the individual to the nation, and in so doing helps to preserve the integrity of the nation itself.[23] One instrument for this integration, but by no means the only one, is the linking of the nation conceptually with the preservation of the individual's rights and freedoms. Through the notion of the private autonomous individual the state is able to mobilize the masses in the service of its own protection and preservation.[24] Here is precisely where the discourse of rights and freedoms is brought into play and the nation becomes an *enunciative modality* for the emergence of political subjects. In fact, as we shall see in the next section, much of modern political identity is informed by reference to a national identity, either positively or negatively.[25] Moreover, this identity is structured and animated by the discourse of threat that we saw take shape in Enlightenment political philosophy.

Enunciative Modalities: From Wilderness to Nation

Foucault would have us make a distinction between the philosophical subject and speaking individuals (speakers of discourse) who become subjects by virtue of the nature of the discourse they speak. Strictly speaking, the philosophical subject never *speaks,* but is only *spoken about.* The philosophical subject can only be the *object* of discourse; it is the attempt by philosophy to ground discourse in some transcendental unity. The philosophical subject is a metaphysical abstraction that tries to explain the pure dispersion of discourse, to serve as its condition of possibility. On the other hand, how do we account for the subjectivity of actual speaking individuals who impress their reality upon us in the form of flesh and blood?[26] The subjectivity of these individuals needs to be explained in terms of what Foucault calls the "enunciative modalities" of their real existence as subjects. Enunciative modalities refer to "the various relations [i.e., *statuses*], the various *sites*, the various *positions* that [a subject] can occupy or be given when making a discourse."[27] The statuses, sites, and positions in relation to the objects of a discursive practice are the possible ways of "being" a subject, determined by discourse. Most commentators have tended to overlook Foucault's thought on enunciative modalities. However, I would argue that it is perhaps the most viable aspect of his work on discourse, especially as regards the practical instantiation of the discursive. In fact, as we shall see, these modalities can serve as a linchpin between the various domains of genealogy, effectually conjoining Foucault's work on discourse, power, and ethics.

The enunciative modality of status refers to *who* is speaking a given discourse. This *who* is less a matter of the identity of the subject than of the right or privilege of the individual to speak. Identity, in fact, is a surface effect or function of this privilege. As Foucault asks, "What is the status of the individuals who—alone—have the right, sanctioned by law or tradition, juridically defined or spontaneously accepted, to proffer such a discourse?" (*AK*, 50). Not everyone can speak a given discourse (or at least not be taken seriously in attempting to do so); the individual must meet certain criteria of acceptance involving such factors as competence, knowledge, institutional support, group affiliation, and the role of the individual in relation to society as a whole. Such criteria and the relations between them are especially evident, for example, in the status of the doctor in society: "Medical statements cannot come from anybody; their value, efficacy, even their therapeutic powers, and, generally speaking, their existence as medical statements cannot be dissociated from the statutorily defined person who has the right to make them . . ." (*AK*, 51).[28]

Subjectivity is also a function of the institutional sites "from which the [subject] makes his discourse, and from which this discourse derives its legitimate source and point of application" (*AK*, 51). Rather than who is speaking, the site refers to *where* the individual is speaking. The place where discourse is spoken determines to a great extent who the subjects are that are speaking; it determines the particular modality of subjectivity that becomes attached to individuals occupying a particular site. Medical discourse, for example, takes place in the institutional sites of the hospital, private practice, and the laboratory, observes Foucault. It is in such sites that medical discourse arises, takes shape, undergoes transformation; it is here that medical discourse has its practical and theoretical points of application. And it is here that the subject we know as the doctor emerges by virtue of occupying these sites in which and from which medical discourse *takes place*.[29]

A third, more complicated enunciative modality of subjectivity refers to the various *positions* the subject may occupy in relation to the objects of a discursive practice itself. This is not so much a question of who or where, but of *how* the subject bears a relation to the pertinent objects of a discourse, objects which are defined in terms of the regularities (sameness of statements) of given discursive formation. For example, sexual deviation is an object of psychiatric discourse. The relation to sexual deviation on the part of the patient-subject might be one of guilt and confession, while the psychoanalyst might bear a relation to this same object as a listening and curative subject.

These enunciative modalities determine the modes of subjectivity that characterize real individuals who speak discourse. "Thus conceived," says Foucault, "discourse is not the majestically unfolding manifestation of a thinking, knowing, speaking subject, but, on the contrary, a totality, in which the dispersion of the subject and his discontinuity with himself may be determined" (AK, 55). On the one hand, then, we have the philosophical subject, a metaphysical spectre which was never more than the object of a theoretical discourse. On the other hand, there are real individuals who become subjects by virtue of having a certain privileged status, of occupying a particular site, and of bearing certain relations to the objects of a discursive practice itself. Occasionally both of these understandings of subjectivity merge, sometimes antagonistically and irreconcilably, in the same subject. Such is the case with the political subject.

The subjectivity of individuals, the so-called speakers and hearers of political discourse, who actually, or even ideally, populate a state, needs to be understood in terms of the enunciative modalities—the statuses, sites, and positions—of their existence as political subjects. Enunciative modalities refer to the ways a discursive practice is attached to bodies in space. This attachment or imposition gives meaning to these bodies as political subjects.[30]

The status of political subjects, the privilege accorded certain individuals to speak certain discourses, is very much a function of the type of political discourse informing the government to which individuals belong. Apart from its institutional machinery, government is a material expression, at least in principle, of a particular discursive practice concerning such ideological elements as representation, the distribution of goods, judicial practices, and the like. Obviously, a democracy will give a different political status to individuals than will a monarchy. There will be different discursive expectations and possibilities in different forms of government. An individual speaking a discourse of governmental accountability might be identified as a democrat in one country and a revolutionary in another, depending on the form of government and the discursive expectations attached to it. Political subjectivity, then, is determined to a great extent by the political structure, to the extent, that is, that this structure is a material expression of a given discursive practice. The status of political subjects is defined by a specific distribution of rights and power that is determined in a given discursive network. Thus, status is, in a way, *assigned* to individuals by virtue of being a part of a state, which is an economy of discursive determinations and delimitations.

Because the political status of individuals is so tied to the discursive practice of a particular form of government, the subjectivity of such individuals will likewise be determined by the various positions they bear in relation to the objects of such discourse. For example, the distribution of goods is an object of the discourse of capitalist democracies; a liberal will bear a different relation to that object than a conservative, obviously. Yet, it is important to realize that such positions presuppose an established discursive practice that provides the various possibilities for subjectival relation to the objects of a discourse. It is the position of individuals in relation to such objects that determines their subjectivity. It is not that we merely *represent* such positions in a discourse; without the discourse, the discursive practice, the various possibilities for subjectivity—of relating politically or ideologically to certain objects—would not be possible.

There are a variety of possible sites from which political discourse may be spoken by real individuals as political subjects. These include the more obvious political institutions such as the floor of the U.S. Senate, the courtroom, and the voting hall. Yet political discourse is also found in the market place; the home, to the extent it is owned property, is subject to taxation, and is protected by law; the battlefield; and the classroom as a site of claims to the right to an education, of controversy over desegregation, and even of the Pledge of Allegiance. Also, the media have always been a particularly influential "site" of political discourse.

If, as Hannah Arendt suggests, modern politics is the more or less peaceful, more or less violent struggle for power, then the enunciative modalities of the modern political subject will be modalities animated by this struggle. The various objects of political discourse, in relation to which individuals are identified as political subjects, are understood in terms of this struggle for power, or more precisely, in terms of a threat to the legitimate limits of power. Rights and freedoms can be taken away, political obligation can be violated, property can be stolen, power is something that can be abused. It is the possibility of such violations which animates the political subject. This does not mean that political subjects live in constant fear, with guns by their door, but it does suggest that everything they do or say or that is important to them *as* political subjects presupposes a discourse in which the concepts of rights, freedoms, property, and power have been given meaning—*value*—by the threat of their loss. Political discourse is a kind of parody of negative theology in that the discursive objects through which it delimits political subjects are precisely those that are defined, or only make sense, in terms of a lack or absence, whether real or potential.

Perhaps the most important enunciative modality of subjects refers to the site of their emergence. Subjectivity is the most defined, the most articulated, where it is bound to an architectural structure or an institution. Here the discourse which delimits subjects can be refined, perpetuated, and put into practice: workers in a factory, soldiers at a military base, patients in a hospital. Yet the most important site of the emergence of modern political subjects is neither a building nor an institution, and it is only by means of an arbitrary delimitation of space that we can even call it a "place." This site, I would contend, is the *nation*, what Benedict Anderson has defined as an "imagined political community."[31]

The nation delimits a space of political subjectivity; it gives subjects an identity by virtue of their identification with the nation: as an American or German, as Japanese or Bengali. It is a place both real and ideal; real to the extent that it designates fixed (or disputed) geographical boundaries, ideal in that it is a place whose boundaries are defined less by fences, rivers, or mountains than by political subjects who share what Walker Connor calls an "essential psychological bond."[32] That bond has less to do with shared language, shared economy, or shared territory than it does with having a common *discourse*— through which certain components are articulated as shared, that is, *national*.[33]

For all the variation in nations and national identities, we see two common themes recurring in national discourse, in the discourse through which a nation defines itself as such, according to Max Weber. The first theme is that of a "common political destiny" and the second to a myth of "common descent."[34] In this sense, a nation has less to do with physical space than it has to do with time. National identity is both constituted and defined by a temporal dimension, by a "presence" that is at once past-prescribed and future-oriented. The latter idea, the myth of common descent, has to do with the idea that the people of a nation share a common genetic origin. This may have something to do with the word *nation* itself, which, as Connor points out, derives from the Latin verb *nasci*, "to be born."[35] For centuries the word *nation* was used almost interchangeably with the word *race*. It was not uncommon, Connor reminds us, to refer to the English or German races rather than nations. However, says Connor, this sense of common origin or descent need not be based on actual historical fact. That would be irrelevant, he argues, to the constitution of a nation and, what amounts to the same thing, its self-recognition *as* a nation. "What ultimately matters is not *what is* but *what people believe is*. And a subconscious belief in the group's separate origin and evolution is an important ingredient of national psychology."[36]

Oddly, however, Connor wants to say that America "is not a nation in the pristine sense of the word" precisely because the American people lack this (sense of) common blood or genetic origin. On the contrary, the discourse through which America is defined is ingrained with both of those elements—the myths of common origin and of common destiny—that Weber ascribes to nations generally. In fact, in the nationalist discourse of the United States, both of those elements are present as two sides of the same coin.

The notion of a common origin is seen not just in the fact that Americans tend to view themselves as a nation of immigrants, all hailing from foreign shores, but that our ancestors, of whatever "blood" origin, faced a hostile and forbidding land, a wilderness full of beasts and savages. Says Frederick Jackson Turner, "the frontier promoted the formation of a composite nationality for the American people. . . . In the crucible of the frontier the immigrants were Americanized, liberated, and fused into a mixed race, English in neither nationality nor characteristics. The process has gone on from the early days to our own."[37] The American myth of descent has to do with a sense of coming from a stock of people who plunged headlong into this wilderness and who tamed it with little more than their own courage, ingenuity, and personal fortitude. Of course, this myth, this discourse, tends to be highly white, male, and Anglo-European. It says nothing of the Middle Passage, of that segment of the population forced to come to America whose lineage was considered dark, alien, and "inferior." Yet in many ways America represents a perpetual frontier, a frontier of spirit rather than of territory. Observes Sacvan Bercovitch, "Traditionally, a frontier was a border dividing one people from another. It implied differences between nations. In a sense, antebellum Americans recognized such differences—their frontier separated them from the Indians—but they could hardly accept the restriction as permanent. This was God's Country, was it not? So they effected a decisive shift in the meaning of frontier, from barrier to threshold. Even as they spoke of their frontier as a meeting ground between two civilizations, Christian and pagan, they redefined it, in an inversion characteristic of the myth-making imagination, to mean a *figural* outpost, the outskirts of the advancing kingdom of God."[38] American immigrants of virtually any ethnic origin, at virtually any historical time, can rather easily appropriate the discourse of frontier spirit in the face of a hostile land and make it a part of their own family history; as such, it belongs with the larger national mythology.

This is in no way at odds with the controversial "Turner Thesis" regarding the closing down of the "real" frontier at the beginning of the twentieth century (even if the thesis were true). In fact, the ideality of the frontier is one main source of its persisting and even flourishing here at the turn of the century. For example, it was a central motif in the literature of immigrants in the twentieth century and is without doubt the dominant trope with regard to space exploration, the "Final Frontier."[39]

Of course, this New World frontier mentality is at the very heart of what I have called savage nobility. The measure of that nobility tends to be the degree to which one is able to tame one's own personal quarter of American wilderness. One of the sad ironies of this mythos is that those who were originally considered "savages" in the conventional sense—I have in mind native American Indians and native Africans, but we could include other groups, past and present—were/are the ones for whom the American landscape was/is the most hostile, the most fraught with danger. Nevertheless, even these marginalized and disenfranchised groups have been able to appropriate the frontier motif of the American mythos by conceiving of their own marginalization and disenfranchisement as a hostile "wilderness" of sorts, to be overcome by personal industry and perseverance.[40]

Thus, one common discursive element that Weber attributes to national identity can be found in a shared sense of the frontier. To be American is to have conquered a hostile wilderness of sorts; herein lies the myth of common descent.

The other common discursive element of a national identity, according to Weber, is a sense of common political destiny. In America this destiny is largely a reflection and a projection of that same frontier mentality—the idea that America is destined to conquer all of the wildernesses of the world, natural, social, moral, political, economic and technological. By the middle of the nineteenth century this mythos would become explicit and would be concretized in the jingoistic discourse of "Manifest Destiny," a term coined by John Louis O'Sullivan in 1845 in a popular magazine with a nationalistic orientation. The notion of Manifest Destiny would be appealed to to justify the territorial expansion of the United States for the next fifty years or more. This expansion was about much more than the acquisition of land, of course. It was about sending a beacon of light into the darkness, of bringing American values and ideology to that part of the world that remained a kind of wilderness, awaiting its penetration, appropriation, and spiritual intubation. This era paralleled the period of high colonialism during which native peoples—savages—would have Western culture imposed upon them in often cruel and violent ways.[41] Yet colonialism proper differed from the expansionist projects of nineteenth-century

America. Americans were "giving" something, not taking it away: namely, freedom and the liberal-democratic values of self-government. Of course, America was willing to go to war with anyone who refused to accept this "gift." And well into the twentieth century, even after harsh political realities brought the expansionist policies of Manifest Destiny to a close, America continued to define itself as a nation in similar terms, that is, not only as the land of liberty, but of its fount and guardian around the globe. Any nation that did not share these values automatically became a threat, and was thus subject to American interventions, in the form of trade, aid, diplomacy, and, if necessary, war.

According to Anthony D. Smith, a demotic *ethnie* moves toward becoming a civic nation when, in addition to economic unity and the identification of a "universally recognized 'homeland,'" its members are turned into "legal citizens by mobilizing them for political ends and conferring on each common civil, social and political rights and obligations."[42] Such a process appears to parallel the establishment of civil society as described in social contract theory, through a similar conferral of rights and obligations. In this sense, to conjoin the discourse of contractual political subjectivity with the discourse of nationhood, it becomes apparent that the (Western civic) nation is not simply the site where the political struggle for power takes place; it *is a place* to the extent that it is animated by this struggle. In fact, it is when this struggle is most intense that political subjects have their most intense awareness of "belonging" to a nation, which in turn intensifies their own sense of "being" a political subject.[43] The plurality of nations in the modern world allows this struggle to have an almost global scope. In this sense, the nation is the very *embodiment* of a discourse of threat; Jack C. Plano and Milton Greenberg have put it, "In the modern era, the nation has provided the unifying concept with which the individual can identify. The results have not always been good, for many national groups have built their unity on a *real or imagined fear* and a shared hatred of other groups or on a desire to bring others under their dominion. The conflicting national interests, which characterize the world's state system, have contributed to the instability of international relations and to the outbreak of wars."[44] It is within the boundaries of the nation that those two political subjects emerge who underline, from mutually opposing vantage points, the integrity of the nation: the *patriot* and the *traitor*. The patriot and the traitor mirror one another, reflecting positively or negatively a translucent danger, played out like a dramatic scene on the vast, politically charged stage of the nation. One is a kind of hero, the other always a villain, but neither makes sense without a country to serve or to betray. "Outside" the boundaries of the nation, on the other hand, we find *allies* or *enemies*: political subjects, or bodies (nations) of political subjects, again which are opposed to each other in terms of the threat they pose to the nation.

The drawing of lines on a map is a political act giving place to subjects who are defined in terms of their identification with, or their relation to, the nation.[45] The relation to the nation can be—from without or within—one of loyalty, or hostility, or even neutrality, but all three of these possible relations presuppose (sometimes concealed and at the extremities perhaps, but there nonetheless) a possible or actual threat to the nation. Does it need to be said that the nation is a condition of possibility for nationalism, the epitome of political threat? Per Plano and Greenberg, "Most modern wars have been products of extreme nationalism in which mass emotional enthusiasm has been marshaled for one nation against another."[46] It seems almost impossible, at some point at least, to define political subjects except in terms of threat. Can this be traced back to a political discourse whose delimitation of the juridical limits of power and political obligation was based on the hypothetical threat of the state of nature? Is it a coincidence that nation-states were officially recognized for the first time by the Peace of Westphalia in 1648, only three years before Hobbe's *Leviathan* was published? Is it an accident of etymology that both *nation* and *nature* are derived from the Latin *natus*, which is the past participle of *nasci*? Could it be that the nation is just a state of nature with a written constitution to sanction its violence?

These questions strike at the heart of modern political identity. In the enunciatve modality of the nation, we see the coalescence of the discourse of threat and disciplinary inscriptions of the body. The Savage Noble is constructed, in part, precisely to be marshaled in service of this "imagined political community" that we call America. Yet of course, human beings are not like modeling clay, inert material passively shaped into this form or that. What contribution does the individual herself make toward her fabrication as an American? What do we ourselves do to in fact *become* an individual?

4

Political Subjectivation and Self-Formation

I have dealt with the modern theoretical constructions that were concerned with the subject in general. . . . I have also dealt with the more practical understandings formed in those institutions like hospitals, asylums, and prisons where certain subjects became objects of knowledge and at the same time objects of domination. Now I wish to study those forms of understanding which the subject creates about himself.

—Michel Foucault, "Truth and Subjectivity"

I must confess that I am much more interested in problems about techniques of the self and things like that rather than sex . . . sex is boring.

—Michel Foucault, "On the Genealogy of Ethics"

Thus far, we have indicated the discursive and nondiscursive practices that delimit certain possibilities for subjectival understanding and configuration. We have, however, left an important dimension of the emergence of the savage noble out of the account: that is, what contribution does the individual herself make toward her constitution as a political subject?

To answer this question we now move to the third phase of Foucault's thought, a phase marked by a transformation in his work on the history of sexuality, on which he was working up to the time of his death. Foucault's work in this area is concerned primarily with the self-constitution of the ethical subject, specifically as it relates to desire and the experience of sexuality, but the models of understanding he provides can be adapted rather easily to the study of the self-formation of the political subject. (In fact, all forms of self-subjectivation may be viewed broadly as ethical activities.) In this chapter, I will highlight Foucault's genealogy of ethics in the later volumes of his *History of Sexuality*, focusing especially on the "technologies of the self" through which individuals constitute themselves as subjects.

Following Foucault's general schema, I will then trace out a technology of the self delineated in one of the most important texts from the liberal tradition, namely, John Stuart Mill's *On Liberty*. Finally, I will sketch out the close affinities between the modes of modern political identity that make up the "Political Spectrum." We shall see that the political spectrum delineates liberals and conservatives through reference to qualitative differences in how these identities understand Mill's foundational value of toleration. However, if we consider the experience of Native Americans, the original Noble Savages, we see that toleration is anything but intrinsically virtuous, that in fact it is morally ambiguous and, potentially at least, politically dangerous.

Technologies of the Self: Sex/Ethics/Politics

There was nearly an eight-year gap between the publication of the first volume of Foucault's *History of Sexuality* and the second, *The Use of Pleasure*. The lacuna is significant because it contained a remarkable shift and transformation in Foucault's project. The first volume, originally published in French as *La Volenté de savoir*, belongs, in both its focus and methodology, with the analysis of power/knowledge relations found, for example, in *Discipline and Punish*.[1] In this introductory volume Foucault lays the groundwork for a genealogy of the "biopolitics" that permeates our modern experience of sexuality. Originally, the later volumes of his proposed six-volume project would elaborate the normalizing effects of this biopower, focusing particularly on modern state apparatuses' concern with the population, and on the "incitement to discourse" about sex and one's sexuality which has proliferated in modern society.[2]

Like the work in discursive regularities and power relations that preceded it, Foucault's project now would also be primarily concerned with the last two or three centuries of our history.[3] Yet Foucault would begin his analysis, in the second volume, originally entitled *Flesh and Body*, with the premodern Christian experience of sexuality.[4] Foucault recognized that Christianity stood at the threshold of our modern experience of sexuality—even more, that it permeated that experience "in depth." On the one hand, the political rationality of "governmentality," which characterized modern interventions into the population, involved an appropriation of Christian pastoral power. Similarly, the incitement to discourse about sex in modern society involved a secularized (and medically sanctioned) appropriation of the Christian confessional and its hermeneutics of desire.

Thus, there were two "prongs" to Foucault's original analysis, both of which led him to a consideration of the Christian ethic of the flesh. This had two important affects on the trajectory of his project. On the one hand, his investigation of the connection between the power relations pertaining to the modern disciplinary state and the Christian pastorate became oriented around "the problematic of governance."[5] That is, he became increasingly preoccupied with "the refinement, the elaboration and installation . . . of techniques for 'governing individuals'—that is, for 'guiding their conduct.'"[6] He began to pose the question of the exercise of power in terms of the question of government. But now *government* took on a broader (and at the same time, a more narrow) meaning for Foucault.[7] Rather than designating a political rationality and technology of power peculiar to impersonal state apparatuses, government referred, in addition, to the ways in which this power made contact with individuals, that is, the techniques for governing the "modes of action" of individuals, of controlling their conduct, of manipulating their behavior, of determining, in fact, the very way they conceived of themselves. What differentiated this from Foucault's earlier analysis of such techniques (in disciplinary practices, for example) was that now Foucault was particularly concerned with the forms and modalities in which individuals themselves appropriate such techniques, how external coercions become "self-control," how government becomes "self-government."

Foucault's turn to governance would alter his approach to the history of sexuality. Recognizing that modern discourse on human sexuality invoked a theme of "desiring man" inherited from the Christian tradition, he came to the conclusion that "one could not very well analyze the formation and development of the experience of sexuality from the 18th century onward, without doing a historical and critical study dealing with desire and the desiring subject."[8] Thus, he resolved to do a genealogy that focused first on the Christian "hermeneutics of desire." This hermeneutics involved certain "practices by which individuals were led to focus attention on themselves," practices designed to make individuals search out "the truth of their being," whereby sinful desires could be recognized and expurgated through practices of confession and penitence. Here Foucault began to recognize "the formation and development of a practice of self."[9] Thereafter Foucault's principle concern would be with such practices or "techniques of the self." That is, "instead of studying sexuality on the borders of knowledge and power,"[10] he would "study the modes according to which individuals are given to recognize themselves as sexual subjects."[11] However, pursuing this line of research took Foucault "farther and farther from the chronological outline" he had originally envisioned. To understand the formation of the Christian ethic of the flesh he found it necessary "to go further back," to the experience of sexuality found in late antiquity, which in turn took him to third- and fourth-century B.C. Greece.[12] This unprecedented expansion of Foucault's historical purview fulfilled an important genealogical requirement.[13] From a practical standpoint, it caused a considerable delay simply because Foucault was neither a Latinist nor a Hellenist and had to work with a whole body of material with which he was, for the most part, unfamiliar.

In any event, before he died in 1984, Foucault managed to complete three new volumes in the history of sexuality: *L'usage des plaisirs*, *Le souci de soi*, and the unpublished *Les Aveux de la chair*.[14] However, these works appeared "in a form that is altogether different" from the one Foucault first imagined (*UP*, 3). In the first place, we find in them a "theoretical shift," away from the manifold relations of power, to the subject. That is, Foucault's project in these works is to identify "the forms and modalities of the relation to self by which the individual constitutes and recognizes himself qua subject" (*UP*, 6). Foucault wants to understand how it is that an individual establishes "a relationship of self with self" through which she forms and identifies herself in particular ways. This is the process Foucault calls subjectivation, a process of self-formation, of appropriating certain beliefs, ideals or ideologies, of adopting certain practices and modes of comportment, of selecting regimes of behavior and rules of conduct through which "a human being turns him- or herself into a subject."[15]

There is another aspect of Foucault's theoretical shift that contributes to the difference in form. In researching the techniques of self through which individuals have historically formed themselves as sexual subjects, he became aware of a recurring dimension of this subjectivation. In spite of the diversity of forms through which individuals have constituted a relationship of self to the experience of sexuality, this experience has always been constituted as a *moral domain*. Why this ethical concern? asks Foucault. Why have we consistently turned sexuality into a moral experience?[16] These questions would come to structure Foucault's inquiry. In fact, he is doing less a history of sexuality than a genealogy of "ethics."

Foucault's use of the term *ethics* differs significantly from that of more traditional Anglo-American philosophy. For Foucault, *ethics* refers to "the elaboration of a form of relation to self that enables an individual to fashion himself as a subject of ethical conduct" (*UP*, 251). To become a subject of ethical conduct requires a complex process of self-formation wherein the individual establishes a *rapport à soi* designating "the kind of relationship you ought to have with yourself."[17] The "ought" of a relation to self is dynamic rather than static; that is, it is not the "ought" that informs a codified set of moral rules or strictures, but rather, it is the "ought" which the individual establishes for herself, an "ought" that gives form to the self, expresses what happens when the self says to itself, "This is what is important to me. This is how I shall act. This is what I shall become." Becoming—or rather, forming oneself as—a subject is a matter of establishing an "ought" in relation to a domain of experience. Or, more precisely, the self's establishing an "ought" in relation to itself defines the domain of experience which the self has as a subject. Foucault shows that the relationship to self can take many forms. It can be governed by the dictates of a rigorous code of behavior but it does not have to be so. Nor is that, strictly speaking, Foucault's concern. Rather, ethics is, in a broad sense and to borrow from the Greeks, a kind of *techne tou biou,* an art of life. Ethics is the way in which individuals give form to their selves, to their lives, by forming themselves as subjects.

The methods of analysis that Foucault employs here could be applied to any form of subjectivity: political, religious, familial. It just happens that he chose sexual subjectivity. Yet what of political subjectivity? Foucault says, "You do not have toward yourself the same kinds of relationship when you constitute yourself as a political subject . . . and when you try to fulfill your desires in a sexual relationship."[18] On the other hand, in the ancient world at least, there was a great deal of overlap in the problematizations that structured both their political and sexual forms of subjectivity. In the classical Greeks we find an "ethics of men made for men" where the individual's ultimate goal was to reach a "point where the relationship with oneself would become isomorphic with the relationship of domination, hierarchy, and authority that one expected, as a man, a free man, to establish over his inferiors" (*UP,* 83). The dimensions of political subjectivity are almost identical to those of one's sexual subjectivity (in that it is structured by virtually the same sorts of problematization). We have, first of all, a "heautocratic structure of the subject" defined by the same role polarities of masculine/feminine, active/passive, ruler/ruled. This, as well, turned on the question of "right use," which was adjusted according to one's status; the standards of appropriate conduct, whether in the domain of sexuality or politics, appealed to a public distinction in which the virtue of moderation was especially expected of "those who had rank, status, and responsibility in the city" (*UP,* 61). In fact, as Foucault demonstrates by citing such works as the *Memorabilia* and the *Republic,* one of the most important principles of government was to develop a "moderate state" in which the passions and desires of the many were controlled and governed by a few exemplary individuals who gained control over themselves. Thus, the ethical work one performed on oneself was designed to acquire not only a self-mastery, but a mastery over others. Says Foucault, "the development of personal virtues, of *enkrateia* in particular, was not essentially different from the development that enabled one to rise above other citizens to a position of leadership" (*UP*, 75). There was, in fact, a continuity and an isomorphism among governing oneself, governing one's household, and governing a city—they were "three practices of the same type." And, finally, the *telos* of the individual is coextensive with that of the state: their fates are intertwined. The freedom afforded to the individual through the cultivation of self-mastery is "indispensable" to the welfare of the state. Foucault quotes, from the *Politics*, "A State is good in virtue of the goodness of the citizens who have a share in the government. In our state all the citizens have a share in the government. We have therefore to consider how a man can become a good man. True, it is possible for all to be good collectively, without each being good individually. But the better thing is that each individual citizen should be good. The goodness of all is necessarily involved in the goodness of each."[19] In a broad sense, the individual's freedom, his mastery of his own passion and desires, was essential to the "well being and good order of the city" (*UP*, 79). In a more narrow sense, however, this freedom was reserved to a mode of political subjectivity that was heautocratic and privileged in character. That is, "in its full, positive form," this freedom referred to "a power that one brought on oneself in the power one exercised over others" (*UP*, 80). The virtue of moderation qualified an individual to exercise authority over others, which was a very important dimension of the individual's freedom. Those who did not govern, in fact, "received their principle of moderation" from those who did; thus, the "nonruler" had less freedom simply by virtue of his subordinate position. All of these concerns are expressed in the "two exemplary moral figures" on which political subjectivity in this period is modeled: (1) negatively by the vicious tyrant, and (2) "the positive image of the leader who was capable of exercising a strict control over himself in the authority he exercised over others" (*UP*, 81).

Later, in the Greco-Roman period to the second or third century A.D., the connection between one's political subjectivity and one's sexual subjectivity will be far less isomorphic and much more problematic. In fact, the collapse of the Greek city-state precipitated a "crisis of the subject" in which the self and its relations to others in the social and political sphere were put into question as never before. This crisis was characterized by a "problematization of political activity" that paralleled the political transformations of this period.[20] The more complex political structure of the state brought about a "relativization" in the exercise of power. For the individual, this manifested itself in a Stoical detachment from one's status as a political actor, reflecting a growing awareness of the factors that were beyond the individual's control. At the same time, the ruler/ruled dichotomy of earlier reflections was replaced with a recognition of the individual's "intermediary" function in the exercise of power. Instead of the classical Aristotelian alternation, one is both ruler and ruled *at the same time*: "Anyone who exercises power has to place himself in a field of complex relations where he occupies a transition point" (*CS*, 88). Where the individual found himself in this complex network of relations was a matter of birth or the artificial status projected onto him by society—neither of which he had any control over. But he could control the quality of the power and governance which he exercised from this position—and it was his moral duty to exercise this power the best way he could. And just as for the earlier Greeks, here also "the rationality of the government of others is the same as the rationality of the government of oneself" (*CS*, p. 89). That is, the object was to control the passions, to cultivate the virtues of discipline and moderation, to develop a self-mastery that would qualify one to govern others. Yet there were two important changes in the relation between self-government and government of others. First, it became less heautocratic, since one had to attend to multiple "levels" in the exercise of power. Second, self-mastery became a much more intense relation to self. This involved a separation, on the one hand, of virtue and the actual ethical work (regimen, ascetic practices) necessary to achieve virtue. On the other hand, while it was recognized that "a whole elaboration of the self by oneself was necessary" for the tasks of governing others, the exercise of power was based on the relationship the individual established (often through an arduous effort and attention to oneself) with himself, which tended to undermine the identification of oneself in terms of one's socially defined political status. Explains Foucault, "From the viewpoint of the relation to the self, the social and political identifications do not function as authentic marks of a mode of being; they are extrinsic, artificial, and unfounded signs" (*CS*, 93). Rather, the true measure of one's integrity, and the true register of one's subjectivity was, for whatever position or status one held, the quality of character the individual constructed for himself through the "cultivation of the self."

The Cultivation of Individuality: J. S. Mill's Manual
of Autonomous Selfhood

In Foucault's analysis of the technologies of the self through which individuals constitute themselves as ethical subjects, he attempts to trace genealogically the cultural patterns that provide frameworks of self-formation for the individuals of a given historical period. He is able to identify such patterns by focusing his analysis on various representative texts, such as Plato's *Republic*, Epictetus's *Discourses*, and Cassian's *Institutiones*. Foucault reads such texts not so much as philosophical treatises in the traditional sense, but rather as "aesthetic manuals," as "manuals for living," as practical handbooks that delineate for the individual certain values, standards, and practices the individual can appropriate in order to define a "style of existence," a mode of being. Reading texts in this way allows Foucault to identify the sorts of problematizations that structure a given form of subjectivation—and thus, to understand the formation of subjectivity under a new dimension. We have seen that in antiquity there was a close connection between forms of political and sexual subjectivity, that the problematizations that structured the self's relation to itself in these domains tended to overlap. Since Foucault was doing a genealogy of the *modern* self, had he been able to complete his project, we might have seen similar connections between modern political and sexual subjectivity.[21]

A genealogy of the modern political subject would concentrate at some point on the texts of the liberal tradition. If we were to analyze such texts as "manuals for living," rather than as juridicophilosophical projects to define principles of justice that govern the exercise of power (the effect of which is to take the political subject as given), we would discover in them models of political subjectivation that become attached to—or are appropriated by—individuals, determining their actions, practices, beliefs, and ideals—that is, models for the constitution of specific modes of being. Such texts generate views about the ways individuals need to comport themselves politically toward the state and toward each other. They provide frameworks of self-formation and identity construction, modes of self-definition and conceptualization. They delineate lines of normativity and abnormality, of social acceptability, of model citizenship and appropriate moral behavior; and they provide points of departure for revolutionary or reactionary personas. Political subjects emerge, in part, as a result of the self-appropriation of concepts generated within the texts of traditional political philosophy, and which are disseminated, in various ways and along various channels, as cultural values. In short, such texts harbor technologies of self through which individuals constitute themselves as modern political subjects.

An exhaustive genealogical survey of such texts, although ultimately necessary, cannot be undertaken here. We can, however, illustrate how a model for understanding this dimension of the emergence of political identity can be derived from Foucault's methods of analysis by focusing on only one text from the liberal tradition, a text from a philosopher for whom "the use of pleasure" has decidedly different connotations: John Stuart Mill's *On Liberty*. By reading this text as a manual of political subjectivation we can identify in it a technology of self representative, in many ways, of the liberal tradition as a whole.

The technologies of self through which individuals constitute themselves as subjects "can be found in all cultures in different forms," says Foucault.[22] Individuals do not so much invent such techniques, although they may give them individual variation; rather, such practices follow patterns that are "proposed, suggested and imposed on (the individual) by his culture, his society and social group."[23] We find certain entrenched patterns peculiar to certain periods in history. In *The Use of Pleasure*, Foucault is concerned with the cultural patterns peculiar to classical Greece; in *The Care of the Self*, with the later Greco-Roman (primarily the Stoic) patterns of late antiquity; and in *Les Aveux de la chair*, with early Christian patterns, especially those peculiar to the monastery. Although they differ markedly in actual form and content, Foucault analyzes such patterns in terms of four major aspects common to all techniques of the self: (1) the ethical substance; (2) the mode of subjection; (3) the ethical work; and (4) the telos.

The *ethical substance* can be defined as this or that aspect of the self that will be the primary object of one's concern—the "prime material" to be worked on. This might be actions or intentions, or desires, or some combination thereof. Foucault calls this the "ontology" of subjectivation in that something is given a reality and made problematic for the individual. In other words, the individual establishes for herself that which she perceives to be the essence of the ethical matter in question. For example, with regard to fidelity, says Foucault, the individual might make desires and his mastery over them the ethical substance; or perhaps one's *feelings* toward one's spouse constitute the true essence of fidelity. We can see already that the determination of the ethical substance requires the determination of a rule, or a precept, or a standard that defines the individual's moral obligations regarding the ethical substance. The way in which the individual determines his relation to such a rule or standard of conduct, and thereby feels obligated to follow it or to live by it, is the second aspect of subjecti-vation: *the mode of subjection*, or rather, put simply, "the way in which people are invited or incited to recognize their moral obligation." The recognition of one's moral obligation (broadly conceived) is a reflection of one's having established a particular sort of relationship to the ethical substance—a relationship of obligation usually predicated on the self-appropriation of a given code or rule of conduct (again, *code, rule*, and the like are broadly and generally conceived and may or may not refer to an actual code or doctrine—they refer more to the relationship established by the individual with himself). A mode of subjection may appeal to divine law, or a sacred text, or some rational principle. For example, one may practice fidelity because it is customary, or because it is "right" or because the Bible says one must, and so forth. The *because* is operative here and designates an active appropriation on the part of the individual. The third aspect of subjectivation is the *ethical work* (*travail éthique*), the work the individual actually performs on himself so that his actions or behavior conform consistently with the relation to the rule or standard of conduct he has established with himself. Foucault calls this ethical work a "self-forming activity (*practique de soi*) or *asceticism* in a very broad sense." It usually involves some sort of regimen or the cultivation of certain habits or the establishing of a routine or exercise; it may be very structured or rather spontaneous in nature. In any case, the main purpose of such activity is "to attempt to transform oneself into the ethical subject of one's behavior." That is, all of this is done for the sake of producing a "certain mode of being" that represents the *telos* of the ethical subject. The telos, or moral goal, of such practices of the self is "the kind of being to which we aspire when we behave in a moral way." For example, the goal of such activities might be to reach a certain kind of purity, or freedom, or virtue, or per-haps mastery of self.[24] In sum, then, the self-formation, or subjectivation, of the ethical subject can be defined as "a process in which the individual delimits that part of himself that will form the object of his moral practice [ethical substance], defines his position relative to the precept he will follow [mode of subjection], and decides on a certain mode of being that will serve as his moral goal [telos]. And this requires him to act upon him-self, to monitor, test, improve, and transform himself [ethical work]" (*UP*, 28). Technologies of the self will be structured in these four ways. What gives content to such technologies and what differentiates one set of such technologies from another is the kind of problematizations that inform them. *Problematization*, for Foucault, refers to a domain of moral valua-tion or valorization wherein certain objects or practices are made the objects of a moral concern. Individuals relate to these things in different ways. Such problematizations give content to the four aspects of subjectivation; in so doing, they structure the self-forming activity of individuals.

Following Foucault, my analysis of *On Liberty* will be structured by focusing on the four major aspects of subjectivation: the ethical substance, the mode of subjection, the ethical work, and the telos of the political subject's self-formation.

Ethical Substance

The ethical substance of *On Liberty*, the "prime material" to be "worked over" in the process of subjectivation, is, of course, freedom, but freedom considered in relation to the exercise of power. Mill distinguishes "civil or social liberty," which is the object of his concern, from the "metaphysical" problem of free will; but it is equally clear that the freedom he has in mind is not so much the collective liberty attributed to a democratic state, but the liberty of the *individual* to pursue certain interests in the civil or social sphere. "The only freedom which deserves the name is that of [each individual] pursuing [her] own good in [her] own way," says Mill, adding the important caveat, "so long as we do not attempt to deprive others of theirs or impede their efforts to obtain it."[25] This caveat shows that Mill's primary concern is with the pursuit of one's own good, rather than with defining what this good might be—the latter, in fact, is precisely what is left to the individual to define. Thus, the understanding of freedom offered by *On Liberty*—a freedom from interference—belongs with what is called in traditional usage "negative freedom," and is to be distinguished from so-called positive freedom.

Negative freedom means, "I am normally said to be free to the degree to which no man or body of men interferes with my activity. Political liberty in this sense is simply the area within which a man can act unobstructed by others."[26] Positive freedom, on the other hand, is identified with the classic Rousseauian project to throw off "the yoke of tyranny" and replace it with a democratic form of government wherein "the people" are masters of their own fate. Liberty in this sense is acquired through certain positive measures, such as the installation of the franchise and various positive political rights, designed "to set limits to the power which the ruler should be suffered to exercise over the community" (*OL*, 2). Positive freedom is the freedom of self-determination generally associated with, and afforded by, a democratic form of government.[27]

Although Mill was an advocate of democracy,[28] he recognized, like

Berlin, that positive freedom was not enough to ensure the freedom of the individual, and that, in fact, positive and negative freedoms often "came into direct conflict with each other."[29] Such conflict can occur in issues settled by popular vote; legitimate minority interests can be overridden by the will of the majority.[30] Thus, the problems of power and personal freedom do not go away with the installation of various democratic mechanisms such as the franchise. Moreover, Mill's sensitivity to the restrictive Victorian and puritanical mores of the time made him aware that there were other ways, besides law and civil penalties, that individual freedom could be impinged, that custom and public opinion could be just as oppressive and coercive as political despotism. We do not really have freedom, says Mill, if everyone is made to live like everyone else.

Thus, the project of *On Liberty* is to find "a limit to the legitimate interference of collective opinion with individual independence" (*OL*, 5). It seeks, in other words, to define an inviolable region of individual liberty, in which one is free to pursue one's own good, to live one's life as one sees fit, free from the interference of law or public sentiment. *On Liberty* delimits three domains of individual freedom: (1) the domain of mind and consciousness, wherein one has complete "liberty of thought and feeling, absolute freedom of opinion and sentiment on all subjects"; (2) the domain of personal lifestyle, wherein each of us has the freedom "of framing the plan of our life to suit our own character, of doing as we like, subject to such consequences as may follow," a freedom that must be respected even when others find our lifestyle "foolish, perverse, or wrong;" and finally (3) the domain of shared interests, which consists in the "freedom to unite" with other individuals "for any purpose" (*OL*, 11–12). The only criterion individuals must meet in order to qualify for the freedom of these domains of conduct is that they be "in the maturity of their faculties," that is, not children or barbarians (or noble savages?). And the only limitation or restriction on doing anything whatsoever within these domains is that the activity not be harmful to others.

The delimitation of an inviolable sphere of individual liberty is designed to give real meaning to the notion of self-government, says Mill. Without such freedoms, even in a democracy, self-government is a misnomer that means, "not the government of each by himself, but of each by all the rest" (*OL*, 4). In order for the individual to be truly self-determining, it is necessary to separate personal concerns from social concerns: "The only part of the conduct of anyone for which he is amenable to society is that which concerns others. In that part which merely concerns himself, his independence is, of right, absolute" (*OL*, 9); two "parts" of political existence separated by a thin juridical line, a line that circumscribes a "free space" in which the individual can conduct his life in any way he sees fit. Even if that conduct is detrimental to the individual's life, even if it would be for his own good, society has no right to cross the line and interfere—society has no *jurisdiction* there. "Over himself, over his own body and mind, the individual is sovereign" (*OL*, 9).

Thus, freedom constitutes the essence of the ethical matter in question in *On Liberty*, the primary object of ethical concern. However, since this freedom is a "negative" freedom, it lacks the substantive quality of, for example, aphrodisia or Christian desire.[31] Negative freedom is an extensionless boundary that must be analyzed in terms of its positive effects: that is, in terms of the two realms it creates, interconnects, and opposes. Negative freedom bifurcates and to some extent polarizes self and society. On the side of society it problematizes the exercise of power; in fact, it functions as a limit in the sense of a restriction or prohibition against the illegitimate excess of power precisely with regard to the individual. On the side of the self, negative freedom acts as a limit in a different sense, that of delimiting a space of activity wherein the individual can create herself, free, as far as is possible, from the interference of the social world. Although it is ostensibly silent on what takes place within this free space, negative freedom nonetheless problematizes for the individual what she thinks, how she lives, and with whom and in what ways she shares her life. In short, it problematizes for the individual her own individuality. In fact, negative freedom has, at bottom, no other purpose than to legitimize a space of emergence for the "private, autonomous individual."[32] We shall see that, in this political atomization of the self, individuality is both a juridico-political category (which problematizes for society the exercise of power), and a mode of being—a relation of self to self which must be cultivated.

Mode of Subjection

In *The Use of Pleasure*, Foucault asks, "To what principles does [the individual] refer in order to moderate, limit, regulate his activity? What sort of validity might these principles have that would enable a man to justify his having to obey them? Or, in other words, what is the mode of subjection that is implied in this moral problematization of sexual conduct?" (53). The same sort of questions can be asked of political freedom. That is, through what principles do individuals recognize their obligation to respect the spheres of political liberty?

On Liberty confronts a social milieu in which the principle mode of subjection is considered by Mill to be an uncritical appeal to custom. Custom, whose influence is manifested in the personal preferences of individuals, serves as a standard against which human conduct is judged. "The practical principle which guides [people] to their opinions on the regulation of human conduct is the feeling in each person's mind that everybody should be required to act as he, and those with whom he sympathizes, would like them to act. . . . The likings and dislikings of society, or some powerful portion of it, are thus the main thing which has practically determined the rules laid down for general observance, under the penalties of law or opinion" (*OL*, 5, 7). It is just this mode of subjection, which sanctions society's interference in the lives of individuals, that *On Liberty* seeks to replace.

Thus, *On Liberty* presents what it considers to be a rational and insuperable principle to regulate both society's and the individual's conduct with respect to the domains of personal freedom. "The object of this essay is to assert one very simple principle," says Mill. "That principle is that the sole end for which mankind are warranted, individually or collectively, in interfering with the liberty of action of any of their number is self-protection. That the only purpose for which power can be rightfully exercised over any member of a civilized community against his will, is to prevent harm to others" (*OL*, 9). The harm-to-others principle repeats, complementarily, the gesture of delimitation found in negative freedom: that is, the bifurcation of self and society, and the problematization of conduct with regard to these two domains. Although it is not a *necessary* correlate of negative freedom, this principle does provide a tangible limit to which both the individual and society can appeal in order to regulate their conduct. On both sides of the line of negative freedom, the harm-to-others principle acts to sanction or condemn any given activity, whether it involves the individual's pursuit of a private good or society's exercise of power. In fact, by reference to this simple principle, appropriate moral conduct can be defined in fairly rigorous (albeit negative) terms for both sides of the political divide. The individual knows, for example, that she is entitled to express her opinions, but not in circumstances where this might provoke a riot. She knows she can unite with others who share her interests, but not when the organization designs to burn people on crosses. She can live her life in a bottle, but not at the expense of her family or creditors. Where the individual's conduct directly affects the lives of others, whether through neglect or abject harm, she can legitimately expect society to deploy its forces. By the same token, the harm-to-others principle not only determines when society can interfere in the lives of individuals, but also, to a great extent, how such interference takes shape. That is, the quality or the nature of the harm dictates the quality of society's retaliation; the greater the harm, the more severe society's reprobation. A criminal might deserve to be punished to the full measure of the law; but the incontinent slob may, at worst, merit only society's disgust and ostracism.[33] At all events, the harm-to-others principle is designed to settle, perhaps only after long and careful deliberation, all matters in which the affairs of the individual come into conflict with those of society.

What sort of validity does the harm-to-others principle have? Mill says that this principle, and the respect for negative freedom that it is designed to preserve, is not justified as a natural right or as a condition of social contract. Rather, respecting the free pluralistic pursuit of individual good, in accordance with the harm-to-others principle, is justified solely on the basis of utilitarian considerations, on the beneficial consequences that will accrue to everyone (as individuals and to society as a whole) as a result. Explains Mill, "I regard utility as the ultimate appeal on all ethical questions" (*OL*, 10). A society that fails to respect the liberty of the individual invites cultural stagnation. Social progress and cultural vitality, on the other hand, are possible only when genius and originality are allowed to flourish free from the yoke of custom and consensual expectation: "The only unfailing and permanent source of improvement is liberty, since by it there are as many possible independent centers of improvement as there are individuals" (*OL*, 67). At the same time, individuals are best served by a free unhindered space of activity that permits them to develop their best human faculties to the fullest. In so doing, human life "becomes rich, diversified, and animating." And this, in turn, is good for society as a whole, for as "each person becomes more valuable to himself," he becomes "more valuable to others" (*OL*, 60).

Alongside these rather grand utilitarian considerations the harm-to-others principle may seem merely instrumental, subordinate to, and given its validity by the great gains to be enjoyed by respecting the spheres of individual liberty. The harm-to-others principle allows a free society to function smoothly as it prevents one individual's pursuit of private good from spilling over and impeding another's. Yet because of the fact that this liberty cannot be defined in specific terms without infringing upon it—that is, no one can be told how to think or live originally without violating the very spirit and intent of the domains of freedom—the harm-to-others principle has a certain functional self-sufficiency and can be justified on its own terms. Utility may be the ultimate appeal, but utility must be necessarily vague (if not silent) when it comes to specifying our moral obligations with respect to individual freedom, simply because it is virtually impossible to

predict (except in broad terms such as "progress" and "human development") what benefits will result from originality and spontaneity. Something like the harm-to-others principle is required to determine, with any
degree of clarity and specificity, what our moral obligations are, to serve as
a touchstone against which to judge the acceptability of our conduct and
the legitimacy of society's exercise of power; but, most important, it must
be a principle the appeal to which does not violate the very freedom it is
designed to protect. It must be a negative, limiting principle rather than a
substantive one carrying its own positive interdictions. In other words, it
must regulate conduct rather than define it. This would seem to imply that,
if one interprets utility in the strict traditional sense of "the greatest good
for the greatest number," one cannot maintain utility as the ultimate appeal
on all ethical questions, and at the same time maintain certain inviolable
regions of individual liberty. At some point the two will come into conflict
with each other. Unlike the utilitarians J. J. C. Smart and R. M. Hare,[34] Mill
avoids this problem (perhaps too neatly) by asserting that respecting
individual freedom is what is best for everyone. Yet this has the effect of
returning the priority of appeal, for all intents and purposes, to the harm-
to-others principle. Thus, as a mode of subjection, the harm-to-others
principle could just as easily be justified deontologically rather than teleo-
logically; it would elicit the same sort of moral observance as a categorical
imperative.

Ethical Work

How does one go about forming oneself as a political subject, according to
On Liberty? What regimen does one follow? What habits does one
acquire? What virtues does one cultivate?

Although *On Liberty* bifurcates self and society, there is no hypostatiza-
tion of society such that it (à la G. W. F. Hegel) transcends the self. Actually, the bifurcation simply reflects the traditional political opposition
between sovereign and subject, whose separation is structured according to
certain arbitrary limits imposed on the exercise of power. In *On Liberty*
this limitation is achieved by reserving an absolutely inviolable region of
personal freedom. Assuming that the harm-to-others principle is respected,
any attempt to dictate coercively what goes on within this region of freedom will always be illegitimate. Moreover, utility demands that society
build provisions for the exercise of this freedom in the political structure,
that each of us respect the freedom of his neighbors. No matter how dis-
tasteful we find their behavior or lifestyle, as long as what they do poses

no harm to us, as long as it does not "affect prejudicially the concerns of others," we have no right to interfere. This applies to each isolated individual as well as to society as a whole.

Thus, whereas for the Greeks the principal virtue to be cultivated was moderation, in Mill's society the principal virtue is *toleration*: it is absolutely "essential that different persons should be allowed to lead different lives" (*OL*, 61). Freedom is meaningless unless we develop a mutual respect for one another, for the inherent integrity of whatever life course each of us chooses. Tolerance may seem like a rather passive virtue; to acquire it does not seem to require the rigorous sort of regimen associated with Hellenic care of the self. Yet, given that custom has been so pervasive in its rule over standards of acceptable conduct, and that "so natural to mankind is intolerance" (*OL*, 8), tolerance demands an active, attentive kind of self-restraint. Custom saps our strength. It causes us "to desire nothing strongly. . . . Its result is weak feelings and weak energies" (*OL*, 66, 67). Thus, the virtue of toleration requires an ongoing struggle with ourselves, with the inclination to accept uncritically the dictates of custom, of received opinion, of our own personal likes and dislikes, a struggle to resist the tendency in ourselves to "prescribe general rules of conduct and endeavor to make everyone conform to the approved standard" (*OL*, 66). Moreover, tolerance requires a certain amount of courage, a willingness to accept the unknown, to give "free scope to variety," to permit experimentation in personal lifestyles.

Without tolerance, there can be no freedom. Yet, strictly speaking, freedom is not the object of tolerance. The object of tolerance is "the cultivation of individuality." Individuality is made possible by the free space of activity opened as an effect of tolerance. Individuality is not, however, something that immediately and automatically springs full-blown the moment society decides to respect certain regions of personal liberty. Individuality must be developed, nurtured, cultivated. "Human nature is not a machine to be built after a model, and set to do exactly the work prescribed for it, but a tree, which requires to grow and develop itself on all sides, according to the tendency of the inward forces which make it a living thing" (*OL*, 56–57). This requires a fairly rigorous attention to self. The self must ask itself such questions as, "what do I prefer? or, what would suit my character and disposition? or, what would allow the best and highest in me to have fair play and enable it to grow and thrive?" (*OL*, 58). Such questions allow the self to prioritize itself, to set itself apart from society and its dictates, to initiate, in short, a process of self-formation whereby one can *become* an individual.

To become an individual one must exercise one's sovereignty over one-self. One must endeavor to actualize the distinctive human faculties of perception, judgment, discrimination, reason, and moral sensibility. These faculties "are exercised only in making a choice" (OL, 56). Choice distin-guishes the true individual from the person who lives in "ape-like" confor-mity to the standards of custom. It is only the exercise of independent choice that cultivates the qualities of authentic individuality. As Mill explains, "He who chooses his plan for himself employs all his faculties. He must use observation to see, reasoning and judgment to foresee, activity to gather materials for decision, discrimination to decide, and when he has decided, firmness and self control to hold on to his decision. And these qualities he requires and exercises exactly in proportion as the part of his conduct which he determines according to his own judgment and feelings is a large one" (OL, 56). An individual is not someone who comes to his or her freedom fully formed. An individual must actively *use* freedom to give shape to her existence. To form oneself as an individual one must actively attend to one-self, to the myriad of capacities and faculties involved in making a choice. Cultivating the faculties and qualities involved in choosing one's own way gives one the strength to resist the dictates of custom and social expectation. In this way the self can become an individual. The shape of individuality is a matter for each of us to decide. In fact, *On Liberty* puts a premium on our forming ourselves of our own design, whatever the result: "If a person pos-sesses any tolerable amount of common sense and experience, his own mode of laying out his existence is the best, not because it is best in itself, but because it his own mode" (OL, 64). Yet however we "lay out our existence," forming ourselves as individuals is a matter of work, ethical work. Individ-uality is a *project* that requires *exercising* choice, *employing* our faculties, *strengthening* our character. In fact, there is perhaps no higher endeavor to which we should direct our energies than the formation of ourselves as indi-viduals, according to Mill: "Among the works of man which human life is rightly employed in perfecting and beautifying, the first in importance surely is man himself" (OL, 56).

Telos

The telos, or moral goal, of subjectivation in *On Liberty*, the "object toward which every human being must ceaselessly direct his efforts," can be summed up in one word: *happiness*. This is the happiness of the fully actualized human being, a being whose moral and mental faculties are developed to their fullest potential, a being characterized by vigor and strength and independence of thought. Happiness is defined as "well-being"—a blissful if not terminal state wherein, finally, "human beings become a noble and beautiful object of contemplation" (*OL*, 60). What it would be like to achieve this state of well-being, this happiness, is not (and perhaps cannot be) expressed in more precise terms, but one thing is certain: happiness can only be achieved by cultivating our individuality. Says Mill, "It is only the cultivation of individuality which produces, or can produce, well-developed human beings" (*OL*, 61). Now we see that, properly speaking, individuality is not an end in itself, but rather, that it is "one of the principal ingredients of human happiness" (*OL*, 54).

Cultivating individuality brings happiness not only to the isolated human being, but to society as a whole. For society, happiness and well-being are defined in terms of progress. Yet progress, like personal happiness, can only be assured by the cultivation of individuality: "The free development of individuality . . . is not only a coordinate element with all that is designated by the terms civilization, instruction, education, culture, but is itself a necessary part and condition of all those things" (*OL*, 54). A free society, a society informed by the virtue of toleration, is at the same time a thriving society, a society pushed forward by the genius, originality, and innovation that springs from the freedom society affords its members.

Thus, just as for the Greeks, the fates of the individual and of the society to which he belongs are intertwined. However, for the Greeks, the moral goal of subjectivation was the freedom that manifested itself in an individual's mastery over self, a freedom/mastery that qualified one to govern the lives of others, (and thus on which the good of the state depended). Now freedom is a means to an end, the necessary condition for the cultivation of individuality, which is in turn necessary to the happiness and well-being of self and society. Where before freedom was identified with the governance of others, now freedom by definition puts itself in opposition to such governance—or rather, it prevents any heautocratic structure of governance by returning, in a unilateral leveling of social relations predicated on certain inviolable spheres of personal liberty, the right of "self-government" to each and every individual.

To summarize: we find in *On Liberty* the determination of an ethical substance—freedom—that problematizes for the self its relation to society as an autonomous individual. This is a binary relation divided precisely along the line traced by negative freedom. Hence, there are two realms of moral concern for the self: one social, one individual. The self determines its moral obligations in regard to freedom by reference to these connected yet decidedly separate realms. The principle or standard to which the self

appeals in order to define its moral obligations with respect to freedom—
or, in other words, the self's mode of subjection—is the harm-to-others
principle, which receives its validity ultimately from utility. This negative,
limiting principle regulates the exercise of power for the self as a member
of society, but it also prioritizes for the self its own individuality, by making
the cultivation of individuality an object of moral concern. Thus, the ethical work for the self, on the one hand, will be to develop the virtue of tolerance, without which freedom as a right belonging to everyone is
impossible. (Tolerance is a social virtue.) Yet the self must also do those
things necessary—exercise choice, develop the distinctive human faculties—in order to become an individual. In this way, the self can achieve the
moral goal of happiness, predicated on the self's cultivation of individuality. In happiness, social and individual concerns are united.

On Liberty marks the threshold, in the nineteenth century, of a subtle
transformation in the experience of political subjectivity. Although it
retains the traditional binary and juridical conception of the exercise of
power, it shifts the locus of this concern away from Sovereignty, away from
the King and to the subject. Or, rather, the experience of political subjectivity becomes one of personal sovereignty, rather than of defining the
obligations of the political subject with regard to governmental authority
(and vice versa). The problematization of negative freedom itself suggests
that a space has opened for the emerging private autonomous individual.
Thereafter, the individual will be the primary object of moral concern in
the political arena. Problems of democracy and representation in regard to
authority will still be of concern, especially when they appear to be threatened (by, for example, the scourge of National Socialism, or what was the
widening shadow of communism), but the problems of individuality—of
what individuals are entitled, or required, to do, to have, to become—will
increasingly define the domain of political experience.

The Political Spectrum: Liberals, Conservatives, and the Ethics of Toleration

> When the Christian majority takes over this country, there will be no satanic
> churches, no more free distribution of pornography, no more abortion on demand
> and no more talk of rights for homosexuals. After the Christian majority takes
> control, pluralism will be seen as immoral and evil, and the state will not permit
> anybody the right to practice evil.
> —Gary Potter, president of Catholics for Christian Political Action

Tolerance. So much of modern political identity is defined by a relation to tolerance. The manner in which tolerance informs, positively or negatively, a particular mode of subjectivity determines to a great extent whether an individual is identified as a liberal or a conservative, as an anarchist or a fascist. Tolerance serves as a practical reference point for placing an individual or group on the political spectrum—to the "right" or the "left" of an imaginary point of neutrality.[35]

Tolerance/interference represents one of the key dynamics in modern political subjectivity, especially to the extent that we conceive of ourselves as individuals. Here I want to examine how this dynamic is played out practically in our ideological oppositions to one another as political subjects. The key point is that our political identities are to a great extent the effect of an arbitrary appropriation. However, this appropriation commits us to certain practices having serious repercussions in the political arena. Moreover, individuals who identify themselves in terms of the political value system they appropriate consider themselves as fulfilling the ethical demands of these value systems; that is, they consider themselves as acting *morally*.

The political spectrum is our contemporary means of identifying particular modes of political identity and of situating such modes in differentiation from each other. Given positions on the political spectrum take their meaning in relation to other positions, defined precisely by degrees of opposition, by shades of ideological gradation. Where points on the political spectrum are defined and given a name—"right-wing conservative," "left-wing liberal," "radical," "moderate"—it is always by reference to this sliding scale of political values. They are category-specific (rather than substantive) designations reflecting the appropriation of a political value system.

Political subjects constitute themselves through an appropriation of a political value system, that is, by establishing a relation to self that incorporates certain principles, beliefs, and practices. These principles, beliefs, and practices, constitutive of an ideology, are defined in terms of problematizations that structure the subject's self-formation. Conventionally, as a means of "ordering things," the political spectrum differentiates political subjects according to more or less identifiable distinctions in the problematizations that inform their subjectivity. In actual practice, however, it is often difficult (for political analysts and philosophers) to define such terms as liberal and *conservative*, to differentiate one political stance (mode of political identity) from another.[36] And yet, those who identify themselves as conservatives have no trouble putting themselves in opposition to so-called liberals (and vice-versa), and of asserting the priority of their political agendas (value systems) over another's. This is, in fact, the essence of politics as it is popularly conceived today. But what supports this oppositional, factional character of modern politics? What can serve as a basis of differentiation between modes of political identity, that would explain their differences and account for, if not justify, their opposition?

When all the ideological baggage is stripped away, perhaps the basic differentiation between modes of modern political identity can be understood in terms of tolerance—the extent to which one justifies, or not, interference in the lives and freedom of individuals. Or, at least, tolerance can serve as a point of departure for understanding this differentiation.[37] A tolerance/interference dynamic informs the political spectrum; it animates specific positions along this line (especially to the extent they can be identified and given a name). It is not that the positions that constitute the political spectrum can be reduced to a tolerance/interference dynamic, by any means, but that dynamic can serve as a kind of prism through which we can better discern the oppositional quality between them. This is not a simple dynamic wherein those on the "left" justify some degree of tolerance and those on the "right" justify some degree of interference. The political spectrum cannot be differentiated in this way. Rather, it is a matter of accounting for the quality of tolerance (or intolerance) that animates a specific mode of political identity. The quality of tolerance refers to whether individuals will be inclined to permit, demand, or forbid interference (social, governmental, or individual) regarding certain objects of political concern (e.g., the distribution of goods, property, taxation, education, welfare, population, sexuality, family, religion, and so on). In other words, will the person be motivated to accept abortion, for example, or will he feel justified in interfering in its practice? Of course, a liberal will react differently (in terms of tolerance) than a conservative. The degree of tolerance is important, but it is a secondary variable, since there can be a high degree of tolerance (or intolerance) on both "sides" of the political spectrum.

Let us begin with the standard opposition between liberal and conservative. Ronald Dworkin defines a liberal as someone who holds a theory of equality that says "that political decisions must be, so far as is possible, independent of any particular conception of the good life, or of what gives value to life."[38] A liberal, then, seeks to preserve the autonomy of the individual to define her own good in life and to see that everyone has the equal opportunity to do so. To achieve this, the liberal prefers an economic market and a representative democracy to other political mechanisms because these "familiar institutions may be expected to provide a more egalitarian division [of social goods] than any other general arrangement" (Dworkin, 66). Any other measures would seem to require imposing some one conception "of what is good in life" on the individual. The liberal, however, recognizes that both a free market and a democracy often function in such a way as to generate inequalities that threaten the equal opportunity of each individual to pursue her own private good. Thus, the liberal advocates certain measures designed to protect "the right of each person to respect and concern as an individual" (Dworkin, 69). The most important of such measures is the adoption of "a scheme of civil rights." These individual rights must be respected even if it requires making reforms in the market, and they cannot be usurped even by the majoritarian decisions of a democracy.

A conservative, on the other hand, follows a different theory of equality, says Dworkin; that is, "the content of equal treatment cannot be independent of some theory about the good for man or the good life, because treating a person as an equal means treating him the way the good or truly wise person would wish to be treated" (Dworkin, 64). To a conservative, the "good" life is equivalent to a "virtuous" life, and political decisions must be such that they foster a virtuous society. A virtuous society, which citizens have the responsibility to promote, is one that rewards, among other things, the "virtues of talent and industry," because it is the cultivation of these virtues that has the effect of supplying "more of what is wanted by other members of the virtuous society" (Dworkin, 72). For this reason, the conservative, like the liberal, highly values democracy and an economic market. Yet, unlike the liberal, the conservative sees less need for civil rights because it is precisely the democratic process that allows the proper virtues to be "legislated into a public morality" (Dworkin, 73). And a conservative will tend to resist any restrictions on a free market because it is this that precisely rewards the virtues of talent and industry. For this reason, the conservative tends to invoke certain "rights to property" that are for him or her as inviolable as the liberal's civil rights. Where problems of inequitable distribution arise, the conservative prefers charity to market reforms and welfare policies, which have the effect of taking from the conservative what he has justly earned. "Justice requires some protection for the successful," says the conservative (Dworkin, 74).

Dworkin gives a fair assessment of the theories of equality which inform the politics of the liberal and the conservative, at least from a conceptual standpoint. Yet as modes of subjection—that is, as the appropriation of principles that determine for the political subject his moral obligations—

they need some qualification. While it is certainly true that the conservative acts on a conception of the good life that he would seek to impose on
everyone, the "good life" for the conservative is most often identified with
the status quo. As Theodor Adorno and colleagues have noted, "Perhaps
the definitive component of conservatism is an attachment . . . to 'things as
they are,' to the prevailing social organization and ways."[39] To the conservative, generally, "what is, is right," and when current social problems
seem to threaten the inherent merit of the existing order of things, the conservative usually reacts in one of two ways. Either he rationalizes such
problems as being "natural," and thinks that it is just a matter of identifying and "getting rid of" of the perpetrators (Adorno, 153–54), or, if the
problems are sweeping in nature, the conservative pleads for a nostalgic
return to "old-fashioned values." The liberal, on the other hand, is characterized by a willingness to resist the status quo, especially when the existing
order fails to respect the right of each individual to pursue her own good,
and to provide an equal opportunity to do so.[40] Yet a liberal could justify
this resistance by appeal to the conservative theory of equality, if the liberal
identifies (as Mill does) the good life precisely with the free pluralistic pursuit of individual good. Considered from the actual processes of subjectivation, however, it is more likely that both the liberal and the conservative
will justify their political agendas by appealing to the standard political
principles handed down to us through the liberal tradition.[41] Both will
defend the freedom and integrity of the individual (as the fundamental
political unit). And both will appeal to some version of the harm-to-others
principle (in defense of the freedom of the individual) in order to define
one's moral obligations. However, the divergences in interpretation on the
part of the liberal and the conservative reveal the fundamental ambiguity in
this principle.

The harm-to-others principle, we will recall, says that we must respect
the freedom of individuals to do as they like as long as what they do poses
no harm to others, that the only time we are justified in interfering with
such freedom is for the purposes of self-protection. Now, the conservative
will interpret this principle "conservatively"—rigidly and to the letter. The
conservative will defend, even more adamantly than the liberal perhaps,
the inviolability of her personal freedom.[42] She will resist anything she considers to interfere with this freedom. But she understands her region of
freedom as a space for the cultivation of certain virtues, such as talent, hard
work, patriotism and love of democracy, family unity, and love of God. She
believes absolutely in the right of each individual to "lay out his existence"
in his/her own way, but she has great difficulty in conceiving of a legitimate

mode of existence that does not try to cultivate these values—hence her "suspicion" of pluralism. In fact, she considers harmful anything, or anyone, which impedes or threatens the cultivation of the proper virtues. This justifies, based on an appeal to the harm-to-others principle, her interference in the lives of others. To that extent (as regards the promotion of a virtuous society), conservatives "treat the lives of other members of their community as part of their own lives" (Dworkin, 72). As regards her own freedom, however, the conservative will tolerate no interference, or at least none that affects her cultivating the proper virtues. She will prefer a laissez-faire market which rewards talent and industry; thus, she will resist such measures as governmental regulation of business, taxation, and welfare reforms. For the conservative, "success tends to be measured in financial terms" (Adorno, 155). Thus, the conservative will tend to be highly protective of her property, which is for her a tangible reflection of her success, that is, of her virtue.[43] The conservative will prefer a merit system to a quota system. She will not necessarily condone active discrimination, but neither will she support affirmative action policies because not only do such policies fail to promote the proper virtues, but they actually punish unjustly those who have such virtues (see Dworkin, 75). More important, such measures represent the most visible examples of interference in the conservative's own domains of freedom. Here the conservative is the first to protest that if she wanted to help those suffering discrimination, she would do so; but no one has the right to force her to adopt such measures. In fact, when the conservative can see no active discrimination, even though she knows such discrimination has occurred in the past, she tends to justify obvious social inequalities by attributing them to a person's own lack of talent or industriousness—that is, under the assumption that "most people get pretty much what they deserve" (Adorno, 155). The conservative's estimation of other people reflects her attitude toward freedom. Freedom is a sacred place for the cultivation of the proper virtues, a place that must be protected at all costs, a place in which each individual can show what she genuinely deserves.

The liberal, on the other hand, can be said to interpret the harm-to-others principle more "liberally"—that is, more flexibly, in the spirit rather than the letter of the principle. He believes in the freedom of each individual to determine his own life. Yet his awareness of social inequities has him inclined to believe that such freedom is meaningless unless each of us has an equal opportunity to take advantage of the same social goods. He sees little value in the "freedom" to be poor, to be illiterate, to be powerless. Thus, the liberal considers it necessary to institute certain social policies, certain structural reforms, designed to correct some of the social imbalances—such as governmental regulation of business, subsidized housing, socialized medicine and education, and the bane of the conservative's existence, taxation—in order to "level the playing field," as is said. This justifies for the liberal a certain amount of interference in the lives of individuals.[44] He is willing to place restrictions on his own freedom as well as that of his more privileged neighbors, at least until such time that unjust social imbalances can be rectified, but he also feels justified in interfering in the lives of those individuals he is trying to help, at least until they "can stand on their own two feet." The social worker is the "patron saint" of the liberal.

The activities of the liberal seem to be informed by a wider, less immediate, more egalitarian (i.e., soft and wishy-washy, in the eyes of the conservative) notion of harm. It is not that he is any less intolerant than the conservative, but his intolerance is directed toward structural imbalances, whereas the conservative's intolerance is more "personal" in nature.[45] This is a qualitative distinction that helps to account for their opposition in the political arena. Yet, genealogically speaking, the liberal and the conservative fall from the same tree. Their self-formation as political subjects merely involves adjustments in the same problematizations: of freedom, of tolerance, of the cultivation of individuality, of happiness. Both liberals and conservatives constitute themselves by establishing a relation to themselves that is structured by these problematizations. They differ from each other because of qualitative distinctions in their interpretations of freedom, of the sort of individuality that freedom is meant to bring about, and—above all—of what they will tolerate for the sake of their freedom.

Once this qualitative distinction has been established, we could go on to (provisionally) draw out a "family tree" of modern political subjects based on the degree of tolerance that informs their self-formation, that is, on the extremes to which they are characteristically willing to go in support of, or in opposition to, the status quo. On the "left," moving further and further away from the center, we would find, respectively, the "activist," the "radical," the "revolutionary," and finally, the "anarchist." On the "right," moving in the opposite direction from the center, we would find the "patriot," the "moral majority member," the "reactionary," and finally, the "fascist."[46] Not surprising perhaps is the fact that the farther we move toward either extreme of the political spectrum, the more intolerance we find informing the modes of political identity. The anarchist beckons to the fascist. But the qualitative difference in the tolerance/intolerance dynamic that structures, respectively, the political subjectivity of the anarchist and the fascist prevents the political spectrum from becoming a political circle, from bending around upon itself and joining at the juncture of extremisms. On the other hand, total intolerance seems to constitute the limits within which modern political subjectivity can manifest itself. Anarchy and fascism stand as finite boundaries at either end of the political spectrum. Political identity, which may perhaps display indeterminable variation within these boundaries, appears to exhaust its possibilities in the excesses of either extreme.

Notice also that it is much more the case that as we move toward the extremes the problem of the State emerges to take precedence over individuality as the predominant moral concern. At the extremes of intolerance, the State constitutes the ethical substance for the self: for the fascist who would return to the State absolute power; for the anarchist who would smash the State to pieces. For the fascist, individual freedom is antithetical to the State and must be suppressed absolutely. For the anarchist, individual freedom is absolutely impossible if the State exists. The purgation, or the liberation, of individual freedom thus constitutes the modes of subjection at the extremes of modern political subjectivity; they define for the self its moral obligations; they justify the excesses of the anarchist's and fascist's respective practices. This requires that the ethical work for both, the means through which they transform themselves into subjects, be one of violence. And, finally, for both, the moral goal of their activities can only be a kind of purity: for the fascist, the purity of the State; for the anarchist, an existence purified of the State.

The State, individuality, freedom, tolerance: these constitute the essential problematizations that structure the formation of modern political identity, at least as it is conventionally delineated by the political spectrum. These problematizations are reflected in texts, such as *On Liberty*, from a tradition that has for centuries now tried to tell us what we *should* be as political subjects. In that sense, political theory has always been involved in "ethics" in the traditional sense. Without doubt one of the principle virtues of that ethics is toleration.[47] Yet, once we get beyond the abstractions of the political spectrum, we see how morally ambiguous toleration can be when applied to real political subjects—indeed, how it can sometimes manifest itself as the worst form of passive-aggressive behavior.

Nowhere has this ambiguity been more prevalent than in the treatment of Native Americans. American Indians were subjected to a policy of segregation almost from the beginning by the Puritans, who forced captured Indians to live separately in what were called "praying towns."[48] This policy became institutionalized with the passage by Congress of the Indian

Removal Act of 1830 under Andrew Jackson. This precipitated the infamous "Trail of Tears," in which fifteen thousand Cherokee were forcibly marched over a thousand miles to reservations in the West. More than four thousand of them would die along the way.[49] The Indian Removal Act has been attributed to "White land hunger and racism," but the act targeted and affected mainly the so-called civilized tribes of the eastern and southeastern United States. Many of these tribes, like the Choctaw, maintained thriving plantations and even owned slaves like their white counterparts. In fact, the Cherokee had given up tribal customs and beliefs in an effort to "make their people culturally indistinguishable from their white neighbors" for more than thirty years prior to the passage of the legislation that would remove them.[50]

This raises some interesting questions: Couldn't legislation have been passed which simply allowed for the purchase of the land from Indian ownership? Why was it necessary to physically remove the tribes? Is there something in the fact that they were placed in the heart of what was then the American frontier, or what remained of it? Why has it proven so difficult to assimilate Native Americans into the mainstream culture? In short, why have Native Americans, more so arguably than any other ethnic bloc, been maintained in social and political otherness?[51]

These are complicated questions with no simple answers. Yet perhaps this state of affairs is due in part to the seminal importance of the Native American's role as Noble Savage to the constitution of our own identities as Americans. The noble savage is not simply the idealized figure of European imagination. From the beginning the noble savage has been our primary, our founding Other. This otherness is both figural, embodied in stale stereotypes and iconography, and practical, through the processes of exclusion and marginalization afforded by the reservation system. Like a prism through which white light is refracted and dispersed into the array of colors we know as the spectrum, the figure of the noble savage is a prism through which Western political identity is confirmed. But, as with a real prism, the white light which is the source of the spectrum is itself invisible, transparent, unseen. To that degree the Savage Noble remains transparent and hence unseen, even though it animates virtually every position along the American version of the political spectrum.

The Savage Noble occupies the privileged position of what Simone de Beauvoir would call "the Subject" or "the Absolute" through which the "Other" is "defined and differentiated."[52] It should be no surprise that the Savage Noble's Others are forced to play outside the political field in which it has dominance and are only given heed to the degree to which they strip themselves down to the barest, most abstract expression of political identity—that is, as autonomous individuals with rights. Only then are they allowed to consort within the privileged space where "all men are created equal." Outside of this space they are subjugated to a form of marginalization that attempts to justify itself under the mantles of "color-blindness" and "tolerance."

We can see now that toleration, contrary to how John Rawls and Mill would have it, is not intrinsically virtuous. In fact, it is amoral; everything depends on how, and upon whom, it is deployed. Yet, what would happen to political theory, to ethics, if it considered political subjectivity not so much in terms of the ideological units of identity that make up the political spectrum, but from the standpoint of the actual processes of subjectivation through which such identities are constituted? From the standpoint of the processes of subjectivation, the whole question of ethics is transformed. It is through the determination of an ethical substance, a mode of subjection, a practice of self, and a telos that an individual forms its identity. More than that, the individual recognizes itself *as such* and is thereby determined in and through that identification. It is the constitution—the self-formation—not simply of a moral or ideological stance, but of a specific mode of being. Thus, it appears that moral claims are always made from the interiority of a particular mode of subjectivation. In fact, a claim to justice and right always attends, and sanctions, the worst political atrocities.[53]

This raises a vital question: If our evaluations of political or ideological positions are always made on the basis of an equally arbitrary appropriation of political values, how are we to condemn (or praise) a given political practice? Does Foucault's approach to ethics plunge us into the morass of moral relativism or nihilism, in other words? In the final chapter, I shall argue that it does not; but, for now, I would like to suggest that perhaps our task is not to condemn a given practice after the fact, but to resist the subjectivational processes that give rise to it in the first place, that give it the appearance of necessity—to deploy, in other words, a genealogically informed and thus subversive attack *against identity* itself.

part 2

Against Identity

5

Governmentality and the Axes of Political Experience

One of Michel Foucault's earliest works, his doctoral thesis, is a translation of Immanuel Kant's *Anthropologie.* The translation is preceded by a 128-page introduction in which Foucault launches a critical inquiry of Kant on the question, *Was ist der Mensch?* One of Foucault's last works is an essay entitled "What Is Enlightenment?" in which he returns to Kant and, in a way, to the same question: What is man? Throughout his career, Foucault maintained a complex, provocative, sometimes volatile relation to Kant. On the surface, this relationship took shape as a destructive critique of *a priori* categories and transcendental unities, a critique of Reason itself, but one completely subversive of the foundational project envisioned by Kant. Yet Foucault was also aware of his debt to Kant for making this possible. Kant stands at the threshold of a philosophical epoch that is constantly putting man into question. Foucault belongs to that epoch, in that he puts the question of "Man" itself into question. There is a sense in which each of the so-called movements of Foucault's thought parallels—in a perverse, anarchistic way, perhaps—each of Kant's three major critiques. First, Pure Reason is parodied and disarmed by adulterated discourses; Foucault's appeal to rarity and exclusion replaces Kant's appeal to synthesis and analyticity. In the second major movement of Foucault's thought, the practical demands of Categorical Imperatives are displaced by the norms and expectations of disciplinary practices; the private sanctuary of conscience is overrun by an external and shameless surveillance. And finally, in Foucault's last work on ethics and subjectivation, the patchwork and arbitrary fashioning of an aesthetics of existence mimics the lawful necessity of critical judgment. Whereas Marx turned Hegel on his head, Foucault turns Kant into comedy, with a Nietzschean laugh that masks an abiding respect.

Up to this point we have dealt separately with each of the movements of Foucault's thought, on discourse, power, and subjectivation, applying each as models for understanding a different dimension of political subjectivity.

However, these three domains "can only be understood in relation to each other, not independently."[1] Thus, the task now is to bring them together, to analyze their complicity and complementarity, to show how they operate with and through one another to constitute the political subject.

A Matrix of Experience

In Foucault's last work he began to recognize the necessity of an analysis that would bring the three main movements of his thought together. He began to speak of the "three axes" of subjectivity, and "the play between types of understanding, forms of normality, and modes of relation to one-self and others."[2] Referring to his previous work he says that he had "emphasized a particular aspect each time," but that it is possible to reread his work in terms of all three.[3] This is not a casual ad hoc juxtapositioning. The discursive formation of a domain of knowledge (such as that of psychiatry) could not "have existed without a whole interplay of political structures and without a whole set of ethical attitudes."[4] In fact, we are not dealing here with three separate domains, but with three *axes* of the same historical configuration.

Thus, we have "three axes whose specificity and whose interconnections have to be analyzed: the axis of knowledge, the axis of power, the axis of ethics."[5] Considered separately from the others, each axis has a specificity peculiar to it in that it puts into play certain analyzable "criteria" that distinguish it from the others. The axis of knowledge, or *truth axis* as Foucault sometimes calls it, puts into play certain criteria that govern the formation and circulation of common statements constituting a discursive practice. This axis delimits a field of concepts, objects, understandings, and representations that purport to explain, under the mantle of scientificity and rationality, what human beings are in truth. The axis of power puts into play the criteria of various rules governing the differentiation of human beings from each other. Through various strategies, apparatuses, and institutions (constitutive of technologies of power), this axis is characterized by certain "dividing practices" that "differentiate the permissible from the forbidden, natural from monstrous, normal from pathological, what is decent from what is not. . . ." Human beings are identified in terms of the place they occupy in the complex web of relations structured by such dividing practices. Finally, the axis of ethics refers to various practices of the self, "bringing into play the criteria of an 'aesthetics of existence.'" Creating an aesthetics of existence is the process of appropriating certain values, practices, and modes of comportment through which individuals fashion a style of living for themselves. Through this, human beings identify themselves as subjects. These three axes constitute "the three fundamental elements of any experience," says Foucault.[6]

The concept of *experience* has had an especially privileged status in the history of philosophy at least since René Descartes, but Foucault redefines the word. It no longer refers to something that a subject *has*, at the interiority of mind or consciousness. Rather, experience is what the subject *is*, understood as an emergence within an historically delimited space boundaried by the convergence of discursive practices, power relations, and modes of subjectivation in their specificity. It is not that the experience of subjectivity is sometimes discursive, at other times effected by relations of power, and still at other times bound to the ways individuals conceive of themselves. Experience is, rather, "the *correlation* of a domain of knowledge, a type of normativity, and a mode of relation to self."[7] The interplay of these three axes constitutes "a matrix of experience" in which a particular, historically defined form of subjectivity can emerge—as an event.[8]

The matrix of an experience of subjectivity can be understood as a domain or space structured by the correspondence and mutual influence of three kinds of register: corresponding to their respective axes we have the interplay of truth, rules, self; of knowledge, technology, modality; of type, norm, relation. When put in these terms we can perhaps see how tenuous and artificial the lines are between the axes, how easy it is for one to slip over and interfere with another. And, in fact, they must be thought about together, without hierarchy or primacy. No one axis is more fundamental than the others or serves as their ground. On the other hand, their convergence gives a specificity to experience that diverges somewhat from that which characterizes each axis when considered separately. That is, there is seldom a perfect mesh among the axes, which often gives rise to an experience that appears inconsistent, or contradictory, or even irrational. This can be seen, for example, in the modern experience of sexuality, in which the dominant discourses speak of repression, but actual practices reflect a widespread preoccupation with sex; where individuals are at once encouraged to denounce their sexuality and to explore it fervently.[9] Foucault would not, and does not, attempt to reconcile such inconsistencies or antagonisms. Instead, he simply notes their occurrence and considers them as part and parcel of a given experience.

How are we, then, to understand the interplay between the three axes? What is the nature of their relation? In what ways do they influence, affect, interfere with one another? First of all, there is "no general law" governing their relationship.[10] There is no transcendental or dialectical principle that reconciles their oppositions and holds them together in a metaphysical unity. The interplay consists rather in a complex, more or less haphazard, network of historical practices, both discursive and nondiscursive. Within this network there are transmissions, transferences, borrowings, usages, employments and deployments, infiltrations and interconnections, mutations, transformations, and instantiations, but also antagonisms, struggles, resistances, cancellations. These have to be taken on their own terms, where and how they install themselves—as the specific historically determined experience which they constitute together.

Let us examine the relation between the axes of discourse and power. Foucault asserts that "relations of power cannot be established, consolidated nor implemented without the production, accumulation, circulation, and functioning of a discourse."[11] This does not mean that discourse is the ground of power or is metaphysically prior to it. Rather, discourse and power "are integrated with one another" in the sense that power is always attended by a set of discursive representations that both sanction and structure the exercise of power. At the same time, power not only distributes discourse in concrete forms in the social body, but in so doing effects new discourse, new discursive expectations.[12] In simple terms, which do not quite capture the richness of the word *savoir*, discourse refers to the production of bodies of knowledge, disciplines, truth. However, "discursive practices are not purely and simply ways of producing discourse. They are embodied in technical processes, in institutions, in patterns for general behavior, in forms for transmission and diffusion, and in pedagogical forms which, at once, impose and maintain them."[13] The "embodiment" of discourse refers to its appropriation and implementation in real social practices: practices that delimit space, determine possibilities, erect hierarchies, define individuals. In such an embodiment we have "the constant articulation . . . of power on knowledge and of knowledge on power."

The phrase "power/knowledge" to a great extent expresses the intimacy of discourse and power relations. Power proceeds through the deployment of various knowledges for the normalization and cohesion of the social body. Knowledge both guides and sanctions practices of subjugation and objectivation that at once govern and define individuals. The production of knowledge, in turn, requires entrenched institutional apparatuses (such as education, science, media) where it can emerge and be disseminated. Knowledge must conform to rules of acceptance, diffusion, and consumption that go beyond the laws of rarity and exclusion governing the emergence of statements within a discursive formation. In fact, the embodiment of knowledge in real institutional and social practices makes it an essential feature of the network of power relations itself. At the juncture of power/knowledge, discourse become "a formidable tool of control and power."[14] Indeed, at this juncture it becomes virtually impossible to distinguish discourse and power since real practices of spatialization and differentiation are immediately and intrinsically animated by discourses that give such practices meaning. The distribution of bodies in space is immediately and inseparably attended by knowledges that explain what these bodies are in truth, what they need, how they should be organized. Truth is not something outside of power; rather, it is the concrete forms effected by the juncture of power and knowledge. Every society is governed by a *regime of truth*, which consists at the same time of (1) "the types of discourses which it accepts and makes function as true," and (2) political structures whose function is to articulate such discourses in concrete forms onto the social body.[15]

One of the concrete forms that power/knowledge gives rise to is the *individual*. The individual is the combination of a set of discursive representations about human activity and existence, and a set of rules, constraints, and practices bearing on undefined bodies. The juncture of power/knowledge delimits a space for the emergence of the individual. This is a relational space, wherein part of the identity of the individual is a function of the place she occupies in a set of rankings and orderings, a set of possibilities for acting and being acted upon. We should not conceive of the individual as an already constituted being who otherwise stands outside the complex of power/knowledge relations. Foucault says that "the individual is not a pregiven entity which is seized on by the exercise of power. The individual, with his identity and characteristics, is the product of a relation of power exercised over bodies, multiplicities, movements, desires, forces" (*P/K*, 73–74). Relations of power, which conjoin a body, movement, desire, force to constitute an individual, "pass via knowledge . . . within forms of discourse" (*P/K*, 69). The individual, then, is not a basic unit. It is a fabrication—a product of specific, historically contingent, discursive and nondiscursive practices that define roles, relations, positions, statuses, freedoms, capacities, natures, even sexuality. Here we should add that the fabrication of individuality has always been accompanied by a concept of *self-hood*, that the individual has a self, that it can be aware *of itself*. This opens up the possibility for processes of subjectivation.

Discourse and power relations bear upon processes of subjectivation in the following ways. Subjectivation is a process of self-formation in which individuals construct an identity for themselves through an appropriation of certain values, practices, regimens, and modes of comportment. This "technology of the self" is a matter of establishing a relation of self with self that involves defining a realm of (moral) concern and determining how one ought to relate to the objects of this concern. In this way the individual forms itself as a subject—and, moreover, recognizes itself as such. Yet, what is the object of this recognition? It is not so much an entity or being present at hand, but a *discourse of truth* about oneself. Embodied in actual practices of subjectivation, such a discourse of truth is not simply a symbolic representation of oneself.[16] A discourse of truth regarding oneself is the circumscription of a space of real possibilities and limitations for the self. An individual cannot conceive of going beyond this space because she is *identical* with the discourse of truth that constitutes the self. In this sense, recognition is at once a determination; identity is a trap.

A relation of self to self can be understood as a "form of reflexivity," says Foucault—that is, as a mode of self-examination and assessment. Discourses of truth can be understood as "forms of rationality," as a thematic complex of representations bearing on common objects and held together by certain principles or standards of organization whose validity is internal to the complex itself. In technologies of the self we have "forms of rationality applied by the human subject to itself."[17] While it is appropriate to speak of a discourse of truth peculiar to the self, the construction of such a discourse involves the application of forms of rationality, or discourses, which come from sources independent of the individual. Religious discourses, discourses of philosophy and medicine, political or juridical discourses, and (perhaps most important to modern subjectivity) the disciplines of the human sciences: such discourses are applied by individuals to themselves in the constitution of themselves as subjects. Such discourses carry their own values, norms, expectations to which, through the process of subjectivation, the individual feels obliged to conform, thus comprising part of the ethical dimension of a relation of self with self. More often than not, however, these discourses are imposed on individuals. Through what channels are these discourses "made available" to individuals? What forces bear on individuals such that they are obliged to appropriate these forms of rationality in technologies of the self?

Forms of reflexivity and discourses of truth are linked by relations of power, says Foucault.[18] In modern society this linkage has been effected most predominantly by the mechanisms of disciplinary power. Techniques of the self "are frequently linked to the techniques for the direction of others. For example, if we take educational institutions, we realize that one is managing others and teaching them to manage themselves."[19] Here we bring into play all the mechanisms of discipline: apparatuses of surveillance and registration, the distribution of bodies in space, the regulation of time and activity, techniques of subjection and individualization. Disciplinary power can be said to proceed through techniques of domination and coercion since it manipulates bodies and controls them. Yet the efficacy and efficiency of these techniques are dependent on technologies of the self whereby individuals take on the norms and rules of discipline and make them part of the constitution of themselves. Thus we have to take into account the "interaction" between the processes by which individuals act upon themselves and the techniques of domination and control peculiar to discipline.[20]

According to Foucault, "The *contact point* at which the way individuals are driven and known by others is tied to the way they conduct themselves and know themselves. This can be called *government*."[21] Here the term government refers not so much to state apparatuses as it does to relations of power in which we find the integration of coercive technologies and technologies of the self. Government, says Foucault, is a question of *conduct*, and this in two senses: a sense of *conduire*, meaning "to lead," and a sense of *se conduire*, the reflexive construction meaning "to conduct oneself." "Perhaps," he explains, "the equivocal nature of the term *conduct* is one of the best aides for coming to terms with the specificity of power relations. For to 'conduct' is at the same time to 'lead' others (according to mechanisms of coercion which are, to varying degrees strict), and a way of behaving within a more or less open field of possibilities."[22] Foucault's play on the word *conduire* expresses the duality of the role or function of government. On the one hand, we have government in the sense of the procedures and techniques for managing, manipulating, and controlling others. At the same time, government refers to self-government—not in the sense of a political right, but much more basic and more literal: the ways individuals attend to themselves, conduct themselves, govern themselves. Government expresses both sides of this relation at once: that the "field of possibilities" for individual attention to self is structured by practices of domination and coercion.

In government there is "the gradual imposition of a whole system of values" that structure the way individuals identify themselves. Thus, government is involved in "the formulation of the truth concerning oneself."[23] That is, it is implicated in the production of forms of reflexivity through which the subject knows itself. Producing a discourse of truth about oneself, through procedures of confession and self-examination, and turning oneself into an object of knowledge (both for oneself and for others) are imposed on the individual as a moral obligation (for example, by Christianity, medicine, psychiatry, education). In this sense, relations of power are involved in the very production of conscience and consciousness.

It is now possible to draw a schematic of a matrix of experience, the modern experience of subjectivity:[24]

MATRIX OF EXPERIENCE

Discourse / Power / Subjectivation

Disciplines / Discipline / Government / Self-Government / Self-Formation

Savoir / Pouvoir / Conduire / Rapport à Soi

Truth / Rules / Ethics

Object / Subject / Self

SUBJECTIVITY

We might observe that this matrix consists of three inverted and overlapping triangles.[25] Each triangle represents one of the three axes of subjectivity. One triangle, which represents the axis of knowledge, has "Disciplines/Discipline/Government" forming its top side. Its other two sides are formed by "Disciplines/Savoir/Truth," and "Government/Pouvoir/Truth," respectively, with "Truth" at the angle of the intersection of these two sides. This triangle can be viewed as encompassing the dynamic of *savoir* and *pouvoir*, of the power/knowledge relations that animate this axis. The middle triangle has "Discipline/Government/Self-Government" as its top side, with "Rules" at its opposite vertex (one could easily replace "Rules" with "Norms" here). This triangle represents the axis of power, which is animated by the relation between power (*pouvoir*) and conduct (*conduire*). Finally, the axis of ethics, or subjectivation, is represented by a triangle with "Government/Self-Government/Self-Formation" forming its top side, with lines running through "Conduire" and "Rapport à Soi," and joining at the angle represented by "Ethics." This triangle can be viewed as animated by the way modes of conduct inform a relation to self. Notice that all three triangles share an element or elements with the other two. The left and middle triangles share "Discipline/Government" and "Pouvoir"; the middle and right triangles share "Government/Self-Government" and "Conduire"; and all three triangles—all three axes—share "Government." Government, in all the richness and complexity of the word, represents perhaps the definitive feature of the modern experience of subjectivity. In government, we have all three axes at play at once, informing an experience of subjectivity in which individuals are at once objects of knowledge, subjected to techniques of control and manipulation, and determined by a notion of selfhood—a form of subjectivity in which we are, at the same time and inseparably, "Object/Subject/Self."

Of course, there is no necessity to these triangles, least of all in their organization as they are presented here. They merely allow us to isolate the factors that permit us to analyze experience in terms of the three axes. Although there is a nonintegrateable difference between the axes, we should at least erase the "slashes" between the elements of this configuration. These elements always function in concert, not simply paralleling each other, but in an interplay defined by their complicity. It is possible to conduct an archaeology of discursive regularities; it is possible to analyze power relations through a genealogy; and it is possible to perform an ethics of modes of subjectivation. Yet these analyses require methodological acts of abstraction that do not really capture the way discourse, power relations, and modes of subjectivation function together. They function together without hierarchy or primacy, and even though these axes are historically contingent, no historical *priority* can be ascribed to one axis over the others. Their relation is so intimate, in fact, that each axis is "affected by transformations in the other two."[26] Nor is there some transcendent force outside or underneath these axes which brings them together and sets them in motion. If anything "holds" them together, it is that each axis is a kind of *problematization*.[27] Experience, then, consists in a series of interrelated problematizations in their concrete forms: systems of representations, institutions, practices.[28] Within the matrix of this experience, of this complex of problematizations, we have the constitution of the human subject, "in its relations to the true, to rules, to itself," all at once.

In modern societies, as Foucault shows, the problematizations constitutive of experience have become much more linked to institutions and institutional practices.[29] This is commensurate with the infiltration of discipline in modern society. The general diffusion of disciplinary mechanisms has had a fundamental impact on our experience as political subjects. The matrix of this experience has been structured by a disciplinary relation to government, or, more precisely, governmentality. At this point, I want to show how political subjects are fabricated through a political technology internal to, and functioning in the interests of, the governmentalized state. This technology is defined by the axial interplay of discourse, power relations, and modes of subjectivation. By understanding political subjects as an effect of this interplay, we will begin to recognize a pernicious antinomy informing their emergence and existence.

The State and/of Governmentality

The three movements of Foucault's thought turn the Kantian question of "What is man?" into the genealogical question, "How does 'man' emerge?" In the same way, and more specifically, the movements of his thought can be brought together to serve as a model for understanding the emergence of the modern political subject. The political subject is taken for granted by traditional political philosophy, whose primary task is to set limits to power.[30] This commits traditional political philosophy to a rather narrow field of concern, namely, problems of sovereignty and legitimation, as if there were a linear relationship between real political freedom and the use or abuse of political power. But this hides a fundamental inconsistency in traditional political philosophy. Neither the question of how political subjects are constituted (of how they emerge in the first place and of how they are maintained in their status as political subjects) nor the question of how power functions can be answered, since both power and the political subject are presupposed by traditional political philosophy, and because, under the contractual view, power and the political subject presuppose one another. That is, if we want to explain power we have to appeal to political subjects who have power, and if we want to explain political subjects it is only by reference to the political power which they may or may not have. Certainly the problems of power and the political subject belong together, but their circular and self-referential juxtaposition in traditional political theory leaves both fundamentally unexamined.[31]

Of course, all political philosophies ostensibly deal with power. From Plato to Machiavelli to John Stuart Mill, power has been of primary concern to political theorists. Yet upon closer examination we find that in traditional political philosophy, and especially in liberal theory, power is probably the most taken for granted and least analyzed of concepts. To be sure, power receives a great deal of intellectual attention and even privilege in the discourses of traditional political philosophy; as, for example, in Mill, who begins *On Liberty* with the declaration that the subject of the essay will be "the nature and limits of the power which can be legitimately exercised by society over the individual."[32] Yet the very way Mill phrases this statement is representative of the narrow conception of power found in traditional political philosophies; that is, an understanding of power primarily in terms of a binary relationship between sovereignty and political subjects. The problem of power for traditional political philosophy has always been a problem of the *balance of power*, the proper distribution of power between the king or governmental authority and the constituency. Thus, power is analyzed in terms of self-determination, representation, accountability, interference, social and economic opportunities, rights, freedoms, and the use of force or coercion over others. These are the true measures of power, says traditional political philosophy, and identifying the proper limits of power is the appropriate object of a theoretical focus.

No one would claim that these are illusory concerns or deny that they have real practical repercussions in society that need to be considered by political theory. Suppose, however, that in reality such things as rights, freedoms, social and economic opportunities, governmental representation and accountability are only the *effects* of power, that they are surface manifestations of a network of relations that make such "indicators" of power possible. If so, then this would leave the problem of power in traditional political philosophy relatively unbroached, its treatment superficial.

Consider the following passage from Isaiah Berlin's *Four Essays on Liberty* (1969), in which Berlin says, "For Constant, Mill, Tocqueville, and the liberal tradition to which they belong, no society is free unless it is governed by at any rate two interrelated principles: first, that no power, but only rights, can be regarded as absolute, so that all men, whatever power governs them, have an absolute right to refuse to behave inhumanely; and, second, that there are frontiers, not artificially drawn, within which men should be inviolable, these frontiers being defined in terms of rules so long and widely accepted that their observance has entered into the very conception of what it is to be a normal human being, and therefore, also of what it is to act inhumanly or insanely; rules of which it would be absurd to say, for example, that they could be abrogated by some formal procedure on the part of some court or sovereign body."[33] This passage contains three classic presuppositions of liberal theory: (1) the political subject as an autonomous individual surrounded by "inviolable frontiers" of freedom (i.e., a classic deployment of the "savage noble" discursive motif); (2) power as something which issues from sovereignty and that may be possessed; and (3) a conception of the State as the seat of sovereignty and bearing a linear, contractual relation of power to the political subject. Let us take each presupposition in turn and examine it with reference to the idea of political identity as the effect of a network of disciplinary power relations.

The first presupposition—the political subject as an abstract, autonomous individual—carries with it assumptions of certain basic rights belonging to the individual and protected by a sphere of inviolability. Whether this concept is based on appeals to a state of nature, or social contract, or the general will, or governmental representation, political subjects under this view are all assumed to have a fundamental identity consisting of the traditional trappings of selfhood: consciousness, conscience, agency; they are only incidentally shopkeepers, physicians, or police officers. Yet strip away the ostensible social identities and all that is left is a metaphysical abstraction. Where are the political subjects valorized by liberal theory? What "frontiers" do they *really* inhabit?

Foucault's analysis of disciplinary practices shows that the political subject is made, not born. Political subjects are produced in a society in which the principal dimension of power is not governmental representation, but disciplinary tactics and apparatuses. The subject produced by discipline is defined with reference "not to the state of nature, but to the meticulously subordinated cogs of a machine, not to the primal social contract, but to permanent coercions, not to fundamental rights, but to indefinitely progressive forms of training, not to the general will but to automatic docility."[34] Disciplinary subjects bear little resemblance to liberal subjects. In liberal theory, the individual is a fundamental unit; in discipline, individuality is a manufactured product of *dressage* and normalization, an *accoutrement* of identity and identifiability, surreptitiously invested in subjected and objectified bodies. The subject does not come full-blown, with certain inherent rights and freedoms to discipline; discipline produces modes of subjectivity through a complex series of meticulous techniques and petty mechanisms. The "rights" and "freedoms" that subjects have are those completely delineated by a disciplinary practice: the "right" to advance in rank, the "freedom" to eat meals at a designated hour, the "liberty" to be trained to be a productive member of society. Even on liberal theory's own terms, the social opportunities, freedoms, and place of subjects are completely tied to the particular disciplinary practices to which they are subjected. Finally, there is nothing abstract or metaphysical about the subjects produced by discipline: they are specific, concrete identities formed and individuated by specific, distinct, refined mechanisms, techniques, apparatuses, and institutions concerned with the smallest gesture, movement, exercise, time, use, and place of the individual. The objectified, individualized, docile bodies of discipline: these are the true "political" subjects of modern society.

No one escapes discipline. There is no free space of autonomy or noninterference that individuals may enjoy. This is for two interrelated reasons. The first is that since the seventeenth and eighteenth centuries there has been a "gradual extension of the mechanisms of discipline . . . throughout the whole social body" (*DP*, 209). Society is now in general a disciplinary society in which discipline has infiltrated almost every aspect of the everyday lives of individuals. Even a casual observation would show that we are subjected to disciplinary institutions from the time we are born. Moreover, Foucault shows that disciplinary mechanisms have spread out from their institutional enclosures, that they have become deinstitutionalized: "One also sees the spread of disciplinary procedures, not in the form of enclosed institutions, but as centers of observation disseminated throughout society" (*DP*, 212). Religious groups, moral factions, charity and service organizations such as the Red Cross and the Salvation Army, social organizations ranging from the Boy Scouts to the PTA, counseling and peer groups, the police, concerned with everything from gambling and prostitution to the raising of children, have spread disciplinary practices directly into the family, the home, the church, the marketplace, to the most scattered areas of social life.

The second reason, which is a reflection of the first, that there can be no space of freedom, in the liberal sense, for the individual, is that to be *individuated* is itself already a mark of discipline's hold on the body. Individualization is a disciplinary form of subjection and domination. It means that the individual has already been marked, trained, differentiated, judged, ranked, is already bound to a disciplinary practice, a function, a use. From this standpoint, to call the individual "autonomous" is a contradiction in terms. For the disciplinary individual, precisely to the extent he is an individual, it is already too late to speak of freedom (in the classic political sense).

This leads into the second assumption of liberal theory, regarding the nature of the power that invests political subjects. In modern disciplinary society, the power that subjects individuals is not a power that issues from sovereignty, not a power that may be possessed or exercised according to the conscious intentions of those who "have power." Disciplinary power is an anonymous network of power relations, a power that is autonomous and automatic, that functions independently of any one individual. We see this most clearly in the type of power that operates in disciplinary surveillance. The pyramidal structure of the disciplinary gaze "makes possible the operation of a relational power" in that the power exercised is a function of the position that individuals hold in relation to one another. As Foucault notes, "By means of such surveillance, disciplinary power became an 'integrated' system . . . organized as a multiple, automatic and anonymous power; for although surveillance rests on individuals, its functioning is that of a network of relations from top to bottom, but also to a certain extent from bottom to top and laterally; this network 'holds' the whole together and traverses it in its entirety with effects of power that derive from one another: supervisors, perpetually supervised. The power in the hierarchized surveillance of the disciplines is not possessed as a thing, or transferred as a property; it functions as a piece of machinery" (*DP*, 176–77). Foucault's description of disciplinary surveillance as "a piece of machinery" is not simply metaphorical. At a basic level, any machine is a structure consisting of various fixed and moving parts. Surveillance is a system of relays, breaks, and connections that puts into play a power effected by the structure itself. This power invests individuals in the sense of their being mediums, channels, points of articulation for the circulation of a power that subjects them all, from the "highest" to the "lowest" in the hierarchy. One cannot point to any one individual and say that this person is the source, the owner, or the initiator of power. One cannot even point to any particular aspect of the framework and say, "Here is power," since we are dealing with a network of relations in which the exercise of power is an effect of the structure itself. Within this structure power is not "wielded" on or against individuals as such; rather, the effect of surveillance is to turn the supervised, perpetually observed individual into "the principle of his own subjection" (*DP*, 203). That is, the individual puts into play the constraints, dictates, norms of discipline, not due to any external force or coercion but freely and without resistance, because she is so deeply embedded in, so complicitous with, the subtle, silent, invisible functioning of this power. Once the structure of disciplinary surveillance is in place—and it comes to be so not so much through conscious intentions, but through a series of relatively disparate tactics and practices—it functions automatically, autonomously, and, most important, *discreetly*, without the individuals fully aware that a certain kind of power is subjecting them.

What is true of hierarchized surveillance in particular is true of disciplinary power in general. It is a power "exercised through its invisibility," a power effected by a whole relational complex of strategies, techniques, and apparatuses, a whole technology of power that in its entirety may seem overwhelming, but in its meticulous operations is subtle, discreet, virtually unrecognizable. This power functions constantly and spontaneously; it controls and coerces through a set of mechanisms built directly into the network itself, mechanisms of objectification, individualization, and normalization.

The liberal, contractual view of power appeals to a notion of sovereignty that still conforms for the most part to its original Latin meaning of "above" or "over." The sovereign is an individual, or group of individuals, who are above all others, supreme in power, rank, or authority. (This is the case even if sovereignty is defined as the "general will" of the people.) It is basically a monarchical view of power. The democratic movements of the

Enlightenment sought to disinvest some of the power of sovereignty and reinvest it in political subjects; but the power that is distributed to individuals in representative government is of the same sort as that previously reserved to the sovereign: a power of self-determination and autonomy, of *personal* sovereignty. Under a contractual ideology and through various mechanisms of legal and juridical reform, power was (supposedly) taken from the sovereign and given, in varying "amounts," to political subjects. The role or purpose of sovereignty was redefined as preserving and protecting the welfare of society as a whole, while at the same time respecting the dignity and freedom of its citizenry. Yet the political power that was distributed to individuals issued, at least in principle, directly from sovereignty. It was still a power that could be possessed and exercised, but now it was, more and more, "in the hands" of political subjects.

Foucault argues that this notion of "sovereign power" did have its historical analogue in society and was, in fact, the principal dimension of power prior to the formation of disciplinary society. Like discipline, but very different in form, structure, and effectiveness, sovereignty was an identifiable technology of power consisting of its own strategies, techniques, and apparatuses.[35] This technology put into play relations of power which were oppositional, confrontational, even violent. The principal differentiation was between an absolute sovereign and *his* subjects (here emphasizing subjects as possessions of the sovereign), who were at the mercy of his benevolence or tyranny. The locus of power was clearly visible and served to polarize the relationship between authority and constituency. This eventually precipitated the reforms, in the name of autonomy and humanity, of such ideological factions as the Physiocrats and the Levellers. These reforms initiated new technologies of power that were ostensibly designed to offset the excesses of sovereignty. But all the while, in the background and on the fringes of society, behind the scenes of the great democratic and humanitarian debates, were developing the subtle, petty mechanisms of discipline that would eventually infiltrate society and supplant the sovereign/democratic technologies as the principal dimension of power.

This leads us into the third presupposition of liberal theory, and of traditional political philosophy in general, regarding the conception of the State as the seat of sovereignty and bearing a linear, contractual relation of power to the political subject. Even if at some point in our history the State did conform (ostensibly) to this model, the State as such no longer exists. Foucault shows how disciplinary mechanisms have infiltrated state apparatuses and changed the face of government in modern society, how sovereignty has given way to "governmentality."

One of the first state apparatuses to undergo a disciplinary transformation was that of the police. Originally a "vengeful arm of the king," and later an instrument of vigilance designed to enforce the codified laws of the reformers, in the eighteenth century the police became one of the most pernicious apparatuses of disciplinary surveillance, deploying a perpetual "faceless gaze," now outside of and free from the enclosed institutions of discipline and bearing on society as a whole: "With the police, one is in the indefinite world of a supervision that seeks ideally to reach the most elementary particle, the most passing phenomenon of the social body" (*DP*, 213–14). The police represents "the infinitely small of political power" in that it permits the transmission of governmental authority to the farthest reaches, the lowest regions of society, filling in the gaps, deploying an "interstitial discipline" that links social spaces together in a patchwork quilt of panoptic power. This is a complex apparatus in that it is "regulated" by legal codes, and the force it wields is at bottom monarchical, but it deploys a surveillance that is disciplinary in its purest form: subjecting through objectification, coercing by making visible.

"The organization of the police apparatus in the eighteenth century sanctioned a generalization of the disciplines that became co-extensive with the state itself," says Foucault (*DP*, 215). How a generalization of this sort was made possible is a complicated issue, but it begins in part with the disciplinary techniques employed by the police apparatus. The police did not simply observe and enforce the law; they *documented* everything and everyone on whom their power was exercised. This resulted in the accumulation of a vast archive of records, reports, registers, "a permanent account of individuals' behavior." Repeating the disciplinary gestures of such institutions as the school and the hospital, this documentation allowed the state to monitor and control its constituency; this gave rise to a number of devices that generalized a political tactic of registration and identification.[36]

Police documentation and registration is coextensive with a fundamental shift in the nature of the State. In simple terms, this shift occurred when the principle concern of the state changed from the *territory,* in which the aim of power was the preservation and protection of the sovereign's principality and to which political subjects were basically subordinated inhabitants, to a prevailing concern with a new object: *population.* As Foucault explains, "One of the great innovations in the techniques of power in the eighteenth century was the emergence of 'population' as an economic and political problem: population as wealth, population as manpower or labor capacity, population balanced between its own growth and the resources it commanded. Governments perceived that they were not dealing simply with subjects, or even with a 'people,' but with a 'population,' with its specific phenomena and its peculiar variables: birth and death rates, life expectancy, fertility, state of health, frequency of illnesses, patterns of diet and habitation."[37] The state's emerging concern with the population is defined by reference to three interrelated areas: the economy, health, and sex. The same demographic changes that gave rise to disciplinary techniques and institutions at the local level caused the state to shift its attention to the production of wealth and the control of disease and sexual practices that affect the size, character, and even morality of those who constitute the body politic. It becomes necessary to take control of the size and distribution of the state's subjects, to exert influence over where and how they work and live, to monitor the quality of their environment, to make inroads into the previously "private" domains of marriage, sexuality, and methods of contraception.

The emergence of population as a political category of primary importance has a double focus, a focus that operates "both at the level of each individual who goes to make up the population, and also the interest of population as such."[38] It will be discovered that the population as a whole "has its own regularities," that it "carries a range of intrinsic aggregate effects" (*GV*, 17). The state will seek to manipulate these effects by implementing certain practices and techniques that affect, for example, birth rates, regional distributions of people, and the flow of capital to designated segments of the population. The individual will become a unit of the population—deserving special attention, but always with reference to the welfare of the larger social aggregate. The practices (as opposed to the ideology) of the state brought to bear on the individual will recognize her, not so much as a person, but as a *body*, whose activities, lifestyle, habits, and relations reflect trends peculiar to particular segments of the population. The power exercised on the individual will be essentially disciplinary in nature, in that it will be characterized by distributions of individuals in space, the control of time and activity, and, above all, the employment of a disciplinary gaze that monitors the individual and "fixes" her place in the broader demographic aggregate of the population.[39]

The shift from the territory to population as the primary target of the state gave rise to a new type of political rationality, says Foucault: that of "governmentality." To explain this rationality, Foucault contrasts the work of Machiavelli and one of his contemporary critics, Guillaume de La Perriere. The politics of Machiavelli's *The Prince*, or at least the interpretations of it that led to anti-Machiavellian literature, posited the sovereign as occupying "a position of externality and transcendence" to his principality. In this perspective, the foundation of sovereignty is the territory, which the sovereign acquires through inheritance or conquest. Subjects are merely inhabitants of the territory, to a great degree as much property of the sovereign as the territory itself. The link between the sovereign and the territory, and the subjects that inhabit that territory, is the principality, understood as the rule the sovereign exercises over a (more or less) defined geographical area, as the relation the sovereign, as ruler, bears to the territory and its inhabitants. This link is a fragile one, says Foucault, constantly threatened from both without and within. The task of sovereignty, the savoir-faire that *The Prince* is written to explain and defend, consists in this, "that the objective of the exercise of power is to reinforce, strengthen, and protect this principality." Thus, Machiavelli's text is concerned with (1) identifying dangers to the sovereign's rule, and (2) with developing an "art of manipulating the power relations that will allow the Prince to protect his principality" (*GV*, 7–8).

It was against the political rationality of *The Prince*, which is a precursor to the juridical conception of sovereignty found in liberal theory to the extent that it attempts to "draw lines" between the power of the sovereign and his subjects, that anti-Machiavellian literature such as La Perrière's *Miroir politique* (1567) arose. This literature attempted to replace the "art of sovereignty" with an "art of government" that would be concerned with all the manifold aspects of the state and not just with the protection of the sovereign's principality. To illustrate the distinction, Foucault quotes from *Miroir politique*, noting that "government is the right disposition of things arranged so as to lead to a convenient end." Foucault interprets "things" in this passage as referring, not simply to the elements which constitute a sovereign's territory, but to "the complex unit constituted by men and things. Consequently, the things which the government is to be concerned about are men, but men in their relations, their links, their imbrication with those other things which are wealth, resources, means of subsistence, the territory with its specific qualities, climate, irrigation, fertility, etc.; men in their relation to that other kind of things which are customs, habits, ways of doing and thinking, etc.; lastly, men in their relation to . . . accidents and misfortunes such as famine, epidemics, death, etc." (*GV*, 11). This notion of government is still very crude, says Foucault, and takes as its model the government of the family (understood under the concept of "oeconomy"). Later, this notion will be taken up by Jean-Jacques Rousseau and François Quesnay and expanded beyond the metaphors of the family and the household; but, although attempts were made (by Thomas Hobbes, for example) to incorporate an "art of government" into a political theory, this view remained peripheral, subordinate, to the juridical view of sovereignty. Social contract theory is designed precisely to strike a compromise between the concerns of government and those of sovereignty, to solicit concern and respect for the rights of subjects who occupy a territory, while at the same time recognizing (under certain arbitrarily defined limits) the authority of the sovereign: "The theory of the social contract will make it possible for the founding contract, the mutual pledge of ruler and subjects, to become a sort of theoretical matrix for the possible integration of the general principles of an art of government. But . . . it remained at the stage of the formulation of general principles of public law" (*GV*, 16). In fact, the model of traditional sovereignty proved to be "too abstract and too rigid" for a model of government to be articulated onto it.[40]

Government finally replaces sovereignty nearly two centuries after La Perriere with the emergence of population as the principal concern of politics. "The population now appears more as the aim of government than the power of the ruler. . . ." (*GV*, 18). This transition was made possible by the convergence of three key historical factors. One factor was the adoption by the state of the archaic Christian model of "pastoral power." Instead of transcendent ruler, the sovereign comes to bear the relation of a shepherd to his flock. The "government of souls" practiced by the Christian Church, designed to lead followers to salvation in the next world, is secularized and replaced with more "worldly aims," says Foucault, such as "health, well-being (that is, sufficient wealth, standard of living), security, protection," in order to achieve a kind of salvation in this world rather than the next. Pastoral power invokes a kind of paradox in that it attributes "as much value to a single lamb as to the entire flock." It is an individualizing power in that it forces the individual to know himself in truth, even as it seeks a self-effacement of that very individualization. In its secular form in the modern state, pastoral power organizes the knowledge of political subjects around two poles: "one, globalizing and quantitative, concerning the population; the other analytical, concerning the individual." Pastoral power brings these two poles together in a change of political emphasis—an emphasis which now focuses on the inhabitants of the state both collectively and individually, rather than on the territory in which they incidentally reside—that will structure the affairs of the state from the eighteenth century to the present day.[41]

The second historical factor that allowed for the emergence of government and its concern with population was the emergence of the modern nation-state in the seventeenth and eighteenth centuries following the

Treaty of Westphalia. The shift to state as nation, rather than principality, gave rise to, and was coextensive with, a number of new "diplomatic-military techniques" designed to preserve the *integrity* of the nation. A nation's integrity is defined in terms of two major interrelated facets, the security of the nation and the identity of the nation. Maintaining the security of the nation requires a dual focus in that threats to that security can come from both without and within. Various "apparatuses of security," such as the formation of standing armies, but just as important, treaties, alliances, and trade agreements (carrying increasingly complex administrative machinery), safeguard the nation's relation to other political bodies. Security is also a matter of great concern within the borders of the nation. But this is not so much a concern with insurrection or rebellion (classic Machiavellian concerns), as it is with matters of health, hygiene, economic stability, crime, welfare, education, "domestic tranquility." It is now recognized that the nation can be undermined from within due to its own internal problems and instabilities. The object of this concern, the target of this governmental intervention, will become the population, with all of its peculiar variables.

The second facet of the nation's integrity centers on its identity. On the international level, diplomatic-military techniques and apparatuses of security contribute toward the preservation of the nation's identity and, to a great extent, its construction. National identity serves as a measure of integrity to the outside world; it is a complex fabrication of ideologies, doctrines, and policies disseminated through various modes of diplomacy and/or techniques of imperialism and colonialization.[42] It is the crux of treaties and agreements, which in turn underline and reinforce the nation's identity, vis-à-vis a relation of mutual recognition with other countries. This face which the nation projects is essential to its integrity as a political body. But it is also necessary to project this face inward, to instill or to discover a national identity in the citizenry. National integrity is a matter of unity.[43] Among the many ways this can be achieved is through the production and propagation of discourses of nationalism, which are disseminated by means of governmental intervention in such institutions as education, at the local level where indoctrinal practices make contact with the individual.[44] Yet any effort to instill a national identity requires a rigorous survey of the social body—the population—to determine its nature and makeup. This leads us to the third historical factor contributing to the shape of modern government (as a disciplinary technology of power), namely, the development and expansion of the police apparatus.

The police, which have their origins in France under Louis XV, play the dual role of serving both as an apparatus of security and of deploying major techniques contributing to the construction of a national identity. In their punitive function, the police exercise a disciplinary surveillance concerned with matters of crime, deviancy, protection, and the enforcement of law; doing so extends the arm of state authority to the local level.[45] Yet, as we have already observed, the police also employ and, in fact, refine the disciplinary techniques of documentation and registration, making it possible to isolate and identify those on whom its power is exercised. This coincides with the development of "a set of analyses and forms of knowledge" that will eventually become organized into that "science of the state" we know as *statistics* (*GV*, 14). Statistics makes possible the production of a whole *savoir* concerning the population. This will serve as the basis for a transition "from a regime dominated by structures of sovereignty to one ruled by techniques of government" (*GV*, 18).

The political rationality that characterizes this transition is governmentality. The historical emergence and convergence of a secularized pastoral power, diplomatic-military techniques, and apparatuses of security such as the police, turns governmentality into a full-blown technology of power, an "ensemble formed by the institutions, procedures, analyses, and reflections, the calculations and tactics that allow the exercise of this very specific albeit complex form of power, which has as its target population" (*GV*, 20). The "governmentalization" of the state consists of a vast proliferation of state administrative apparatuses and widespread bureaucratization. There is a virtual explosion of offices, branches, divisions, bureaus, agencies, and institutions that function as the instruments of governmental intervention into the affairs of the population. This intervention is essentially disciplinary in character.[46] Above all, government institutes apparatuses of writing that would make those found in the school, the barracks, or the hospital pale by comparison.[47] Through the disciplinary techniques of registration and the constituting of files, government individualizes and categorizes whole segments of the population. It is on the basis of the knowledge and data provided by this documentation and registration that services and policies are meted out at the local level by governmental offices. Intervention also occurs through governmental regulation, which operates a disciplinary gaze over such everyday activities as those regarding work, health, and the exchange of goods and services. Another disciplinary aspect of governmental intervention is that it contains its own "infra-penalty"; punishment practices (such as fines, levies, seizures, audits, the withholding of services or benefits) that bear only a cursory relation to more traditional juridical and legal measures and are far removed from the violent spectacle of the sovereign's wrath. These practices are designed to be corrective, with the welfare of the population as a whole as its target. Finally, governmental intervention is disciplinary in the sense that the power it exercises is characterized by its invisibility. Although it often proceeds "through large-scale campaigns," it is most effective when the population is "ignorant of what is being done to it" (GV, 18).

All this makes the relation of the state to political subjects very complex and tends to undermine the presuppositions of liberal theory on this issue. While it is true that modern liberalism comes to be organized around the problem of "too much government,"[48] which is manifested by subjectival divisions (such as liberal/conservative, left/right) defined in terms of the political stance subjects take on the limits of governmental intervention, the appeals made on behalf of particular political positions still refer to the old model of the State (as the seat of sovereignty, which, it is presumed, has the power to control the nature and extent of governmental intervention), and are structured on the binary, juridical model of social contract (i.e., appealing to the delimitation of mutual rights and powers). However, the state no longer (if it ever did) bears such a relation to political subjects. The analysis of governmentality shows that it is a technology of power that transcends the office of sovereignty. It is characterized by a network of power relations that—like the disciplinary practices which spawned it—function independently of any one individual or body of authority. The relation of political subjects to government is not a contractual one; it is a relation of subjection and subjugation to an anonymous mosaic of governmental procedures and practices; a relation of absorption and indoctrination, of individualization and categorization, of subordination to demographic aggregates, of subtle coercions and procedural manipulations. Whereas the instruments of sovereignty were the laws of the land, which solicited obedience from political subjects but which also served as a link to sovereignty that subjects could prioritize and use as a basis for the prevention of abuses of power, the instruments of government, by contrast, consist in "a range of multiform tactics" that presuppose the complicity of the subjects on which they are applied, and from which subjects cannot simply decide to withhold their involvement (GV, 13).

And yet, even with the ineluctable transition to government and governmentality in the eighteenth century, for traditional political theory "the problem of sovereignty was never posed with greater force than at this point" (GV, 18). This arguably continues to be the case. The juridical, contractual view of sovereignty and political subjectivity still found in contemporary liberal theory fails to address the problems of power posed by the governmentalized state and disciplinary society. In this sense, liberal theory is *anachronistic*, appealing to notions of power and political subjectivity that no longer apply. Thus the question remains: Why is it that liberal theory retains such strength and apparent viability? Foucault addresses this problem in the following way: "Impossible to describe in the terminology of the theory of sovereignty from which it differs so radically . . . disciplinary power ought by rights to have led to the disappearance of that grand juridical edifice created by that theory. But in reality, the theory of sovereignty has continued not only to exist as an ideology of right, but also to provide the organizing principle of the legal codes which Europe acquired in the nineteenth century, beginning with the Napoleonic Code. Why has the theory of sovereignty persisted in this fashion as an ideology and an organizing principle of these major legal codes?" (*P/K*, 105). In modern society, the principle dimension of power consists of disciplinary techniques and mechanisms, including those employed by the governmentalized state to control and manipulate the population. The relation of political subjects to this power is not contractual; the appeal to rights and mutual obligations does not apply. Disciplinary power, says Foucault, is "absolutely incompatible with relations of sovereignty" (*P/K*, 104).[49] Yet the traditional conception of sovereignty and its contractual relation to political subjects still persists. Why?

The main reason for this, suggests Foucault, is that the contractual theory of sovereignty itself serves a disciplinary function; that is, it serves to *conceal* disciplinary coercions and modes of domination by deflecting attention away from them. "The theory of sovereignty, and the organization of a legal code centered upon it, have allowed a system of right to be superimposed upon the mechanisms of discipline in such a way as to conceal its actual procedures, the element of domination inherent in its techniques, and to guarantee to everyone, by virtue of the sovereignty of the State, the exercise of his proper sovereign rights" (*P/K*, 105). A more or less fictitious relation of sovereignty actually serves to disguise the real mechanisms of power that subject individuals. The theory of sovereignty provides an outlet through which political subjects can appeal, in the name of rights and liberty, without upsetting the meticulous network of mechanisms and relations that really dominate and control them. However, Foucault is quick to point out, disciplinary power is not the way the sovereign now exercises and maintains control over his subjects. On the contrary, it is the "closely linked grid of disciplinary coercions," as *opposed* to sovereignty, which acts "to assure the cohesion" of the social body (*P/K*, 106). At the same time, the ideological conception of sovereignty, which animates political subjects in terms of universal norms and absolute rights, allows the network of disciplinary relations, through which subjects are really and materially effected, to function unmolested.

The Political Technology of Individuals

It is no coincidence that the emergence of the political subject of contract theory coincides historically with a transition to an "art of government" and its concern with population. It is no accident that the private, autonomous individual comes on the scene at almost exactly the same time as the entrenchment in the social body of the techniques of individualization peculiar to discipline and governmentality. In fact, the individual with rights and freedoms is in actuality produced through a "political technology of individuals" operating within the modern state itself. Asserts Foucault, "I don't think that we should consider the 'modern state' as an entity which was developed above individuals, ignoring what they are and even their very existence, but on the contrary as a very sophisticated structure, in which individuals can be integrated, under one condition: that this individuality would be shaped in a new form, and submitted to a set of very specific patterns."[50]

Ideology posits the individual as an autonomous being (or a being worthy of autonomy) in contradistinction to the state. In Western societies, this is the basis of legislation, which proceeds, Foucault says, from the idea "of the Citizen, of the Individual . . . that all citizens have equal rights."[51] In actuality, however, individuals are fabricated by a political technology consisting of mechanisms and procedures internal to the state itself. The patterns according to which this political technology shapes individuals are those that meet the needs and requirements of the political rationality of governmentality. In fact, one set of these patterns is precisely that of the private, autonomous individual of the ideology of right. This form of individuality plays an important role in the maintenance and preservation of the governmentalized state.

We have already observed that the political rationality of governmentality consists of a concern for the population, that it incorporates a secularized version of pastoral power with its concern for the individual (as a member of the population), and that, above all, it infiltrates the social body through mechanisms and apparatuses that are essentially disciplinary in character. Governmentality is involved in, or proceeds through, all those petty mechanisms of surveillance and normalization that take hold of individuals and define them. It utilizes all those objectivizing and dividing practices that bring bodies of knowledge to bear on bodies in space in order to give them their own identity, their own pathology, as living human beings.[52]

We should add that governmentality is informed by a "new relationship between politics and history." We can best understand this new relationship by considering how governmentality emerges within and comes to invest the enunciative modality of the nation. Within the state there is a growing sense of its existence as one nation among many, that it is in competition with other nations, informed by an appreciation for the history that binds nations, positively or negatively, together: "Politics has now to deal with an irreducible multiplicity of states struggling and competing in a limited history."[53] The task will be to know how the nation-state should be governed in order to be sustained. This will require identifying and developing the state's strengths. Government will be concerned with individuals only insofar as they add or subtract to the strength of the state. Explains Foucault, "From the state's point of view, the individual exists insofar as what he does is able to introduce even a minimal change in the strength of the state, either in a positive or in a negative direction."[54] In this sense, the state's concern with the individual is instrumental and impersonal.

We have to be precise when defining the nature of this concern. To say that it is impersonal does not mean that it is necessarily "inhumane." Governmentality is characterized by a recognition that the strength of the state and the welfare of individuals are intertwined. This is manifested by an increasing tendency on the part of the state to take care of the lives of individuals: to become involved in the administration of food production and distribution; to see that individuals have adequate housing, education, employment; to provide health care and medical assistance, Social Security, insurance, and other support measures. In fact, it can be said that government becomes concerned with the very happiness of individuals, but this is far less an altruistic concern than it is a concern for the preservation and strength of the state. That is, government is concerned with the happiness of individuals because this is "a requirement for the survival and development of the state.... People's happiness becomes an element of state strength."[55]

The concern that government has for the "happiness" of individuals requires, obviously, "an increasing intervention of the state in the life of individuals."[56] This intervention becomes so pervasive, in fact, that it becomes the object of political and philosophical debates regarding the proper limits of governmental interference.[57] These debates, these discourses, are made on behalf of a private, autonomous individual who has the right that her freedom, her property, her very lifestyle will not be violated, or at least unduly restricted, by the excesses of governmental intervention.[58] This form of political subjectivity—this "cult of the individual"—is not simply a theoretical object of a political discourse; it is played out in real enunciative modalities of the self. It informs the political spectrum and is the crux of the ideological conflicts between liberals and conservatives. Real political figures emerge in the space opened by the problems, by the problematization, of (governmental) interference and individuality.

But the "concern" of governmentality for the lives of individuals has little to do with so-called individual rights. The problems of intervention and interference posed by the exercise of this concern cannot be addressed by ideological appeals to right. This is not simply because the power peculiar to governmentality is a relational power permeating the entire social body and not a power issuing from a central governing body to which such appeals could be made; it is also because the interventions of governmentality are of a sort that only recognize the individual as part of a population, not a private autonomous individual with rights. The knowledge it brings to bear on the individual is that of statistics and the human sciences, not that of ideology. The mechanisms and apparatuses of governmentality are designed for ensuring the docility of individuals, not for respecting their rights. Even in those institutions—such as the courts and other lawmaking bodies, which seem to be erected expressly for protecting the rights of individuals, of "defending" society as an agent of right—we find underlying their juridical reflections a penal machinery (e.g., the police, prisons, punishments, registrations) that puts into play "a justice which is given the task of watching over a population rather than that of respecting the rights of subjects."[59] In governmentality, law is always subordinate to order.

This is not an "evil" or malicious refusal on the part of governmentality to respect the rights of individuals; it is rather that governmentality refers to a structure and a rationality to which the appeal to right simply can have little effect. It is not set up for an effective recognition of individual rights precisely because it works from an entirely different form of individuality. Yet the existence of juridical, legislative, and democratic institutions seems to pose a problem. They cannot be separated from governmentality since we are dealing with a technology of power and political rationality that characterizes the entire modern state. What place could such institutions, which seem to work from an ideological rather than a statistical notion of individuality, have in the governmentalized state? We have already framed this question in terms of power: that the juridical, binary conception of power actually acts to conceal disciplinary mechanisms of control and coercion.[60] Now let us pose the question in terms of the private, autonomous individual: What "use" might governmentality have for such a notion?

The efficacy of disciplinary mechanisms is a direct reflection of their success in producing *docile* bodies, individuals who do not only not resist the techniques and practices that control them, but actually take on the norms and expectations of discipline and make them part of their own ethical relation to themselves. Yet in any power relation, says Foucault, there is always the possibility of resistance.[61] The disciplinary mechanisms of governmentality are able to function more or less smoothly because they are able to channel such resistance, where it arises, toward objects that do not really touch on the ways individuals are managed, controlled, and defined. Governmentality is able to control the shape and degree of resistance precisely through the notion of the private autonomous individual. Individuals who conceive of themselves in this way direct their resistance toward sovereignty and couch it in terms of democratic representation and the recognition of rights; but sovereignty does not control governmentality.[62] Even more important, consider what it is that we are really doing when we assert a right. Let us set aside the rights to freedom of speech and democratic representation; these are really just rights to assert a right.[63] When we assert a right we are usually concerned with addressing some issue or situation bearing directly or indirectly on the quality of our lives. We may assert a right to work or to be treated fairly in the workplace; we may assert a right to education and the equal opportunity to advance along with our peers; we may assert the right to be treated humanely by the police and the courts. Other rights may bear on issues of health care, the protection of the environment (which affects our health), or the equitable distribution of social resources. When we assert such rights we think we are exercising our autonomy as political subjects, as separate individuals. In actuality, are we not really asserting the right to come under the governance of precisely those institutions and apparatuses where discipline grabs our bodies and subjects them to its normalizing practices? We might also ask, by what means are the discourses of right made available to individuals so that they may identify themselves in terms of autonomy?[64] Are they not manufactured in the same institutions and disseminated through the same cultural channels as the discourses of the human sciences?

In fact, governmentality has a real stake in the perpetuation of the private autonomous individual. This form of subjectivity is articulated right onto disciplined bodies, as a cloak, a veil. In this way, political rights and freedoms become tied to normalization and pathologization. Rights and freedoms tend to diminish to the extent one deviates from the norm. For example, the madman of the asylum has fewer rights than the sane person. The criminal is entitled to less freedom than the law-abiding citizen. By invoking pastoral power, society justifies its restrictions by claiming that it is for the individual's "own good," as well as for the good of society, of the general population. This articulation of right onto normality has the effect of turning rights and freedoms into measures of rank and hierarchy, thus becoming completely absorbed in disciplinary indices of individuality.

In the juncture between the governmentalized state's concern for the welfare and happiness of individuals on the one hand and the governmentalized state as nation deploying individuals as instruments of its preservation in war on the other, we have a strange modern paradox, a paradox that only accents the radical indifference the state has for the rights of subjects, for the subjects of right. "The coexistence in political structures of large destructive mechanisms and institutions oriented toward the care of individual life is . . . one of the central antinomies of our political reason," says Foucault.[65] Yet it is an antinomy that pervades our experience as political subjects. In this antinomy we see how a discourse of right can be used by structures that fundamentally ignore rights, how promises of autonomy are bound to practices of domination. This is the antinomy of government, an antinomy hinging on the duplicity of government. In fact, it is the hinge, the gap, the space of our emergence as modern political subjects.

The political subject that rises from this space—or, more precisely, the form of political subjectivity that is erected upon this space—is perhaps best understood as a kind of *arsis*. From the Greek, *arsis* literally means "a lifting up." In classical poetry, it refers to the unaccented part of a foot of verse; but due to a misunderstanding of original Greek usage it came to mean the accented part. The antinomy of the experience of modern political subjectivity is to hold this relation at once, of being accented and unaccented at the same time, based on a misunderstanding of its usage, a misunderstanding effected in fact by the technology that uses it. Made the measure of ideology, but measured in fact by the scales of discipline and statistics, raised to the pedestal of right, but erected by a technology which turns rights into an instrument of domination, the political subject is the living embodiment of a modern contradiction.

Thus, political subjects emerge in the governmentalized state through a political technology of individuals that is involved in the fabrication of their political identities and that integrates them in the social body. We are deceived if we think of this integration in contractual terms, as effected and held together by the recognition of rights. Rather, it "is the effect not of consensus but of the materiality of power operating on the very bodies of individuals."[66] This power proceeds via discourse, in the knowledges it brings to bear on bodies in order to govern them, and in the discourses of truth it makes available to, or imposes on, these bodies in order that they may govern themselves. The interplay of these factors produces the forms of individuality that we recognize as political subjects. Thus, the political technology of individuals brings into play, into an *inter*play, all three axes of subjectivity. Together they constitute the matrix of our modern experience of political subjectivity.

We must be suspicious of the generality of this claim. We cannot ignore the specificity of even a single political subject. Nor can we underestimate the effect a single political subject can have on the experience of the social body as a whole. Mahatma Gandhi, Martin Luther King, Fidel Castro, Napoleon, Betty Friedan, Magda Portal, Evita Perón, Nelson Mandela: these names represent singular forms of political subjectivity that had a profound impact on the political bodies to which they belonged. And there are always lesser-known figures who exert a similar influence. Yet if we were to extend or compress our analysis to this very fine, minute level of the single political subject, we would find that they are produced from the same determinative factors, that their political subjectivity is the effect of an interplay of the three axes of discourse, power, and subjectivation. Of course, we would have to be very specific in our analysis, taking into account the institutions through which they had been channeled from birth through adulthood, the discourses and bodies of knowledge they had been exposed to, the value systems they had felt obliged to appropriate; but we would also have to examine the extent to which their influence was due to possibilities already present in the social structure itself. We must be careful not to impute a political movement or struggle to the will of a single dynamic individual. We have to ask, through what processes of integration were individuals bound, as political subjects, to their projects? Moreover, we have to ask if what they are doing does not fulfill the design and expectations of a technology in which they are already thoroughly imbricated. Does their resistance end up being reintegrated into the social body without upsetting the basic structure? Do the movements they put into play end up repeating the same gestures or following the same dictates of the existing rationality? We have to entertain also the possibility that such exceptional figures are merely names for a form of resistance, a form of political subjectivity, waiting to erupt from the meshes of the social network all along. In short, we must resist the romance of resistance we all too easily attach to certain dynamic and charismatic individuals. We have to resist the metaphysics of subjectivity, wherein individuals are constituted by spirit or will. We have to ask, instead, through what political technology were these individuals fabricated, and what function might they serve in the interests of this technology itself?

6

"The Most Perfect Freedom"

The Indians, their old masters, gave them their choice. . . .
They chose to remain; and the reasons they gave me would
greatly surprise you: the most perfect freedom. . . .

—Michel-Guillaume-Jean de Crèvecoeur,
"Distresses of a Frontier Man"

Any consideration of political identity must at some point take up the question of freedom. As I have already observed, traditional political philosophy tends to approach the issue of freedom from the standpoint of power. As such, it tries to identify principles of justice that will place limits on the exercise of power. In so doing it seeks to acquire freedom for the political subject. Liberal theory tends to understand freedom in one of two ways, in terms of either "positive" freedom or "negative" freedom. Jean-Jacques Rousseau is typically understood as advancing a version of the former, while Robert Nozick defends a version of the latter. However, freedom isn't so much about power as it is about *identity*. Moreover, as I demonstrate in this chapter, what Rousseau and Nozick are in effect articulating are not so much principles of freedom as modalities of political subjectivity. In fact, Rousseau and Nozick, positive and negative freedom, *together*, delimit the conceptual space in which modern political subjects understand their relation to freedom. This is a "polarized" space in which subjects are bound to a form of identity and to a set of subjectival constraints.[1]

Michel Foucault avoids the philosophically suspect opposition between positive and negative freedom, and offers instead an understanding of freedom that approaches this issue of identity in a way that is simply unavailable to more traditional political philosophies. There are two avenues of such freedom: one might be called "strategic" freedom since it consists in engaging relations of power in a subversive or disruptive way; the other is a form of freedom through *counter-memory*, which is related to Nietzsche's notion of *aktive Vergesslichkeit*, or "active forgetting." Both avenues of freedom are opened up not by ideological appeals to rights or even by revolution but by a genealogical critique of political identity itself. Genealogy disrupts the political technology of individuals that binds them to an identity. By identifying points of weakness in structures of domination, genealogy opens a space of concrete freedom for political subjects, a freedom from (a specific expression of) political subjectivity effected by a subversion of its necessity. We shall see that freedom through genealogy is to be understood very differently from the concepts of positive and negative freedom found in the liberal tradition. Somewhat paradoxically, however, it is with regard to freedom that Foucault's thought has perhaps the most potential value while being at the same time at its most vulnerable to criticism.

On the Polarities of Political Freedom: Rousseau and Nozick

Consider two statements, one well-worn and still enjoying popular currency, the other known as well, perhaps, only in the professional circles of political philosophy:

> Man was born free, and everywhere he is in chains.
> —Jean-Jacques Rousseau, *The Social Contract*

> My property rights in my knife allow me to leave it where I will,
> but not in your chest.
> —Robert Nozick, *Anarchy, State, and Utopia*

These statements, separated by a span of two centuries, represent the conceptual borders of Western notions of political freedom. They mark the positive and negative poles of our experience as free political subjects.

The first statement, from Rousseau, is uttered from the heights of a discursive practice still resonant with the memory of a State of Nature, still governed by the ominous figures of Sovereignty and Absolute Monarchy. But from these heights, Sovereignty will fall—or rather, it will collapse, through a usurping act of *contraction*, only to rise once again as the General Will: "As nature gives every man an absolute power over all his limbs, the social pact gives the body politic an absolute power over all its members; and it is the same power which, when directed by the general will, bears, as I said, the name of sovereignty."[2] In the collapse of sovereignty in the general will there is no loss of power or force, only a loss of caprice and particularity. For the general will conforms to a law of perfect rationality, a

law carrying the moral force of truth, whose absolute authority over isolated individuals derives from the necessity of their union in a social contract. In fact, their union *is* the sovereign: through social contract the
plurality of "private persons" becomes the unity of "the public person,"
whose will the fragmentary individual is compelled to obey.

And yet, this same compulsion is also the principle of the individual's
freedom. The individual's relationship to the body politic of the public
person is that of *citizen*. As a citizen the individual is at one and the same
time a nodal point of power and the source of her own subjection. That is,
citizens, says Rousseau, "are sovereign in the one aspect and subjects in the
other" (61). The subjected-sovereignty of the citizen is brought about by a
"total alienation" of the individual's rights to the public body, but this
alienation of rights creates a condition of perfect (political, if not economic) equality between the citizens of the state. This equality is the measure of the individual's autonomy. That is, "each giving himself to all, gives
himself to nobody" (18). In social contract, individuals put themselves
under the "supreme direction" of the general will, which is the expression
of their union as citizens. Submission to the general will is a submission to
the dictates of reason itself. As such, this submission represents freedom
from the tyranny of subjective whim and inclination on the part of other
individuals or groups who might be more powerful. In social contract,
then, "we gain the equivalent of all that we lose, and more power to preserve what we have" (18).

The freedom that the individual enjoys under the direction of the general
will is precisely and most literally a *political* freedom—freedom as a product of convention and bound to a political structure, to a set of political
(contractual) relations. This freedom is to be distinguished from the "natural liberty" that individuals enjoyed in the state of nature. Society has
long since corrupted the happy existence of the noble savage in the state of
nature.[3] Society has long since crushed the natural independence of the
individual, who is now chained to a state of conflict, struggle, inequality,
isolating competition, and domination.[4] This condition of virtual slavery
permeates the social body as a whole; the Monarch is only the figurehead
of the individual's corruption and oppression. Submission to the general
will through social contract restores to individuals the freedom they lost as
a result of their entrance into society. However, it replaces their natural
freedom with a conventional liberty altogether different from the freedom
they experienced in the state of nature as noble savages. That is, the individual is now "free" to be a rational being, which is to say, free to live in
accordance with the dictates of the general will.

How does one know what the general will requires? Through pure democracy; a simple majority serves as the sovereign expression of the general will: "That a will may be general, it is not always necessary that it should be unanimous, but it is necessary that all votes should be counted; any formal exclusion destroys the generality" (28). The tabulation of votes gives rise to a decree that has all the canonical authority of law. Individuals are bound as rational beings to respect such law. Where they do not, the community is justified, under the terms of social contract, to wield its collective power against them. However, this coercion is for the sake of restoring to the individual the rationality he denies in the refusal to obey the general will, that is, it is for the sake of restoring to the individual his freedom: "Whoever refuses to obey the general will shall be constrained to do so by the whole body; which means nothing else than he shall be *forced to be free*" (22; emphasis added).

There is no contradiction here. The freedom to do as one wants independent of societal constraints has been lost, lost absolutely and forever, but individuals can acquire a new freedom through democracy. Through the vote, individuals have a voice in the determination of the obligations and constraints to which they will be subjected. In this way individuals immerse themselves in a generality that serves as the principle, the rational principle, of their subjection. Yet this subjection is at the same time a freedom—a freedom from arbitrary coercions and particular power, but this freedom is first and foremost a *positive* freedom of self-determination (wherein *self* refers to a public self to which the individual belongs).

For Rousseau, social contract is the condition of the individual's freedom from societal oppression. In the political structures predicated on this form of social contract, sovereignty and government are fundamentally separated. Sovereignty is reserved solely to the general will; the government becomes simply an "intermediate body" for the administration of the general will's laws. "To be legitimate, the government must not be combined with the sovereign power, but must be its minister."[5] To be sure, government and sovereignty have been separated in the modern state. Moreover, government has indeed become our "minister," in that it governs us in accordance with the rationality and dictates of a pastoral power. These "facts" already inform *The Social Contract*, although that may not be readily apparent since it founds government on a notion of "legitimacy" and charges it with the "maintenance" of our liberty. On the other hand, Rousseau advocates measures Foucault would recognize as *disciplinary* in character, measures that seem to be justified not so much by reference to the ideology of right, but to the dictates of governmentality. Or perhaps it would be better to say that these measures represent the subordination of the ideology of right to governmentality, which has the effect of giving governmental coercions the air of legitimacy.[6] Yet the notion of government as minister and administrator of our everyday lives is, strictly speaking, of secondary importance in *The Social Contract*. Its primary concern is with defining and creating the social and political conditions where government can have such a role. At this point it confronts a situation in which the social contract has not yet been realized in society. The general will has not yet been established as the principle of sovereignty. In order for the general will to have free expression, the first and primary obstacle to be overcome is Absolute Monarchy. Sovereignty must be wrested from the King.

For Rousseau, democracy is the ideal form of state. It is so perfect, in fact, that only gods are worthy of it.[7] Democracy is impractical for the real world of politics, but the general will requires democratic expression. Rousseau solves this problem through his separation of sovereignty and government. The general will's laws will arise through democratic participation and will have complete sovereign authority. Still, the government that administrates these laws onto the social body need not be democratic; citizens need not have a say in the ways they are actually governed, as long as it is in accordance with the laws and spirit of the general will. Nevertheless, none of this can be realized as long as sovereignty remains the capricious privilege of the monarch. Thus, Rousseau becomes a reluctant philosopher of *revolution*.

Since the eighteenth century, freedom has been bound conceptually to revolution.[8] Political freedom is always democratic freedom, and democratic freedom is always attended by a discursive memory of struggle, of conflict, of revolt against an oppressive ruler. Revolution continues to inform our subjectival relation to freedom. The threat of political tyranny and oppression animates our experience as subjects; it binds us to the nation as the home of our democratic liberty. Freedom through revolution is, thus, a *unifying* freedom, a freedom that joins subjects together through a recognition of their equality, of their common mission toward a free and democratic polity, of the necessity of their interdependence in the preservation and maintenance of the democratic state. In this sense, the general will still flows through our bodies and attaches us to the body politic, with a promise of liberty conditioned upon a contractual absorption in a national identity.

Yet this is only one dimension of our modern experience of political freedom. This brings us to the second of the two statements with which we began. This statement, from Nozick's *Anarchy, State, and Utopia*, makes no explicit reference to freedom. This "omission" is appropriate because the understanding of freedom from which it proceeds differs significantly from Rousseau's statement. That is, it is informed by a conception of negative, rather than positive, freedom—a freedom from interference similar to that articulated and defended in John Stuart Mill's *On Liberty*.[9]

Let us highlight the key words in this statement. In the density of these words we can glimpse the negative freedom which animates them and which sanctions their utterance:

> *My* property rights in *my* knife allow *me* to leave it where *I* will, but not in *your* chest.[10]

When compared to the first statement, from Rousseau, we can see a dramatic semantic move from generality to particularity. The generic and categorial "man" has become the specific and empirical "I." The third-person and nominative "he" has been replaced by the first-person and accusative "me." Most important, we have the interjection of possessive pronouns, "My" and "your," which now seem conspicuously absent from Rousseau's statement. We should also mark the appearance here of "property rights" and "allow" and "will." These introduce the notions of ownership, legitimacy, and intentionality. A figure is taking shape here who no longer defines his freedom by reference to a collective body, but instead to individual rights. A public freedom is being supplanted by a private autonomy. Ownership and property are taking precedence over citizenship and community. Finally, we should not overlook the interpolation of "but" in the second clause of the statement. This disjunctive, conditional "but"—as opposed to the conjunctive and combinatory "and" of Rousseau's statement—performs a syntactical operation of immense importance. It expresses the juridical *limits* of my freedom. My freedom is based on personal rights that allow me to do anything *but* that which interferes with your freedom. In this tiny word, we have a fundamental separation of distinct political beings.

Notice also that the limitation on personal freedom is expressed, appropriately enough, in terms of *harm*. I am at liberty to live as I please as long as what I do does not harm you, and vice versa. Of course, such harm does not have to be anything as extreme as a knife in the chest. In fact, under negative freedom any interference can be interpreted as harm, just as any harm can justify interference.[11] At any rate, the point is that the very conditionality of such formulations presupposes politically and ontologically separate human beings. Negative freedom is a freedom of separateness.

The movement from generality to particularity expressed in these two statements from Rousseau and Nozick reflects the historical transition from positive to negative freedom, and the increasing concretization of the political subject. In fact, negative freedom opposes itself to any public unity, such as the general will, and to any mode of political subjectivity associated with it. Says Nozick, "There is no *social entity* with a good that undergoes some sacrifice for its own good. There are only individual people, different individual people, with their own individual lives."[12] Whereas positive freedom requires the contraction of sovereignty, negative freedom requires its fragmentation. Sovereignty must be broken up and dispersed to the concrete units of individuality representing the "separate persons" of the state. My autonomy extends as far as the limits of my personal sovereignty. And because my power is relatively weak precisely due to this separateness, I require certain fundamental rights (regardless of on what such rights are based) to protect me against unjustifiable coercions and social inequities, which I always interpret as an interference in my own personal freedom. This requires that I reject the "total alienation" of individual rights demanded by a political absorption in the general will. I must retain the right of individual dissension against the social body, if necessary. I am entitled to a degree of self-determination regardless of what is dictated by the general will, by the public self. Such is the measure of my autonomy, and of my integrity, as a separate human being.

The freedom expressed in Nozick's statement is thus that belonging to the private, autonomous individual. *Belonging* is the key word here, because the index of this freedom is propriety. For the private autonomous individual the primary issue with regard to freedom is not monarchy or absolutism, but distributive justice. The problem is to define the proper limits of what I owe the community and of what the community owes me. Real freedom is personal freedom, a freedom based on entitlement, on the delimitation of inviolable spheres of individual existence.

Traditional political philosophy debates the compatibility of negative and positive freedom.[13] These debates tend to turn on the issue of equality, of whether or not the equality promised by positive freedom is obtainable, or even desirable, if we are genuinely committed to the negative freedom of private autonomy. Yet, outside of these juridical reflections, we can see that the modern experience of political subjectivity is animated by both positive and negative freedom at the same time. Far from canceling each other, or of one canceling the other, positive and negative freedom are two poles whose contact charges our experience with an energy and a tension: between polity and property, between equality and autonomy, between citizenry and individuality. This tension, this energy, opens and delimits the space of our emergence as free political subjects.

Are there, however, any conceptions of freedom available to us as political subjects other than or beyond the narrow, polarized dichotomies of positive and negative freedom? Foucault offers us an understanding of freedom that addresses the connection of freedom to identity in a way that traditional notions of political freedom do not. For this freedom, "a demanding, prudent, 'experimental' attitude is necessary; at every moment, step by step, one must confront what one is thinking and saying with what one is doing, with what one is."[14] Freedom, in Foucault's sense, is not a state or a telos, not a private right or a public unity, but an ongoing practice, a way of thinking, and a space of activity, that is constantly attenuated to the play of forces which circumscribe individuals.

Countering Memory: Different Freedoms/Freedoms of Difference

"I firmly believe in human freedom," says Foucault.[15] Perhaps this statement sounds strange coming from a philosopher whose work seems bent in its entirety on convincing us of our thoroughly determined situation. How is freedom possible for human beings whose very existence is linked inseparably to a matrix of anonymous forces, to a network of coercions and practices of domination, which seem to dictate our every move, our every thought? It seems almost contradictory to say, on the one hand, that we are an effect of an interplay of ubiquitous power relations, and to hold out the possibility of freedom in the face of such a seemingly comprehensive determination. Foucault himself says that "power is co-extensive with the social body; there are no spaces of primal liberty between the meshes of its network."[16] If this is true, then in what sort of "human freedom" can Foucault believe?

There are no spaces of primal liberty just as there is no primal subject to which such liberty could inhere. The possibilities for subjectivity are a direct reflection of what the social network allows. On the other hand, we "should not assume a massive and primal condition of domination," either, says Foucault.[17] That is, the matrix of experience in which the subject emerges is not fixed and immutable in its determination of the subject. Rather, it is a *relational* matrix; the relations that determine the subject can always be channeled in other directions, subverted, changed. In other words, there is always the possibility of freedom with regard to a set of relations that subjects individuals, that determines what they are *as subjects*.

There are two avenues of such freedom, both of which are opened by a genealogical critique of the matrix of our experience as subjects. One avenue, which I shall call a "strategic" freedom, concerns power and the disciplinary character of modern society. Foucault's shift in perspective from power as *Recht* to the "manifold relations" of power commits us to rethinking the notion of political freedom. That is, instead of mounting juridical oppositions to the structures and forces that dominate us, we have to understand the way techniques, mechanisms, and apparatuses of power infiltrate society and attach themselves to human beings.[18] What are the prospects of effecting change in this disciplinary structure? What do various structures make possible? What types of change do they invite? In other words, this avenue of freedom involves identifying and putting into play certain specific strategic responses to the network of power relations that subjects us. The problem is to develop possible strategies against our subjection, to open up new possibilities of subjectivity.

Still, strategic freedom is meaningless unless it is informed by what Foucault calls "counter-memory." As an avenue of freedom, counter-memory bears directly on the processes of subjectivization. That is, we constitute ourselves as political subjects, in part, through an appropriation of discourses of ideology and modes of self-comportment. In fact, the appropriation of an ideology (the possibilities for which are delimited by discursive practices and power relations) is what constitutes an individual *qua* subject; but more than that, individuals are determined in and through their recognition of themselves as subjects, governed by this more or less arbitrary appropriation of an identity for themselves. The constitution of a political identity entails an individual being deeply embedded in a constellation of beliefs, practices, relationships, and ways of thinking: a specific mode of being.[19] We are circumscribed and determined by the type of political identity we become. Counter-memory in a sense liberates us from a particular mode of subjectivity in that we come to recognize the optionality and nonessentiality of a particular way of being. Through counter-memory, we disinvest ourselves from the power that a particular constellation of meanings once held over us. By means of genealogical accounts of that constellation, we distance ourselves from its authority.

Both strategic freedom and counter-memory are designed to liberate us from certain forms of subjection. One bears principally on institutionalized practices, the other on practices of the self (to the extent that these can be separated), but these freedoms require each other in order to be effective. Both are informed by a genealogical critique of our experience as political subjects. Together they constitute a double-edged sword of freedom, a freedom made for *cutting*.

Counter-Memory

"Whenever man has thought it necessary to create a memory for himself, his effort has been attended with torture, blood, sacrifice," observes Friedrich Nietzsche.[20] Memory, for Nietzsche, refers to the more or less violent imposition of values that become fixed, obligatory, "unforgettable." Memory is the first condition for the establishment of conscience, which consists in the recognition of a moral constraint. Through memory we are bound to a set of moral obligations, the "forgetting" of which sanctions a possible punishment. Memory is a form of confinement, a subtle but incarcerating restriction on our freedom—which is not a right, but simply our freedom to be *otherwise*.

Foucault's *counter-memory* is very close to the Nietzschean idea of "active forgetfulness" (*aktive Vergesslichkeit*).[21] Counter-memory consists of essentially forgetting who we are. It is a forgetfulness of essence, of necessity, of the moral and ontological obligations that bind us to an identity. There is freedom in forgetfulness. Counter-memory holds us at a remove, a distance, from ourselves; not in the traditional sense of self-reflection, but of wrenching the self—this identity—apart, through an incision, a cutting that makes the self stand naked and strange before us across an unbridgeable divide, a gap of *difference*. Counter-memory dislodges the propriety of *our-selves*. The self, as a coherent identity, becomes foreign through counter-memory. We cannot remember what it was that compelled us to act, believe, *be* a given way. Counter-memory dissolves this compulsion, this determination, this *subjection*. The power of identity is suspended through a forgetfulness of its necessity—a freedom is opened within the space of a difference that no identity can constrain. This difference always plays outside the limits, outside any delimitation of being. Counter-memory thrusts us into this uncharted world, where a memory makes no sense, where play is the order of the day, where lightening and chance disintegrate the heavy and solid, the *identical*.

Counter-memory bears directly on processes of subjectivation, on the techniques of the self through which we constitute for ourselves an identity. "Counter-discourses" anticipate a subjectival freedom of open possibilities by opposing themselves to the discourses of truth through which we recognize ourselves as subjects.[22] These counter-discourses, the discourses of genealogy, lift the burdensome obligations imposed on us by such a recognition. As a forgetfulness of these obligations, counter-memory always takes the form of a transgression. It invites condemnation even as it refuses to be held accountable. Yet there is freedom in this refusal, in this transgression—for those who have the stomach for it.[23] There is always an essential risk involved in refusing, in forgetting, one's identity.[24]

Counter-memory is not a form of consciousness. It is nothing, really, except the effect of a certain kind of description of ourselves, a description of the historical ontology of ourselves as subjects. This description has been closed off and denied by power/knowledge relations, excluded and made peripheral by certain dominant discourses and entrenched scientific-philosophical enterprises that bind us to a conception of what we are in truth. Counter-memory counters, or suspends, the power of identity through genealogical accounts of its constitution. Genealogy effects "the systematic dissociation of identity" by revealing its radical contingency, its historicality and utter lack of essentiality. The purpose of genealogy, says Foucault, "is not to discover the roots of our identity, but to commit itself to its dissipation."[25] Genealogical critique is an *exposition* of our history as subjects that has the effect of *dis-posing* subjectival constraints by *ex-posing* the contingency of their *imposition*. Genealogy turns the firm *posture* of the self-identical subject into the mere *posing* of a pretentious display.

Genealogy proceeds through "dissension" and "disparity." Wherever "the self fabricates a coherent identity," genealogy puts into play a subversive counter-analysis that "permits the dissociation of the self, its recognition and displacement as an empty synthesis."[26] Genealogy disturbs, fragments, displaces the unity of subjectivity. It cuts through the oppressive, assimilating density of Truth and discovers in this beguiling haze that subjectivity is nothing more than a colorful *mask*. Who we are, what we are, is a mask displayed for public viewing and examination, for person-al subjection and ethical subjugation. Genealogy cuts through this mask, only to make another discovery. Behind it there is no essential identity, no unified spirit or will, no naked subject stripped of its colorful dress. Rather, there is only a matrix of intersecting lines and heterogenous congruities, an arbitrary and historically contingent complex of discursive and nondiscursive practices. Asserts Foucault, "If the genealogist refuses to extend his faith in metaphysics, if he listens to history, he finds that there is 'something altogether different' behind things; not a timeless and essential secret, but the secret that they have no essence or that their essence was fabricated in a piecemeal fashion from alien forms."[27] Contrary to what René Descartes or John Locke would contend, unity (whether of consciousness proper or the continuity of personal experience) is not the essence of subjectivity. Unity is a mask for an interplay of anonymous forces and historical accidents that permits us to identify subjects, to identify ourselves, as specific human beings. Unity—identity—is imposed on subjects as the mask of their fabrication. Subjectivity is the carceral and incarcerating expression of this imposition, of the limitations drawn around us by discourses of truth and practices of individualization; but seen through the "differential knowledge" of genealogy, the identity of subjectivity collapses.

Counter-memory through genealogical critique is a transgression of limits. As such, it opens onto a possibility of freedom. Genealogy permits us "to separate out, from the contingency that has made us what we are, the possibility of no longer being, doing, thinking what we are, do, or think." In this sense, genealogy gives "new impetus, as far and wide as possible, to the undefined work of freedom."[28] The freedom offered by counter-memory is a kind of parodic reversal of negative freedom: it is not a freedom *from* interference, but *for* it—for disruption, for displacement, for violating those inviolable spheres of liberty that serve as the limits of our subjection. It is not a freedom *for* individuality, but *from* it—a freedom from individualization, from the practices and discourses which bind us to our own identity as individuals. It is not a freedom against the *office of government,* but against *governmentality*—against a rationality that imprisons us in the cellular space of our own self-government. At the same time, the freedom of/through counter-memory is a form of mimetic play with the notion of positive freedom whereby citizenship is unwrapped like a cloak from the politicized body.

In simple terms, it can be said that genealogy "enables one to get free of oneself."[29] That is, by exposing the nonessentiality of the limits imposed on us through the constitution of a self, it opens the possibility of going beyond those limits.[30] This opening is a kind of fracture, at once an open space and a breaking free of the constraining power inherent in identity and identification. In this sense, genealogy opens up "a space of concrete freedom, i.e., of possible *transformation*."[31] This notion of fracture allows us to define freedom more precisely, to gauge whether or not a genuine space of freedom has been opened for us. Freedom, concrete freedom, is a space of possible transformation. Unless we are free to transform ourselves, to be other than the identity dictated for us by some extraneous rationality, we have no freedom. Even the most violent forms of resistance against subjection accomplish nothing if they do not gain this freedom, do not open a space of possible transformation—which means nothing more, and nothing less, than the possibility of being otherwise. Something very like this point is made by Dennis Altman with regard to the Stonewall riots of 1969 and the militant Gay Liberation Front that emerged from them in the early 1970s. In one of the seminal texts of what would later become known as Queer Theory, Altman rails against the limited vision of a political movement that sought for gay and lesbian people little more than an expansion of rights and the "liberal tolerance" of the homophile community: "Homosexuals can win acceptance as distinct from tolerance only by a transformation of society, one that is based on a 'new human' who is able to accept the multifaceted and varied nature of his or her sexual identity. That such a society can be founded is the gamble upon which gay and women's liberation are based; like all radical movements they hold to an optimistic view of human nature, above all to its mutability."[32]

This requirement that we are only genuinely free if we able to transform ourselves is recalcitrant.[33] It is crucial to understand, however, that what is being required here is *not* a freedom to transform ourselves in accordance with some global or teleological model of a more "genuine" form of subjectivity. This freedom does not consist (as it does in *On Liberty*) in replacing one form of subjectivity for another that is supposedly "truer" or more fulfilling to human nature. Not only is this illusory and unobtainable, it would also amount to a cancellation of freedom, a reimposition of subjectival limitations and expectations. Rather, the freedom opened by countermemory is a freedom of permanent transformation, of always being able to become other than what we are.

Strategic Freedom

"What I mean by power relations," says Foucault, "is that we are in a strategic situation towards each other."[34] This situation is not so much a matter of being "trapped" or hopelessly oppressed, but of having one's possibilities for action, for existence, structured and determined by the position one holds in a network of relations. This position is strategic in that one can always affect the status of given power relations, either by contributing to their maintenance as they are, or by struggling against them. There can be imbalances of power, wherein one's possibilities are extremely limited, but there are *always* possibilities of resistance, of changing the relations of power. Notes Foucault, "We cannot jump *outside* the situation, and there is no point where you are free from all power relations. But you can always change it."[35]

A common objection against Foucault's claim that power is everywhere is that, if this is true, then there can be no freedom.[36] However, Foucault does not claim that power is everywhere, if one means by power a univocal exercise of force, coercion, or privilege that crushes or suspends freedom wherever it installs itself. Rather, Foucault's claim is that power *relations* are everywhere. In fact, it is not incorrect to say that every *where* is an enclosure of power relations that delimit space and structure the possibilities for action within that space. While it may be the case that such possibilities are extremely limited and asymmetrical, they are by no means permanently fixed or intransigent. If they were, this would not be, strictly speaking, a power relation.[37] This distinction between power and power relations is crucial. It allows Foucault to say that "if there are relations of power throughout every social field it is because there is freedom everywhere."[38]

Power (as Foucault understands it) consists in relations of reciprocity, of mutual subjection and determination. Even where power relations produce an asymmetrical situation of domination and oppression, the exercise of power presupposes subjects who are free to act in compliance with its mandates. Even more basically, it presupposes individuals who could act otherwise, and whose present situation—that is, the empirical fact that they act or behave in a given way—is the result of an imposition of requirements and expectations of what they may do, of how they may act. That is, a requirement is imposed on these individuals *not* to act otherwise, which carries an implicit and most probably suppressed understanding that they could. Observes Foucault, "When one defines the exercise of power . . . one includes an important element: freedom. Power is exercised only over free subjects and only insofar as they are free. By this we mean individual or collective subjects who are faced with a field of possibilities in which several ways of behaving, several reactions and diverse comportments may be realized."[39] In any power relationship, even the most oppressive, submission is always potentially a refusal to submit. Power relations are dynamic and unstable; they are "changeable relations, i.e., they can modify themselves, they are not given once and for all."[40] There is always the possibility, by definition, that the parties involved will act in ways other than that prescribed for them. This would have the effect of altering or even reversing a given power relation. Still, the possibility for this does not have to be imported from outside the power relation; it is already there, constitutively, all along, precisely because the parties involved have freedom. This is not a metaphysical freedom, not a right, but merely possibilities individuals have by virtue of being in a power relation—nothing more. "There cannot be relations of power unless the subjects are free," says Foucault.[41] Even the most effective coercion presupposes a suppression of freedom. Coercion, in whatever form, oppresses, not so much an individual but possibilities for free action. Domination makes no sense apart from a freedom it seeks to control. *Control* is the key word here, because unless a form of domination eliminates *all* possible action (which would mean the end of a power *rela-*

tion), freedom is still and always present and can turn itself against the domination that controls it. In other words, freedom can always take a form, not of submission, but of *resistance*.

"In the relations of power," Foucault tells us, "there is necessarily the possibility of resistance, for if there were no possibility of resistance—of violent resistance, of escape, of ruse, of strategies that reverse the situation—there would be no relations of power."[42] Resistance is inherent to any power relationship, not foreign to it. Resistance is one of many possible expressions of freedom. However, in situations of effective domination, freedom does not manifest itself as such. Even so, the latent possibility of freedom makes every power relationship, even the most oppressive, one of "reciprocal incitation and struggle," of constant provocation.[43] Maintaining a given power relation requires a constant struggle against an actual or potential resistance. There can be no relation of power without freedom, and there can be no freedom unless subjects can act otherwise, that is, resist a given relation of power. In this sense, even the most submissive subjects provoke a struggle against their possible resistance. This is constitutive of what it means to be dominated.

Resistance "does not predate the power it opposes. It is co-extensive with it and absolutely its contemporary."[44] Because resistance is constitutive to any power relation, even the most limiting, this means that there is always the possibility of changing a given power relation. "At the heart of power relations and as a permanent condition of their existence there is an insubordination and a certain essential obstinacy ... there is no relationship of power without the means of escape or possible flight."[45] The problem is to turn this inherent obstinacy into an active resistance. This will make it possible to gain freedom, not from power relations in their entirety, but from a given, specific relation of power. In fact, it is better to say that the problem consists, not in gaining freedom, since that is already essentially there; rather, the problem is to change, subvert, or reverse a given power relation, and this by making freedom take the form of a resistance.

Resistance is often associated with global theories of revolution; but resistance as it is meant here refers to something much less ambitious, much less sweeping with respect to the situation it opposes. That is, opposition takes the form of strategic responses which recognize that resistance "relies upon the situation against which it struggles."[46] This entails that the possibilities for resistance will always be necessarily limited by the situation (i.e., power relation) to which one is subjected. The radical specificity of our subjection requires a "local and regional" struggle against power, a specific and immediate response, exploiting possibilities for oppositional action given by the power relation in spite of itself. In short, freedom has "to be pursued at the level of gestures, practical actions, and in relation to specific situations."[47]

Our position is always strategic with regard to any relationship of power, which gives us at least a potential opportunity to change the power relationship, to free ourselves from a particular mode of subjection; but what specific strategies should we adopt in order to capitalize on our strategic position? What should be the specific forms of our resistance? The most basic requirement for an effective resistance is to understand what it is, precisely, that one struggles against. Properly speaking, our struggles should be "against subjection, against forms of subjectivity and submission" asserts Foucault. The source of our subjection and subjugation is not the state (as a central governing body), not an elite group, a class, or an economic relation. Rather, it is an anonymous technology of power. As Foucault see it, "This form of power applies itself to immediate everyday life which categorizes the individual, marks him by his own individuality, attaches him to his own identity, imposes a law of truth on him which he must recognize and which others have to recognize in him. It is a form of power which makes individuals subjects."[48] In other words, it is the complex matrix of disciplinary power against which we need to mount our resistance. Our struggles must be "antidisciplinary" (to the extent that this is possible) in that they resist the forms of subjection, of subjectivity, imposed on us by disciplinary inscriptions. The possibilities for free action are directly, almost linearly, related to our identities as individuals, to how we are identified, by ourselves and others, in a relational and hierarchical complex of rank and statistical gradation. Through power/knowledge relations, discipline "forces the individual back on himself and ties him to his own identity in a constraining way."[49] Our identities are to this extent the result of disciplinary mechanisms of normalization and individualization. Thus, the object of our resistance will be "to refuse what we are"—that is, to break through, to fracture, the limitations imposed on us by a disciplinary ascription of our own identity.

What can be done against the disciplinary mechanisms and power relations which subject us? Is there any recourse besides juridical, rights-based appeals to sovereignty?[50] Foucault offers us no easy, formulaic answers. Resistance has to be specific and appropriate to the situation it opposes. It may require calculated retreats, compromises, temporary submissions. The most basic form of resistance would be a simple refusal: "To say no is the minimum form of resistance."[51] Such resistance can have a significant impact on the powers that be. Moreover, it can open up other possibilities for strategic resistance. Resistance can also take the form of "confrontation strategies," which can take shape as direct challenges, and can be more or less violent. Even when such confrontations are ineffective, they can make it possible to identify strengths and weaknesses in a given power relation, which can be used strategically in future attacks. Another possible form of resistance would be various "subversion strategies," which operate by using the dictates of a given power relationship against itself, but without outright opposition. Even the appeal to rights can be effective in suspending or even upsetting relations of power, provided that such an appeal is recognized *as a strategy*, that it is raised in response to a specific practice, and that it does not end up perpetuating or reinforcing a particular disciplinary coercion, or of setting up a new one in its place.[52] Whatever its form, any strategy of resistance will have as its aim, ultimately, to refuse a certain form of subjection which limits the possibilities of what we can *be* as free human beings: "The political, ethical, social, and philosophical problem of our day is not to liberate the individual from the state and from the state's institutions, but to liberate us both from the state and from the type of individualization which is linked to the state. We have to promote new forms of subjectivity through a refusal of the kind of individuality which has been imposed on us for several centuries."[53]

Promoting new forms of subjectivity requires resisting entrenched relations of power. This does not mean we can ever be completely free of power relations. On the contrary, the best we can do is to replace one power relation with another. The best we can hope for is a power relation with fewer constraints and more open possibilities for free activity, for expressions of human subjectivity.[54]

Is this what Michel-Guillaume-Jean de Crèvecoeur was seeking when he resolved to remove himself and his family from so-called "civilized" society and to live among the Indians? To justify and explain this apparently audacious decision, Crèvecoeur appealed to the experience of countless white European settlers who had been captured and forced to live with their Native American captors. Later, when given the opportunity to leave, he says, "they chose to remain." The first and principal reason Crèvecoeur gives for these settlers choosing to stay with their "savage" brethren was that they experienced "the most perfect freedom."[55] We might ask, what does Crèvecoeur mean, here, by *freedom*? And how is it more "perfect" than other forms of freedom? Is this positive freedom or negative freedom? We might be tempted to dismiss this as neither, and to say that it merely refers to some romantic idealization of Native American life. Perhaps. But suppose we look upon it as a form of counter-memory. What these settlers were refusing by living with the Indians was a certain set of subjectival constraints, a form of identity. Similarly, Crèvecoeur was attracted to this choice because he found himself caught in the middle of a power relation that threatened his life. Moreover, he articulated this threat in terms of the imposition of certain forms of identity by the factions involved, as either traitor or spy. His decision to join a Native American tribe was strategic in that it would distance him from that threat, but, more than that, it opened a space of distance from these forms of identity to which he had been confined. In fact, he would shake off his former Western identity and adopt a new one: "According to their customs we shall likewise receive names from them, by which we shall always be known."[56] In that sense, perhaps the "most perfect freedom" of which Crèvecoeur speaks refers to a space of possible transformation.

Freedom and the Politics of Transformation

Foucault's reflections on counter-memory show that freedom is not so much an issue of power (as it is conventionally understood in traditional political philosophy), as it is of *identity*. Rousseau and Nozick are attempting to elaborate views of political freedom that would liberate the political subject from any arbitrary and excessive exercise of power; but in actuality, they are articulating forms of political identity: the citizen and the autonomous individual, respectively. Both of these identities are best understood in terms of subjectival constraints and determinations through which otherwise meaningless bodies are bound to, and identified in terms of, a set of political (i.e., power) relations. As I argued earlier, both positive and negative freedom are subsumed—in a sense, conscripted—by the disciplinary agendas of a governmental rationality. Moreover, this subsumption is so subtle, so thorough, so efficient that those who are subjugated are not even aware of it. In fact, the success of this disciplinary-identificational machinary is such that those subjected to it assume they are free (in the ideological senses elaborated by Rousseau and Nozick). In this sense, identity is an instrument of power. That is, it is through identity that power is channeled and manifested as this or that political personage: sovereign/subject, master/slave, capitalist/proletarian, liberal/conservative, noble savage/ savage noble, and so on. Counter-memory allows us to break through, to fracture these identificational determinations and to permit a possible transformation by attending to the power relations through which such identities are both constructed and sustained.

A typical, if simplistic, criticism of this view often takes the form of a question: "If freedom through counter-memory is to be understood as a 'freedom of permanent transformation,' what if I want to transform myself into a tyrant—an Adolf Hitler or Pol Pot, for instance? What's to prevent me from doing so?" The obvious reply to this question is, "Nothing"—provided the social conditions (i.e., power relations) are there to permit you to do so. But do not expect me to freely submit to your tyranny. Any form of subjectivity that designs to dominate or crush others must expect strategies of resistance—violent resistance—to oppose it. Such a resistance does not have to be justified on the basis of transcendental ethical principles (the apparent lack of which motivates the above objection.) It does not have to be *justified* at all. At no point have I argued that freedom is a matter of right or entitlement. The important question here is whether one wants to transform oneself in a way that invites, or requires, active resistance or not. This is the unavoidable question we all must face, every day, as *political* subjects.

Interestingly, almost the same sort of objections were raised against Jean-Paul Sartre and existentialism. In *Being and Nothingness*, Sartre could largely dodge charges of moral nihilism by claiming that he was doing an "ontology," not an ethics; but later, in his famous public address, "Existentialism Is a Humanism," he tried to address such criticisms by insisting that "existentialism is optimistic, it is a doctrine of action."[57] However, this characterization of existentialism was more asserted than it was argued. It was really Simone de Beauvoir who addressed the issue of the possibility of an ethics from an existential point of view directly in her book, *The Ethics of Ambiguity*. In this work, Beauvoir offers an ethics of radical freedom in which freedom founds itself as a value and as a principle of ethical choice:

By turning toward this freedom we are going to discover a principle of action whose range will be universal. . . . Freedom is the source from which all significations and all values spring. It is the original condition of all justification of existence. The man who seeks to justify his life must want freedom itself absolutely and above everything else. At the same time that it requires the realization of concrete ends, of particular projects, it requires itself universally. It is not a ready-made value which offers itself from the outside to my abstract adherence, but it appears (not on the plane of facticity, but on the moral plane) as a cause of itself. It is necessarily summoned up by the values which it sets up and through which it sets itself up. It can not establish a denial of itself, for in denying itself, it would deny the possibility of any foundation. To will oneself moral and to will oneself free are one and the same decision.[58]

To the degree to which this freedom *founds itself* as a value, and is not based on some transcendental ground or source, I think that an ethics such as Beauvoir's is compatible with Foucault's project and could be effectively articulated onto it, provided that Beauvoir's emphasis on the individual is properly informed by a genealogical understanding of the individual's emergence and constitution.[59]

Foucault's genealogical analyses reveal that "the self is not given to us"—there is no essential identity around which discourse, power relations, and modes of subjectivization revolve, but rather the subject is an effect of their interplay. This recognition of the subject as historically contingent effect, rather than essential, metaphysical entity, leads Foucault to a Nietzschean conclusion, that "we have to create ourselves as a work of art."[60] We have to become involved in an ongoing process of creative self-transformation, of self-overcoming, in a genuinely Nietzschean sense. Yet when Foucault says that we have to create ourselves, he is not expressing this as a moral demand; it is, rather, a description of our situation. Constituting ourselves as subjects is a creative endeavor that involves giving meaning—style—to our existence, whether we recognize it as such or not. And Foucault is also extending an invitation: he is inviting us to open a space of freedom for ourselves, a freedom that consists in affirming ourselves "as a creative force."[61] In abandoning any notion of metaphysical essentiality or anthropological necessity regarding who and what we are, we are able to recognize the creative contribution of the subject in the process of his or her own self-formation. This recognition itself is a kind of liberation, a distancing from the processes of subjection and subjectivization, through which the power of a particular identity is suspended. In the affirmation, not of a discourse of truth about ourselves as "creative beings," but of creative *activity* in and for itself, recognition is no longer a determination. Through this affirmation, identity becomes a game, in which the relationships we have to ourselves are not of unity and coherence, but of difference and creation. In this way subjectivity becomes, not a limitation, but an *art*.

Perhaps all this sounds too playful for the serious business of politics. In fact, this is just the sort of play required to break through, to fracture, the most oppressive forms of political subjection. A whole range of social problems, from limitations on social opportunities to declarations of war, are in part attributable to processes of subjectivization. The constitution of a political identity for ourselves involves the appropriation of values and beliefs that commit us to certain practices—practices that have real political consequences. We alternately lament or praise such consequences with little or no sense that their source lies in part in the arbitrary appropriation or imposition of an identity. We condemn the persecution of minorities, for instance, but how often do we ever really question the endemic processes of differentiation and identification that divides human beings along lines—limits—of race and gender? War is the most tragic of human dramas, we say, even when it is "necessary" to secure our liberty, but to what extent is this necessity tied to an arbitrary drawing of lines—limits—on a map, to the contingency of a national identity that marshals troops for its perpetuation? The bigot and the dictator are micro- and macro-symbols of our political subjection. We raise our opposition against them willingly, enthusiastically, thinking that freedom consists simply of overcoming their petty, or global, tyrannies. We never think to overcome a much finer, more pervasive, less violent but more pernicious, quotidian form of subjection; that is, we never think to overcome our*selves*. Political subjectivity is played out every day in struggles of domination and submission. Real freedom, concrete freedom, consists in fracturing the political identities—our liberalism, our conservatism, our patriotism, our individualism—through which we are bound to, limited by, rationalities that make these struggles necessary.

If we can come to recognize the optionality and lack of necessity of given forms of political subjectivity, we might have a point of departure for changing (overcoming) certain kinds of real political relations. If this sounds utopian or idealistic, we have only to consider that most if not all political conflict in this half-century can be understood as clashes of identity. Most political movements in the last forty years in the United States can be understood in these terms.[62] Such movements have been (to some degree) successful in upsetting certain entrenched political identifications that had been the basis of their subjection and domination. The resistance that such movements have raised against their subjection is predicated on a refusal of a subjectival conceptualization and its limitations. Moreover, we have seen evidence that such refusals have gained wider social acceptance; they increasingly infiltrate the social structure through institutionalization and demarginalization. Of course, there are backslidings and retrenchments on a fairly regular basis (consider recent legislation to ban gay marriages, or the platform statement of Southern Baptists that wives "submit graciously to the servant leadership of their husbands"). Still, in many instances the political battles over identity—women in the military as a policy (though, of course, in practice sexual harassment and discrimination are still very prevalent), for example—have at least lifted such movements from the shadows and given them an air of legitimacy.

This fact alone should make us suspicious, however. Too often strategies of resistance are no more than *liberation* movements—such as popular feminist, civil rights, and gay rights movements. Such movements are often animated by a metaphysical or juridical conception of what it is for human beings to be free.[63] These conceptions are themselves imported from traditional notions of what it is to be a political subject, of what it is to be human. But, as Seyla Benhabib observes, the form of political subjectivity assumed by the liberal traditon is "disembedded and disembodied," and, as such, "cannot do justice to those contingent processes of socialization" through which one "becomes" a self.[64] Foucault's reflections on discourse, power relations, and modes of subjectivation not only confirm this point but complicate it exponentially. Any political theory that would hope to offer an adequate view of freedom must address itself to this complexity, which means attending to the manifold processes through which political identities are constituted. This would place an enormous burden on political philosophy and would no doubt alter both its project and its trajectory. It is not clear that the juridical, rights-based notion of political identity found in the liberal tradition could be sustained against a genealogical critique, except perhaps as a strategy. In fact, it seems likely that our conception of political freedom would be transformed, irreversibly. If political identity is a fabrication of anonymous technologies, and if the liberal, juridical notions of freedom propagated by philosophers like Rousseau and Nozick are actually imbricated in these very technologies, then genuine freedom is only possible through a genealogical critique of identity itself. This freedom would be strategic in that it would carve out spaces of thought and action made possible by (a given set of) power relations themselves; and, above all, it would be transformative in the aforementioned sense that counter-memory, an effect of genealogical critique, makes it possible to suspend the power of a given identificational determination, possible to be other than what we presently are.

Nonetheless, it is precisely Foucault's thinking on power relations and the formation of identity as they regard the notion of freedom that tends to attract the most intense criticism. The more sophisticated versions of such criticism are not easily dismissed, in part because they claim to be based on internal inconsistencies in the Foucauldian project itself. Such criticisms—versions of which can be found in Jürgen Habermas, Charles Taylor, Nancy

Fraser, Alasdair MacIntyre, Michael Walzer, and Richard Rorty, among others—appeal to certain self-referential and even paradoxical elements in Foucault's thought that threaten its validity and intelligibility. Such criticisms are so common as to be suspicious. In fact, due to the frequency of such charges and because of the apparently insoluble problem on which they are based, I think that the phenomenon these criticisms collectively address deserves a name: "the Foucault Conundrum." In the last chapter I respond to these criticisms. I also try to anticipate what a postliberal, postnational, genealogically informed political theory would look like. We already have many robust models of such a theory, and, although there are many important differences between them, what they share in common is the insight that political theory addresses itself properly, not to rights, power, or government, but to the question of identity.

Genealogy and Other-Politics

Conclusions, Implications, Applications

Jeremy Bentham is kept in a large mahogany cabinet at the University of London. His skeleton is dressed in the eighteenth-century garb of a gentleman scholar. A wax head with glass eyes stares fixedly from the recesses of the cabinet, reproducing the perfect philosophical countenance. On special occasions, such as ceremonial dinners, Bentham's tomb-cell is opened and he is displayed for public viewing. There he sits sternly, silently, without protest as the eyes of curious onlookers fall upon him and examine him. Perhaps he reflects on the twisted irony of his situation: Bentham, the father of the panopticon, caught forever in perfect docility, in the clutches of an assessing gaze.

This macabre scene challenges our firmest, our most cherished beliefs about the human subject. In the case of Bentham, we have a subject whose reality has become that of *display*. Displayed in his case, Bentham represents the epitome of disciplinary constraint. The most asymmetrical of power relations holds Bentham, individualizes him to the point of absurdity, and allows him to perform his function, that of icon. Bentham is the ideal political subject because he performs his function with an absolute minimum of resistance. In perfect silence, he reflects the essence of our subjection.

Our Cartesian heritage inclines us to resist the attribution of subjectivity to this figure. This cannot *really* be Jeremy Bentham, we would object. It cannot be the human subject known in life as Jeremy Bentham. But then, what do we mean when we use this dense, treacherous little word, *really*? Certainly the same bones that now fill the period clothing and support the wax head of this figure *really* at one point occupied the flesh of the person known to all and sundry as Jeremy Bentham. Of course, we never appeal to such lowly matter as flesh and bone when defining the personhood of someone. Plato taught us better than that. We all know that what is really essential to a person is *spirit*. With death the spirit leaves the body— whether it continues in another form is a matter for theologians to decide—and the person ceases to exist. Thus, as much as it may look like Bentham, and despite the fact that it contains the very same skeleton, wears the very same clothes, has the same face, this figure cannot *really* be Jeremy Bentham.

Let us be good philosophers and employ our best Cartesian doubt regarding this matter of spirit. What if Bentham were really still alive and "inhabiting" this figure, except that he was being particularly taciturn? How would we tell the difference? Certainly not by reference to spirit. We can't *see* spirit, and even if Bentham were to speak to us, we still couldn't be sure this was not a cleverly constructed automaton. We have another recourse: the *cogito*. If Bentham thinks, then Bentham exists. But surely Bentham doesn't think—his head is now made of wax. To confirm this, just to make sure we aren't being deceived, we could melt his head. Watching it change color and texture as it spattered on the floor, we could see for ourselves that it contained no gray matter. Of course, the fact that Bentham no longer thinks does not mean he doesn't exist. He *does* exist—or at least this figure exists, which has his bones, wears his clothes, and displays his countenance. How is that different from when he was, so to speak, "alive"? Thus the question remains: Is this *really* Jeremy Bentham?

The appeal to spirit—or consciousness, or ego, or thinking, or will—to capture the essence of subjectivity is the grist for daydreaming lens grinders. Such notions are predicated on an act of abstraction that thrusts the subject into a metaphysical void, giving it a universality that makes it formless, odorless, colorless, utterly unrecognizable. Such notions can tell us nothing, absolutely nothing, about the reality of *Jeremy Bentham*, alive or dead.

Thus, let us replace our Cartesian doubt with Nietzschean suspicion. Let us ask different questions: Has any subject ever been understood apart from a discursive milieu that gives him *meaning*? Has any subject ever been understood apart from a structure of power relations that determines her *place* in the world? Has any subject ever been understood apart from a set of practices through which he fashions a specific *mode of being*? These questions, which belong together, do not appeal to the interiority of a private world, but to a radical exteriority of historical contingencies. When applied to the question, "Is this *really* Jeremy Bentham?" they alter it completely; it becomes a question that must be analyzed in terms of certain privileged discourses (e.g., those of biology, medicine, theology), in terms of certain entrenched institutional practices, rules, regulations (e.g., those of rank, authority, normalization), and in terms of certain identifiable, and identifying, ways of conducting oneself. Even more, it is in terms of the correlation of these factors that we define the reality of Jeremy Bentham.

This is the approach that must now be brought to bear on the question of the political subject. That is, political subjects are the effects of an *interplay* of discursive practices, power relations, and modes of self-formation; political subjects are the products of a *correlation* of processes of rarity, of exclusion, of appropriation; political subjects are *fabrications*—not entirely unlike the figure that now stares grimly from his mahogany cabinet.

The work of Michel Foucault allows us to understand political identity, not in terms of a metaphysically given entity, but as a fabrication, a construct. In general terms, Foucault's work allows us to see political identity as discourse-specific and historically contingent: it varies according to the interplay of discursive regularities, regional practices, disciplinary effects, and modes of self-problematization. The political subject emerges within the space of this interplay. Considered in terms of this interplay, the notion of the political subject as a fundamental and essential identity animated by spirit or will becomes suspect. Rather, the political subject is an effect, an *arsis*, erected in a matrix of experience that thrusts onto undefined bodies the mask of their own identity. In this sense, political subjectivity is "an historical event, one which [is] not at all necessary, not linked to human nature, or any anthropological necessity."[1] The self-identical subject of traditional political philosophy emerges from genealogical analysis shattered, dispersed, and exposed as a reticulated convergence of lines of power, of discursive limits, of self-limitations.

Genealogy exposes the nonessentiality of the political subject through a historical analysis of its constitution. The exposure of political subjectivity is effected by recognizing in it the axial interplay of discursive practices, power relations, and processes of subjectivation. Yet what is exposed in this analysis is not the "origin" of the political subject, understood as the transcendental conditions of its appearance. Rather, what genealogical critique exposes is the *Entstehung* of the political subject, its *emergence* as an event. As Foucault explains, "Emergence designates a place of confrontation but not as a closed field offering the spectacle of a struggle among equals. Rather, as Nietzsche demonstrates in his analysis of good and evil, it is a 'nonplace,' a pure distance, which indicates that the adversaries do not belong to a common space. Consequently, no one is responsible for an emergence; no one can glory in it, since it always occurs in the interstice. In a sense, only a single drama is ever staged in this 'nonplace,' the endlessly repeated play of dominations."[2] Here we have, arguably, one final reversal of Jean-Jacques Rousseau. Rousseau's history of the origins of the political subject appeals to the notion of origin as *Ursprung*, which Foucault describes as "the meta-historical deployment of ideal significations and indefinite teleologies."[3] Genealogy as the parodic pursuit of *Entstehung*, by contrast, undermines any notion of necessary origination. The event of the political subject's emergence is the effect, rather, of pure play and raw contingency, of the "play of dominations." The space of the political subject's emergence refers not to the firm ground of historical necessity, but to a "non-place," to a space of "pure distance" opened and bordered by the accidental junction and concurrence of more or less random phenomena. Political subjects emerge in the "interstice," between discourses of right and disciplines of subjection, between the polarizing demands of positive and negative freedom, between citizenry and individuality, between unity and pluralism, between the antinomic concerns of a governmental integration.

This interstice, this space of axial interplay, is not unlike Jeremy Bentham's mahogany cabinet at the University of London. In their own way political subjects are like Benthams—identities pieced together from alien forms, fabrications of anonymous technologies. In the interstice of the political subject's emergence we can see discourse at play, animating and giving meaning to an otherwise meaningless figure. In this interstice we can see power extending its web, encircling the body and cloaking it in the constricting fabric of its own identity. In this interstice we can see the subject at work on itself, dutifully fashioning the dress of its stylized display.

We see subjection in this interstice, we see domination and oppression; but we also see freedom, a persistent obstinacy that holds the promise of new possibilities, of new beginnings. This freedom, this resilience, gives life to the subject—it extends itself in the form of pure force and desire, seeking limits only for the sake of transgressing them. "It is through revolt that subjectivity . . . introduces itself into history and gives it the breath of life."[4] The political subject is at bottom nothing more than the envelopment of freedom, a circumscription of a persistent resistance. The story of freedom's relentless struggle to escape its bonds is the story of history itself. By listening with a suspicious ear to this story, the genealogist not only exposes the nonessentiality of the emergence of the political subject, but also of those philosophical discourses which make the political subject the central figure of a juridical reflection. In particular, the discourses of the liberal tradition are shown to be replete with metaphysical biases and presuppositions regarding the political subject. We see this most distinctly in the liberal tradition's conception of the political subject as a concrete, ontologically distinct unit of individuality. This unit is invested with rights, freedoms, obligations, animated by the spirit of Sovereignty, protected by inviolable spheres of liberty, bound in a contractual relation to society, possessed of a proprietous power. Foucault's work undercuts the authority and essentiality of all such claims and assumptions informing the discursive practice of the liberal tradition.

It is not just a matter of dismissing these discourses, however. Foucault's work shows that they are imbricated in the anonymous technology of power/knowledge relations that turns individuals into subjects and puts them in the service of the rationality of governmentality. These discourses provide value systems and frameworks of conceptualization that individuals can appropriate in the production of a discourse of truth about themselves, a discourse that serves as the principle of their subjection as it binds them to the constraints of a self-identification. Thus, more is going on here than a "positivistic" dismissal of a useless metaphysics. On the contrary: the problem is to show how this metaphysics is used, effectively, as an instrument of subjection and subjugation.

The Foucault Conundrum

Putting the problem this way allows us to address some possible objections. The first objection that I would like to consider is one which might be raised from the liberal tradition itself. That is, traditional political philosophers may or may not deny that they are dealing with a political subject as a pregiven metaphysical entity. Yet even if they are assuming such a political subject, these philosophers might say, in the end it does not matter because their real concern is with defining the principles of political justice that would permit political subjects to live together in peace, harmony, and, if possible, mutual prosperity. In fact, such an objection is voiced explicitly by John Rawls, who says, "One might say that our ordinary conception of persons as the basic units of deliberation and responsibility presupposes, or in some way involves, certain metaphysical theses about the nature of persons as moral or political agents. Following the precept of avoidance, I should not want to deny these claims. What should be said is the following. . . . If metaphysical presuppositions are involved . . . *they would not appear to be relevant* for the structure and content of a political conception of justice one way or the other."[5]

From this standpoint it does not really matter how the political subject is actually constituted, because we will always find ourselves dealing with already-constituted, or pregiven, political subjects. The problem is to identify and establish the political conditions necessary for governing the subject's relations with other subjects, with government, and with other nations. Given the real world of politics, the best way to approach this is by reference to rights, freedoms, obligations, sovereignty—all of the elements of what have been disparagingly labeled "juridical reflections."

This objection undermines itself from within. It conceals an implicit premise that cannot be articulated without the whole argument collapsing. This hidden premise is that these "juridical reflections," which are justified as being necessary to addressing the real world faced by already-constituted political subjects, can be somehow separated from the constitution, the emergence, of the political subject; but this is demonstrably false. Says Seyla Benhabib, "In the final analysis, conceptions of self, reason, and society and visions of ethics and politics are inseparable."[6] The problem of showing how the political subject is constituted is not an extraneous or purely academic enterprise. Such an analysis reveals that the juridical reflections of the liberal tradition are themselves involved in, contributing factors to, the constitution of the political subject. It shows how such reflections are instrumental to techniques of subjection and domination. Thus, the emergence of the political subject and the attempt to define her rights, freedoms, and political obligations *cannot* be separated. The liberal tradition's juridical, rights-based appeals to sovereignty have been complicitous with and inseparable from our emergence as political subjects.

A variation of the first objection might take the following form: even if everything is conceded to a Foucauldian analysis regarding the emergence of the political subject, it is still necessary that certain rational principles of political action be identified, to give impetus and direction to resistance, to keep the subject from becoming immobilized by a kind of moral inertia that results from the lack of objective normative standards against which a given state of political subjugation could be judged. Something very like this objection comes from Jürgen Habermas, who contends that Foucault's critique of our subjection is so successful that it deprives us "of the normative yardsticks" that would be required to get free of it.[7] Indeed, this objection is very common; it is raised by a number of critics as diverse as Nancy Fraser, Richard Rorty, Charles Taylor, and Michael Walzer. This objection is so common, in fact, that perhaps the dilemma that it is meant to identify deserves its own name: "the Foucault Conundrum."

I agree with Honi Fern Haber that the criticism of Foucault about his alleged lack of normative standards tends to miss the point.[8] However, although the criticism may miss the point with respect to Foucault's project, the concern that motivates the criticism is a legitimate one. It is reasonable to desire that political theorists, if Foucault can be characterized as such, tell us how we *ought* to act with regard to the forces that subject us.

And, although Foucault insists that this is not his role as an intellectual, this insistence itself leaves Foucault vulnerable to a stronger version of the Foucault Conundrum criticism from Alasdair MacIntyre that challenges the intelligibility of the whole genealogical project. In the discussion that follows I shall consider each point in turn.

It is true that Foucault closes off any transcendental appeal to reason by which we could identify what Habermas calls "yardsticks," or normative standards, since he shows that there are only finite, historically contingent *rationalities*. It seems to be possible, through genealogy, to recognize the force or compulsion of such rationalities, but doing so seems to cut us adrift from rational standards altogether, in the sense that we have no means by which to condemn the powers that subject us, nothing on which to base the judgment that we ought to resist it. Thus, we find ourselves immobilized. We could resist a given form of rationality, but only by putting ourselves under the subjection, the normative dictates, of another form of rationality. Surely this is not the freedom promised by Foucault's "counter-memory." Thus, it would seem that there can be no freedom from our subjection.

However, there is a false assumption here. This argument assumes that one must *first* identify a normative standard *before* one can mount a resistance, and thereby get free of a mode of subjection. It assumes that an "ought" is necessary to condemn a rationality, to say that it is wrong, before—and on the basis of which—one attempts to get free of it. This assumption is false for two reasons. First, it erroneously separates freedom from the recognition that one is dominated; but since freedom, as Foucault understands it, consists simply in the opening of new possibilities, this recognition is itself a kind of freedom, at least in the sense of a distancing of oneself from the necessity of one's subjection. Of course, the argument asserts something else; it says that such a recognition is impossible without a normative standard that allows us to see that the domination is "wrong" and that one "ought" to resist it. However, no such "ought" is required. In fact, Friedrich Nietzsche would argue to the effect that such "oughts" are, if not superfluous, then at least derivative.[9] That is, an "ought" is always produced as a "symptom" of a situation that must be dealt with (or not), but which in itself has no moral value one way or another—or at least no *intrinsic* moral value. The moral value of a given choice extends from the context in which the choice is made and through which an "ought" is articulated. Moreover, the historical contingency of moral "oughts" need not count against the rationality of abiding by them, nor should the apparent

lack of transcendental or *a priori* normative standards lead to moral inertia. Such standards are always context-bound and historically contingent,
but that fact, in itself, does not count against their legitimacy.

Perhaps an analogy will help to explain this. Suppose someone holds her
hand directly above the flame of a candle. Experience tells her that if she
leaves her hand there, it will be burned. Is an "ought" really necessary to
tell her what to do here? Is it necessary to say to her, "You *ought* to remove
your hand, friend, or you will be sorry"?[10] She will find out what her options
are in short order. But whether she "ought" to move her hand or not will
depend on the reasons her hand is there in the first place; the point is that
no "ought" is required beforehand to tell her what she *might* do. Similarly,
experience—this time referring to genealogical history—can tell us the story
of dominations and subjections. No extraneous normative or rational standards are required to recognize dominations and subjections as such. We
need only appeal to the amoral, arational standard of freedom—of open
possibilities, of possible transformations. This would not be a transcendental appeal, since freedom is immanent to any power relation. We do not need
to get outside the situation in order to recognize our subjection. One can
recognize domination against the "standard" of open or closed possibilities.
This recognition, which is made possible by genealogical critique, is morally
neutral with regard to whether one "ought" to resist. One is faced with an
arbitrary choice, but it is no more arbitrary than the domination itself. A
point conceded by the objection we are considering (at least as I have set it
up) is that there are no transcendental normative standards; but this is a
double-edged sword. This means that there is no transcendental basis for
saying that it is better to be dominated than it is to be free. Yet one *can*
recognize one's subjection. When this subjection is judged against the immanent, neutral standard of open possibilities, is it really necessary to say that
one "ought" to resist it? The choice, though arbitrary, is clear: accept your
subjection, or resist it—move your hand, or let it burn. The argument
erroneously assumes that unless we can identify some transcendental normative standards, we will be immobilized, that is, forced by inertia or lack
of direction to accept our subjection. But, in fact, it is only the requirement
of such normative standards itself that immobilizes us, since it precludes an
arbitrary response to an arbitrary situation. The reality of it is that we
choose freedom, or not, everyday.

As I have already mentioned, one major problem with criticisms of the
sort discussed above is that they are based on a misrepresentation of
Foucault's project. These criticisms are predicated on the assumption
that Foucault wants to condemn the power/knowledge regime. Because he

lacks the normative standards by which to do so, it is contended, this makes his philosophy politically conservative. That is, we are forced to accept our subjection with little or no hope of changing it. This is mistaken. Foucault's object is not to condemn the network of power/knowledge relations; his object is to expose the interplay of determining factors constituting this network as the source of our emergence as subjects. This exposure, this critique, has the effect of opening up new possibilities for subjects, in the sense that the recognition and understanding of their subjection can be used tactically in order to resist it. Whether they will resist it or not is an arbitrary (though not necessarily irrational) choice, and Foucault is adamant in his conviction that his role as an intellectual is not to tell them whether they should or should not resist it.[11] His role, rather, is to show subjects where their freedom lies and to expose points of weakness in the structures that dominate them. In this sense, Foucault's philosophy is far from conservative. In fact, it is ideologically neutral, but effectually radical and activistic. Says Foucault, "My point is not that everything is bad, but that everything is dangerous. . . . If everything is dangerous, then we always have something to do. So my position leads not to apathy but to a hyper- and pessimistic activism."[12]

Everything is dangerous—resistance as well as submission. Resisting one's subjection involves an essential risk, not simply in the sense that it invites the forces of retaliation against one's insubordination, but also, and more important, perhaps, it involves the risk of cutting oneself loose from a source of comfort and sustenance. "Relations of power are not bad in themselves," says Foucault.[13] Relations of power are at play in the constitution of all that we deem good or worthwhile in society. Thus, there is a risk, a danger, involved in resistance; but there is also a danger in accepting uncritically and without question our received values and political structures. Foucault feels that "the ethico-political choice we have to make everyday is to determine which is the main danger."[14] Like Nietzsche, Foucault wants to activate an abiding suspicion. This suspicion requires a recognition of the contingency and lack of necessity of things. But it also requires an active engagement with the powers of subjection, not from the standpoint of an anarchistic nihilism, but of challenging the forces that make us what we are. This is a suspicion which courts danger, that flouts limits, which transforms transgression from an occasion for moral condemnation into an instrument of possible freedom.

Nevertheless, any "instrument" may be used for good or ill. We normally want to know how that instrument "ought" to be used. In this sense, the objections from Habermas, Fraser, Rorty, Taylor, and Walzer about the apparent lack of normative standards in Foucault are legitimate. On the other hand, it would just be wrong to assert that Foucault's work lacks ethical import, or even that it fails to provide some sort of ethical direction.[15] In fact, many critics suggest that the basis of such an ethics lies in freedom.[16] And yet, at present any ethical direction Foucault offers us is largely implied. Thus, one might want an ethics where that direction is made more explicit, where an "ought" is prescribed in a more conventional sense. Still, it is not clear that such a prescription is even possible within the discourse of genealogy; it may be that such an ethics is precluded on genealogy's own terms.

In fact, before we can lay the Foucault conundrum to rest, we have to consider a more serious version of it that comes from Alasdair MacIntyre, who refers to the conundrum as Foucault's "self-engendering paradox." What is at stake here is not simply genealogy's difficulty in offering us normative direction, but the rationality of the entire genealogical project. Says MacIntyre, "The insights conferred by this post-Nietzschean understanding of the uses of history are themselves liable to subvert the project of understanding the project. . . . Hence once again it seems to be the case that the intelligibility of genealogy requires beliefs and allegiances of a kind precluded by the genealogical stance. Foucault's carrying forward of Nietzsche's enterprise has thus forced upon us two questions. Can the genealogical narrative find any place within itself for the genealogist? And can genealogy, as a systematic project, be made intelligible to the genealogist, a well as others, without some at least tacit recognition being accorded to just those standards and allegiances which it is its avowed aim to disrupt and subvert?"[17]

Although MacIntyre leaves open the door to the possibility that some future genealogy might be able to answer the questions he raises in some adequate and internally consistent way, the "responses so far," he says, have only confirmed genealogy's "progressive impoverishment."

At first, MacIntyre's criticism may look devastating. For MacIntyre, genealogy's strength is also its fatal weakness, its successes a harbinger of its eventual failure. That is, the genealogical critique inaugurated by Nietzsche in the nineteenth century has been successful in subverting and undermining what MacIntyre calls the "encyclopaedic" understanding of truth and the possibility of rational inquiry. However, for MacIntyre, what genealogists like Nietzsche and Foucault did was—like philosophical Frankensteins—create and release a critical juggernaut that would eventually turn back against its creators.

MacIntyre frames the "self-engendering paradox" of genealogy in terms of a series of unacknowledged—and unacknowledgeable, from the standpoint of genealogy—contradictions. MacIntyre asserts that the very intelligibility of the genealogist's project rests on a commitment of the genealogist "to standards at odds with the central theses of the genealogical stance." In particular, genealogy's attempt to decenter and deconstruct the self of Western metaphysics can make sense only to a self that is in fact "persistent and substantial."[18] Thus, genealogical texts end up subverting themselves, in the ironic sense that their success, their intelligibility, relies on appealing to the very same sort of standards and assumptions they sought to undermine in the first place.

However, what MacIntyre refers to negatively as "self-subverting," other commentators, such as Bernd Magnus, have called "self-consuming concepts."[19] These concepts are part of the very methodology of genealogy and indeed most post-Nietzschean forms of inquiry. These are concepts that the genealogist appeals to provisionally in order to critique a tradition, but which are then subjected to the same sort of critique in order to avoid repeating the same metaphysical gestures as the tradition they are critiquing. For example, Nietzsche appeals to the "will to power" to critique Western morality in *Beyond Good and Evil*. At first sight, will to power looks like some sort of metaphysical postulate in the conventional sense. Yet, by the end of *Beyond Good and Evil*, we see Nietzsche turning his critical suspicion against his own thoughts, and in so doing, attempting to effect their erasure.[20] We see something like this self-consumption of concepts in Jacques Derrida and his notion of *différance*, which he says is "neither a word nor a concept" but which nevertheless for us "remains a metaphysical name." At some "strategic point," says Derrida, *différance itself* will have to be deconstructed.[21] Something very similar is going on in Foucault. Analogous to Magnus's idea of "self-consuming concepts," Charles Scott says that a certain kind of "recoil" occurs with many of Foucault's ideas: "In [*The Order of Things*] the knowledge developed by the genealogical study has the effect of coiling again the various discursive and epistemic strands and forming a springing, self-overcoming movement whereby the truth of this knowledge is relegated to a lineage that is itself now in question."[22]

In fairness, MacIntyre to a degree acknowledges this erasure or self-consumption in Foucault's thought, and he locates it correctly, I think, in Foucault's appeal to masks. However, he is nonetheless persistent in his suggestion that even, or perhaps especially, this appeal to masks only underscores the paradox: "For in making his or her sequence of strategies of masking and unmasking intelligible to him or herself, the genealogist has to ascribe to the genealogical self a continuity of deliberate purpose and a commitment to that purpose which can only be ascribed to a self not to be dissolved into masks and moments."[23] For MacIntyre the main problem with genealogy comes down to the issue of personal identity, both in terms of the genealogist having a self in the conventional sense that her own language cannot accommodate, and also the "continuity within discontinuity" that such a self implies. MacIntyre contends that behind the discourses of genealogy, behind the masks of the genealogist, there is a "shadow narrative" of heroic exploits, and that this shadow narrative points to a "narrator behind the masks," that is, it points to "a stable and continuing referent for the 'I.'"[24] Moreover, it is only through the assumption of such a continuing self that some notion of accountability makes sense; and it is only by appeal to such a notion that the genealogist can be *held accountable*, in terms of intelligibility, of being able to "make sense" to herself and to others, and in moral terms, through which genealogical thinkers such as Martin Heidegger and Paul de Man might be held accountable for their ties to National Socialism, for example. Both of these last points obviously have serious repercussions for whether or not genealogy can be a viable form of political inquiry or critique, one that doesn't compromise its own claims, either morally or epistemologically.

MacIntyre suggests that the genealogist's reliance on masks, through which the genealogist is able to employ personal pronouns but in a provisional, highly encumbered sort of way, "presupposes just that metaphysical conception of accountability"— and hence of selfhood—"which genealogy disowns."[25] In his discussion of the genealogist's reliance on masks, has MacIntyre left something out? It is not just the genealogist who wears a mask. Personhood, self-identity, is itself a mask, a mask we all "wear" of necessity precisely to the extent that we are persons. Bentham's wax head is a symbol of that necessity as well as of its historical contingency. The "I" *is* the mask, not that which lies behind it.

In a 1980 interview for the Paris newspaper *Le Monde*, Michel Foucault did something rather unusual for a professional philosopher—he insisted that he be interviewed anonymously. This particular interview was one in a weekly series, extending over a period of five years, devoted to Europe's top intellectuals. But this time, at least, the readers of this series would have no "name" by which to orient themselves. "Why did I suggest that we use anonymity?" Foucault remarks in the interview. "Out of a nostalgia for a time when, being quite unknown, what I said had some chance of being heard. . . . A name makes reading too easy."²⁶ Foucault's gesture says something about the way in which a name can mark more than just a person, more even than an *oeuvre*, a body of written works that transcend their author. A name represents the condensation of an entire milieu of interpretations, critiques, sentiments, preconceptions, and expectations. This milieu tends to determine beforehand the possibilities for engagement with a given author or thinker. The interview in question was later published under the title "The Masked Philosopher," but Foucault's gesture of anonymity can be interpreted as a kind of "unmasking," the stripping away of this dense and cumbrous mask designated by the name, the milieu, of Michel Foucault. However, he does this, not in order to reveal the real "truth" of his thought and work but, rather, to open up new and different possibilities for encountering his thought.

When Foucault refused to identify himself in the *Le Monde* interview, he could be construed, as I said, as unmasking himself, not in order to reveal the "true" Foucault behind the mask, but rather of making possible the formation, through discourse, of a new mask, one that would be fashioned through the narrative engagement with the interviewer initially and then embellished and expanded by the larger public domain in which that discourse would circulate. Thus, to assert that personhood is itself a mask does not rule out the possibility of speaking of an "I"—nor does it prevent the "I" from speaking. To say that the I—the subject—is an effect, not the agent, of discursive and nondiscursive practices that exceed the I on all sides does not thereby rule out the possibility that the I might speak *as an I, as a self*. Obviously, it does speak.

The genealogist differs from the Thomist in rejecting the grounded or foundational, epistemological or metaphysical, "given-ness" of the I. Instead, the genealogist attempts to show how the I is *given over*, bound to and effected by anonymous factors that precede it and sustain it as such. As Heidegger said in *Being and Time*, we are "thrown" into a world which is "always already" there. In a similar sense, we are always already identities, subjects, persons—it would otherwise of course be impossible to recognize ourselves as such or to anguish over what we "really" are as persons. But that concession does not entail the metaphysical assumptions regarding personal identity that have reigned from Plato to Parfit.

As for the issue of accountability, once it is conceded that the genealogist can employ the language of conventional selfhood on occasion without thereby being involved in a contradiction, and since selfhood of whatever form always presupposes a larger community informed by shared standards both of morality and intelligibility, then it follows that the genealogist's project cannot only make sense to that community, but that its success or failure can be judged, legitimately, by the very same standards that the genealogist would otherwise call into question. For the genealogist knows that while any stance is provisional and historically contingent, intelligibility—*sense*—often requires that some stance be made. This possibility of taking a stand—of appealing to standards through which an assertion is made or a conclusion is drawn—is not ruled out by the genealogist. It does not entail a contradiction if the genealogist on occasion feels compelled to appeal to such standards in order to render his or her own project intelligible, in spite of the fact that the genealogist is always suspicious of those standards, sensitive to their historicality, and watchful of the play of heterogeneous and hegemonic forces that such standards both stem from and perpetuate. On the other hand, the genealogist retrieves marginalized discourses and local knowledges, and may even experiment in genre in order to demonstrate that there are more ways to "make sense" than by the quasi-Socratic method of appealing to standards. As MacIntyre himself observes, perspectivism is not tantamount to relativism or moral nihilism. Nor is the genealogist an habitual perpetrator of the genetic fallacy. In fact, what the genealogist shares with the philosopher of tradition (and not with the encyclopaedist—as both are defined by MacIntyre) is an understanding and appreciation of history, for what has come before. This permits a kind of genealogically informed consideration of different standards, of different normative and conceptual schemes. Through a process of evaluative judgment based on the "experience" derived from genealogical retrieval, one is able to say not which set of standards is better in any ultimate or ontotheological sense, but merely which one is *preferable*, based on an understanding of what such schemes have committed us to in the past. On the other hand, new ways of thinking might emerge precisely through the genealogical critique of the old. But it is largely by the fact that we are able to better appreciate the old that the new reveals itself, offers itself as a choice. This no doubt is not what the Thomist philosopher has in mind. To the Thomist, what the genealogist offers us is at best some form of meager pragmatism. Perhaps. But, the genealogist would reply, this is not offered as one set of standards over or against all the others, as an option we may simply choose. Rather, the genealogist compels us to recognize that that is all we ever had in the first place. This does not mean that we cannot come to reasoned judgments or that we cannot be held accountable for acting upon (or failing to act upon) those judgments. Likewise, the genealogist's recognition of the contingency of moral stances does not mean that we must be frozen by moral inertia or that we cannot be politically active. On the other hand, the genealogist does tend to complicate all of these issues immensely. That is, there is no pure form of subjectivity in the Cartesian sense, no pristine rationality in the Platonic sense, no unadulterated notion of accountability in the Kantian sense, no simple notion of guilt in the Judeo-Christian sense, and, moreover, no possibility of freedom in either a positive or negative sense that doesn't supplant one set of power relations for another. Thus, any form of political activity that is predicated on a Cartesian, Platonic, Kantian, Judeo-Christian, Hobbesian, or Rousseauian understanding of selfhood or subjectivity is going to be suspect. Nevertheless, what the genealogist shares with the existentialist is the insight that we must deal with our facticity as it presents itself, and that *at this juncture in our history* the problematizations of rationality, accountability, and freedom are an essential feature of the matrix of experience in which our subjectivity is at present defined. The genealogist recognizes that necessity even as he or she points toward the possibility that things might be otherwise.

Political Theory on the Horizon

To label Foucault's philosophy as "conservative," "liberal," "radical," or "anarchistic" is to place it under the dictates of precisely those sorts of juridical and ideological oppositions that he would seek to dissolve. "We must escape the dilemma of being either for or against," says Foucault.[27] The oppositional and antagonistic predilections of our standard political identifications blinds us to the network of anonymous and *disinterested* factors that cause such identifications to arise in the first place. By identifying ourselves in these ways, under these labels, we only unwittingly contribute to the perpetuation of the present power/knowledge regime. If our task is to change it, or even some portion of it, we have to "set aside" our political identifications. We have to suspend this power that binds us to an arbitrary political identity committed to defending ideological principles. As Foucault notes, "One must pass to the other side ... by trying to turn off these mechanisms which cause the appearance of two separate sides, by dissolving the false unity, the illusory "nature" of this other side with which we have taken sides. This is where the real work begins."[28] Yet, modern political subjectivity has been invested through and through with this necessity of taking sides. It is an essential feature of the discourse of threat that at once isolates us to a private autonomy and binds us to a national identity. It is the practical expression of a binary, juridical conception of power that obligates us to sovereignty and is justified on the basis of right. It is the ethical substance of a technology of self that gives rise to fragmentary individuals who define friends or enemies according to whether they cross an arbitrary ideological line. This burdensome, agitating, fragmenting, oppositional gesture, this taking of sides, pervades our experience as modern political subjects. It is played out in our institutions and on our battlefields. It structures our courts, our government, our policies and agendas, our diplomatic relations and military alliances. In the nuclear age it represents the ultimate threat. Thus, in so many ways, this taking of sides is the essence of politics today. On one level, of course, we know this, but is it necessary? How much violence could be avoided without it?

It is important to understand that when Foucault says we need to abandon this dilemma of taking sides, he is not calling for some humanistic "laying down of arms" after which we become united in an international brotherhood (or sisterhood, or some vapid combination thereof). His is not the typical Marxist project of establishing a more harmonious global community. Nor does Foucault think that overcoming this dilemma is a matter of attacking ideology per se, or of "raising consciousness." He realizes that ideology and consciousness are merely surface effects of a vast relational matrix. Nothing will be changed unless we direct our energies toward this matrix. Thus, when Foucault calls us to the "other side" he is inviting us to escape the limits of an identificational determination in which taking sides is made a requirement. *Outside* of this determination, the necessity of ideological opposition is effectively and actively forgotten.

Of course, there is always more work to do. Political philosophy can help to guide this work, but only if it resists the desire for closure that informs utopian teleologies or the attempt to lay down first principles of political justice. Above all, it would have to be a philosophy that is no longer "erected around the problem of sovereignty."[29] Perhaps Foucault's work on discourse, power relations, and modes of subjectivation can serve as a basis for constructing a new political philosophy. Such a philosophy would have to break free from the narrow confines of right and sovereignty that delimit the discourses of the liberal tradition. In order to understand our emergence as political subjects, and to trace out the possibilities of getting beyond our subjection, this new philosophy would have to extend its critique to the farthest reaches, the darkest corners, of our history and culture. It would have to apply itself to areas not immediately recognized as political: to family, religion, sexuality, morality, art, literature, science. It would be a philosophy that could cross (out) national boundaries, since it would no longer be tied to an ideological interest, and apply itself to political subjection elsewhere: in Eastern Europe, Northern Ireland, the Middle

East, for instance. We can only begin to imagine of what such a philosophy would consist, and the monumental task that would always be placed before it.

Indeed, the enormity of the task that is placed before political theory by genealogy indicates that the time for grand totalizing theory is long past. Instead, we have seen in the past decade or so a plethora of politico-theoretical discourses that have moved from the margins and fringes of academe into ever-increasing prominence. These discourses fragment and disperse what had been a theoretical monolith. I have in mind, among others, the discourses of political feminism (particularly of the postmodern variety), postcolonial theory, and multiculturalism. These discourses differ from those of traditional political philosophy in that the issue of identity is problematized in a different way, both conceptually and methodologically. It is not that traditional political philosophy cannot mark the difference between the Western white male and his Others, but that difference tends to be marked in terms of economic, social, and power imbalances. More-over, traditional political philosophy attempts to address those imbalances in typically juridical ways, by appealing to principles of distributive and compensatory justice, for instance. Traditional political philosophy lacks the conceptual machinery required to recognize the way that those imbalances are tied inseparably to cultural identity itself; it also lacks the methodological tools necessary to effect a deconstruction of those identificational constraints. Not to be reductionistic or to obviate some important differences between them, but what postmodern feminism, postcolonial theory, and multiculturalism have in common is that they can be said to marshal a critique against identity itself, against entrenched forms of cultural, social, and political identification and conceptualization, in ways that could never be available to more traditional political theory. What all three also have in common is that they address themselves to the acts of violative (and often violent) appropriation through which in part such identities have been constituted.

For example, such a recognition will lead Luce Irigaray to observe that femininity is a "construct," produced and defined through "male systems of representation." Under such a condition a woman has an identity in only a derivative sense. Constrained to such a relation, "she has no 'proper' name," says Irigaray.[30] The same could be said of all the victims of racism, anti-Semitism, and colonialism, of homophobia and xenophobia. They too have no *proper* name—though their history *as* victims has been a dramatic, and dramaturgic, attempt to acquire such a name, to achieve, to be conferred, nothing short of legitimacy.[31] Theirs is a history of name-calling and misidentification: "nigger," "kike," "spick," "fag." Of course, even apparently neutral, purely referential designations are likewise historically contingent and value-laden. From "Negroes" to "blacks" to "African Americans," "Indians" to "Native Americans," "Hispanic" to "Latino," from "queer" to "gay" to "queer" again, the names, chosen or imposed, are as much political gestures as taxonomic ones. Usually names are the *nomina* of familiarity, but in this case the names are inflected with the otherness and fractious alterity that preceded them.

Traditional feminism tries to "liberate" women by invoking the basic tenets of liberal theory—rights, freedoms, personal sovereignty, justice—and does so on behalf of a genderless abstract individuality. A classic example of this is the *Declaration of Rights and Sentiments*, drafted and signed by Elizabeth Cady Stanton, and others, in 1848 at Seneca Falls, New York. This document borrows both the language and format of Thomas Jefferson's Declaration of Independence to assert the rights and equality of women. Postmodern feminism tends to be suspicious of such liberation movements and especially of the form of political identity presupposed by them. Echoing Foucault, Irigaray says, "It is not a matter of toppling that order so as to replace it—that amounts to the same thing in the end—but of disrupting and modifying it."[32] This disruption proceeds not so much through marches and protests, but through a number of much more subtle tactics and strategies, one of which is mimicry, which consists of, as Irigaray notes, assuming feminine identity *deliberately*: "[this means] to convert a form of subordination into an affirmation, and thus to begin to thwart it. Whereas a direct feminine challenge to this condition means demanding to speak as a (masculine) 'subject,' that is, it means to postulate a relation to the intelligible that would maintain sexual indifference."[33] Through mimesis, identity itself is turned into a political strategem whereby what had been invisible and taken for granted is now *re-presented* in such a way that it is rendered visible and, as such, problematic.[34] Because femininity refers to a cultural construct rather than to an essence, it cannot be sustained without transformation once it is subjected to this sort of hyperreflexive exposure. A kind of dehypostatization of identity occurs, somewhat ironically, through a "playful repetition" of identity itself. It is such genealogical and deconstructive gestures, not juridical claims to rights and equality, that informs a "politics of difference" of the type advocated by Irigaray.[35]

Similarly, contemporary multicultural theory resists the politics of assimilation that has been the typical response to racial and ethnic conflict. The politics of assimilation works, like traditional feminism, by invoking the rhetoric of equality; through this rhetoric it attempts to assuage the conflict by glossing over the differences between cultural groups. Multiculturalism, on the other hand, understands itself as "a politics of recognition," and what it attempts to recognize are precisely those differences that traditional approaches would like to ignore. More conservative versions of multicuturalism, such as those advocated by Charles Taylor and Michael Walzer, have primarily targeted the academy, in particular the curriculum and canon formation, and they do so by appeal to liberal democratic ideals.[36] More radical projects of multiculturalism are based on a recognition that the issue of cultural diversity is an issue of cultural identity, and that little will be changed simply by having students read a few representative authors. Rather, these more radical versions of multiculturalism direct themselves, on the one hand, to the experience of what it is to belong to a particular racial or ethnic group, to the experience of cultural *difference* itself, and, on the other hand, to the cultural machinery in which such identities are constituted.[37]

A particular conception of identity is at stake here. Is cultural identity to be understood as pristine though adulterated (and hence, in principle at least, recoverable—the classic Rousseauian lament), or is it produced through adulteration itself? Nowhere has this question been more important or more controversial than in postcolonial theory. Nicholas Thomas, for example, asserts that for postcolonial discourse, "recovering or reinstating the subjectivity of the colonized is claimed to be a central aim."[38] Homi Bhabha, on the other hand, challenges the possibility of retrieving any such pure identity. Instead, we need to understand cultural identity in terms of what Bhabha refers to, in *The Location of Culture*, as cultural "hybridity." Says Bhabha, "Colonial culture is articulated as a *hybridity* acknowledging that all cultural specificity is belated.... Cultures come to be represented by virtue of the processes of iteration and translation through which their meanings are vicariously addressed to—*through*—an Other. This erases any essentialist claims for the inherent authenticity or purity of cultures.... It is in this hybrid gap ... that the colonial subject *takes place*."[39]

The term *hybridity* conveys the sense that a union of sorts has occurred, a union that effects a sort of transformation of the principals involved, that whatever the conjoining entities in question were before, they can no longer be so understood. In fact, postcolonial theory addresses itself properly, asserts Bhabha, not to the space from which the colonizer proceeds and extends itself, nor even to an original space of colonization. Rather, what issues from the union of colonizer and colonized is a "Third Space" peculiar to both in their complicity: "It is that Third Space, though unrepresentable in itself, which constitutes the discursive conditions of enunciation that ensure that the meaning and symbols of culture have not primordial unity or fixity, that even the same signs can be appropriated, translated, rehistoricized, and read anew."[40] Essentialist notions of cultural identity in a postcolonial world are inconsistent with the idea of cultural hybridity, which brings into relief both the imperialist interventions and the native responses through which such identities have been constituted.

Gayatri Spivak generally shares Bhabha's reservations regarding the possibility of subjectival retrieval; she likewise rebukes any nostalgia over a "lost" subjectivity. In fact, her emphasis on the "epistemic violence" done to the subaltern subject by the very postcolonial critic who would seek to understand her casts doubt on the possibility of a retrieval or translation of any sort. "Can the subaltern speak?" asks Spivak. No, she answers, "there is no space from which the sexed subaltern can speak."[41] Can the postcolonial critic speak for her? Only by an intervention that is in its own subtle way also a form of colonization, suggests Spivak. However, Bhabha has shown that there *is* a space from which the subaltern can speak—the "Third Space," the space in which the subaltern emerges as such in the first place. This is a space that postcolonial theory doesn't so much translate as it delimits and demarcates. And what it brings into relief is an act of mutual transformation and even procreation, but also of violence and violation.

The colonized world of which, and to a degree for which, Bhabha and Spivak speak is a violent world, as is shown clearly in the seminal work by Frantz Fanon, *The Wretched of the Earth*, from which Bhabha draws. Fanon describes a world wherein the hands of African dissidents are routinely chopped off, a world in which the lips of Angolan malcontents are "pierced in order to shut them with padlocks." Violence, suggests Fanon, is at the very heart of the relationship between colonizer and colonized: "Their first encounter was marked by violence and their existence together—that is to say the exploitation of the native by the settler—was carried on by dint of a great array of bayonets and cannon. . . .The violence which has ruled over the ordering of the colonial world, which has ceaselessly drummed the rhythm for the destruction of native social forms and broken up without reserve the systems of reference of the economy, the customs of dress and external life, that same violence will be claimed and taken over by the native."[42] The violence that Fanon describes and suggests is constitutive of the relationship between native and settler is echoed in Spivak's description of group rape, which she says is expressive of the acts of colonial conquest itself.[43] It was through such acts, says Jean-Paul Sartre in the preface to *The Wretched of the Earth*, that Europe "created a new breed, the Greco-Latin Negroes."[44] To be Other, then, in relation to the colonizing subject, is to be *known*, identified, in the most proprietary of ways; it is to be owned, co-opted, possessed, and dispossessed in the same moment. It is to have one's identity imposed upon one in the most violent and violative of ways.

To the extent that postcolonial theory attempts to trace out the history and character of this imposition for the sake of altering its trajectory, it can be said to be, at some level, a discourse of *reparation*. Consider, for example, Bhabha's anticipation of an "*inter*national culture," based on cultural hybridity, wherein "we may elude the politics of polarity and emerge as the others of our selves."[45] What *post*colonial theory speaks for and about is that form of identity that colonial culture itself would call "the noble savage." Yet postcolonial theory does not attempt to liberate the native from colonial power by turning him or her into the reverse, namely that abstract unit of free individuality that I have called the Savage Noble. If postcolonial theory is effective in bringing about a change in the relationship between colonizing Subject and colonized Other, it is not by appeal to rights and freedoms in a juridical sense, nor through retrieval of a lost identity, but rather through a genealogically informed critique of the mechanisms through which such identities have been created.

This brief canvassing can only demonstrate in some small fashion the many ways that postmodern feminism, multiculturalism, and postcolonial theory mark the horizon toward which political theory must advance. For the juridical reflections of traditional political philosophy, these (relatively) new "political" disciplines install critical, genealogically informed reflections on identity. Slowly, begrudgingly, traditional political theory has come to tolerate these theoretical upstarts. Indeed, few scholars today would feel it necessary to offer a justification for their existence in the academy. But what has yet to happen fully is for the insights of postmodern feminism, multiculturalism, and postcolonial theory to reverberate back upon more traditional political theory and thereby disrupt, suspend, *question* the form of political identity that has long remained invisible, transparent—namely, the autonomous individual, the Savage Noble—within it, to show that that identity, too, is a construct, is one form among diverse others, to show how the American nation-space is itself a "Third Space" inhabited by "hybrid" forms of identity.

Although it is difficult to trace the direction of influence, it is no coincidence, I think, that the mythos of savage nobility that took shape during the colonial period in America coincides with the height of social contract discourse and its appeal to a state of nature. The state of nature is the theoretical counterpart of the real wilderness in which the new "American" identity was forged. That identity, it turns out, is hybrid, born from the marriage of American Indian and European—not a simple mixture or composite, but something altogether new, something qualitatively different. Even the space upon which this new identity emerges is transformed: from wilderness to frontier and, finally, to nation. We may conceive of this space, the space of emergence for modern political identity, as a "Third Space" formed by the collision of American and European cultures. This would give new meaning to Frederick Jackson Turner's classic statement that "the frontier is the outer edge of the wave—the meeting point between savagery and civilization."[46] The frontier is what happens to the wilderness on its way to becoming a nation, a body politic of civil laws, of civilized peoples, but also of the disciplinary practices peculiar to governmentality. The colonist "tames" the wilderness; but in doing so he transforms himself. He becomes the Savage Noble, and the civil laws of his civilized society must be such that they reflect and support his autonomous individualism. A closer look at this individualism shows that it actually functions as the ideological shield of the mechanisms through which we are really and materially subjugated to the amorphous mass of the population and the dictates of the governmentalized nation-space.

Notes

Preface

1. Says Foucault, "The failure of the major political theories nowadays must lead not to a nonpolitical way of thinking, but to an investigation of what has been our political way of thinking during this century." See "The Political Technology of Individuals," in *Technologies of the Self: A Seminar with Michel Foucault*, edited by Luther H. Martin, Huck Gutman, and Patrick H. Hutton (Amherst: University of Massachusetts Press, 1988), 161.

Chapter 1: Introduction

1. Peter Gay claims that, although "most of his readers believed—and there are those who still do—that Rousseau championed the 'noble savage,' . . . this notorious phrase does not appear in his writings." Introduction to Jean-Jacques Rousseau, *Basic Political Writings* (Indianapolis: Hackett, 1987), viii. Yet while the terms as such may or may not appear together, they certainly appear in close enough proximity to warrant the attribution of them to Rousseau. See, for example, *The Discourse on the Origin and Foundation of Inequality among Mankind*, in which Rousseau remarks on how "the multitude of naked savages despise European pleasures and brave hunger, fire and sword, and death itself to preserve their independence." Only a paragraph separates this from a passage in which Rousseau describes this desire for liberty as "the noblest faculty of man." *The Discourse on the Origin and Foundation of Inequality among Mankind*, in *The Social Contract and Discourse on the Origin and Foundation of Inequality among Mankind*, edited by Lester G. Crocker (New York: Simon and Schuster, 1967), 232–34. We shall see that, for Rousseau, this is just one of many faculties which contribute to the nobility of the savage.

2. Jean-Jacques Rousseau, *Discourse on the Origin and Foundation of Inequality*, 200.

3. Says Rousseau, "In proportion as [man] becomes sociable and a slave to others, he becomes weak, fearful, mean-spirited, and his soft and effeminate way of living at once completes the enervation of his strength and of his courage. . . . All the comforts with which men indulge themselves . . . make them degenerate more markedly." *Discourse on the Origin and Foundation of Inequality*, 184–85.

4. Although Christopher Columbus brought several "Indians" back with him to Spain forcibly in cages, he described them as "very gentle" people who "love their neighbors as themselves." Yet by 1609, Richard Johnson would describe them as "wild and savage." In fact, throughout the greater part of the seventeenth century most colonists, and especially the Puritans, viewed the Indians as "cruel, barbarous, treacherous, and lazy." See Ronald Takaki, *A Different Mirror: A History of Multicultural America* (Boston: Little, Brown, 1993), 30–39.

5. All the quotations here, including the translations of Buffon, are from Thomas Jefferson's *Notes on the State of Virginia* (1785), "Query VI," reprinted in *The Heath Anthology of American Literature*, vol. 1, 2nd ed., edited by Paul Lauter (Boston: D.C. Heath and Company, 1994), 894–900.

6. Gabriella Ibieta and Miles Orvell, eds., *Inventing America: Readings in Identity and Culture* (New York: St. Martin's Press, 1996), 458.

7. Heckewelder, quoted in ibid., 461.

8. Says Geoffrey Rans, "the figure of Natty Bumppo was responded to by an appreciative public both in the U.S. and abroad. . . . For Europeans, the appeal of Cooper's fictions lay in his evocations of the American landscape and of characters like Natty and his Indian companions Chingachgook and Uncas, who seemed to embody the Romantic ideal of man in harmony with Nature, the Noble Savage," "James Fenimore Cooper 1789–1851," in Lauter, ed., *The Heath Anthology of American Literature*, 1327.

9. James Fenimore Cooper, from *The Last of the Mohicans* (1826), chapter 1 reprinted in Lauter, ed., *The Heath Anthology of American Literature*, 1335; emphasis added.

10. Says Slotkin, "If the first American mythology portrayed the colonist as a captive or a destroyer of Indians, the subsequent acculturated versions of the myth showed him growing closer to the Indian and the wild land. New versions of the hero emerged, characters whose role was that of mediating between civilization and savagery, white and red. The yeoman farmer was one of these types, as were the explorer or surveyor and, later, the naturalist. Yet it was the figure of Daniel Boone, the solitary, Indian-like hunter of the deep woods, that became the most significant, most emotionally compelling myth-hero of the early republic. The other myth-figures are reflections or variations of this basic type." See his *Regeneration through Violence: The Mythology of the American Frontier, 1600–1860* (Middletown, Conn.: Wesleyan University Press, 1973), 21.

11. Frederick Jackson Turner, *The Frontier in American History* (New York: Henry Holt, 1920), 30, 4, emphasis added.

12. We could comment on the fact that these icons are "to a man" white, male, and of European descent. We should also make a distinction between the figures of an American mythos and the philosophical form of subjectivity that underlies that mythos. For a discussion of the former and the influence such figures continue to have on the American sense of selfhood, see Richard Slotkin, *Gunfighter Nation: The Myth of the Frontier in Twentieth-Century America* (New York: Harper Perennial, 1993).

13. The notion of "hybridity" is borrowed from Homi K. Bhabha, *The Location of Culture* (New York: Routledge, 1994). I will discuss this issue more thoroughly in chapter 7.

14. Michel Foucault, "Revolutionary Action: 'Until Now,'" in *Language, Counter-Memory, Practice*, edited by Donald F. Bouchard (Ithaca, NY: Cornell University Press, 1977), 221.

15. Says James Wiser, "The celebration of the autonomous self is characteristic of the modern age in general." See his *Political Theory: A Thematic Inquiry* (Chicago: Nelson-Hall, 1987), 92.

16. Both Edward Burke and Alexis de Tocqueville saw the individual as a threat to the unity and welfare of the commonwealth. In the years immediately following the French Revolution it was referred to, more often than not, in negative and disparaging terms. "It was the disciples of Claude Henri de Saint-Simon, who were the first to use '*individualisme*' systematically, in the mid-1820s. . . . They used '*individualisme*' to refer to the pernicious and 'negative' ideas underlying the evils of the modern critical epoch." Steven Lukes, *Individualism* (Oxford: Basil Blackwell, 1973), 6–7. Wiser finds one of the earliest expressions of "postfeudal individualism" in the writings of Pico della Mirandola in 1484. Wiser, *Political Theory*, 91–92.

17. Michel Foucault, "Truth and Power," in *Power/Knowledge: Selected Interviews and Other Writings, 1972–1977*, edited by Colin Gordon (New York: Pantheon Books, 1980), 117.

18. Foucault, "Nietzsche, Genealogy, History," in *Language, Counter-Memory, Practice*, 147.

19. Foucault, "Structuralism and Post-Structuralism: An Interview with Michel Foucault," *Telos* 55 (spring 1983), 201.

20. I believe that the historical theme I schematize above is in the background of liberal theory generally. Perhaps its most explicit expression is found in Benedetto Croce's *History as the Story of Liberty*, translated by Sylvia Sprigge (New York: W. W. Norton, 1941). As Croce himself observes, "Hegel's famous statement that history is the history of liberty [was] spread throughout Europe by Cousin, Michelet, and other French writers" (59).

21. Michel Foucault, "The Subject and Power," in Hubert L. Dreyfus and Paul Rabinow, *Michel Foucault: Beyond Structuralism and Hermeneutics* (Chicago: University of Chicago Press, 1982), 212.

22. The notion of necessity to which I appeal here is not, of course, that of logical necessity. Rather, the term is relative to the apparent givenness, or unquestioned entrenchment, of the concept of political individuality. By revealing the historical contingency—and, thus, lack of historical necessity—of that concept, it makes it possible to realize that we might conceive of ourselves otherwise, which might in turn alter the way we think about the political.

23. Says Foucault, "I think I would distinguish myself from the Marxist and the para-Marxist perspectives. As regards Marxism, I'm not one of those who try to elicit the effects of power at the level of ideology. . . . Because what troubles me with these analyses which prioritize ideology is that there is always presupposed a human subject on the lines of the model presupposed by

classical [i.e., Enlightenment] philosophy endowed with a consciousness which power is then thought to seize on." See his "Body/Power," in *Power/Knowledge*, 58.

24. The more prominent adherents of communitarianism include Alasdair Mac-Intyre, Michael Sandel, Charles Taylor, and Michael Walzer. See Sandel, ed., *Liberalism and Its Critics* (New York: New York University Press, 1984), part 2, and Walzer, "The Communitarian Critique of Liberalism," *Political Theory* 18, no. 1 (February 1990), 6–23. For an excellent critical assessment of communitarianism as it pertains to both liberalism and postmodernism, see Seyla Benhabib, *Situating the Self: Gender, Community and Postmodernism in Contemporary Ethics* (New York: Routledge, 1992) especially chapter 2. Although I make liberal theory the object of genealogical critique here, this project should be distinguished also from recent attacks on liberalism found in so-called new conservative political thought. See, for example, Robert Devigne, *Recasting Conservatism: Oakeshott, Strauss, and the Response to Postmodernism* (New Haven: Yale University Press, 1994). In fact, I will argue that conservatism and liberalism fall from the same tree, genealogically speaking, and that they both appeal to or presuppose very similar notions of metaphysical and political individuality as the objects of their respective juridical projects, however their programs and policies may differ otherwise.

25. See, for example, Jean-Marie Auzias, *Michel Foucault: Qui Suis-Je?* (Lyon: La Manufacture, 1986); Gilles Deleuze, *Foucault*, translated by Sean Hand (Minneapolis: University of Minnesota Press, 1988); Didier Eribon, *Michel Foucault*, translated by Betsy Wing (Cambridge, Mass.: Harvard University Press, 1991); James Miller, *The Passion of Michel Foucault* (New York: Simon and Schuster, 1993); Clare O'Farrell, *Foucault: Historian or Philosopher?* (London: Macmillan, 1990); Garth Gillan, "Foucault's Philosophy," *Philosophy and Social Criticism* 12 (1987), 145–55.

26. Michel Foucault, "Truth, Power, Self: An Interview with Michel Foucault," in *Technologies of the Self: A Seminar with Michel Foucault*, edited by Luther H. Martin, Huck Guckman, and Patrick H. Hutton (Amherst: University of Massachusetts Press, 1988), 9.

27. This sort of approach leaves one vulnerable to two types of criticism, one having to do with the "proper" interpretation of Foucault's thought, the other with its proper application. While not trying to insulate myself from either of these two types of criticism, I would like to suggest that oftentimes the critical question for a project such as this should be whether or not my appropriation of some aspect of Foucault's thought *could* be used or applied, directly or derivatively, in the ways that I attempt.

28. Michel Foucault, "On the Genealogy of Ethics: An Overview of Work in Progress," in Dreyfus and Rabinow, *Michel Foucault: Beyond Structuralism and Hermeneutics*, 237.

29. Michel Foucault, "What is Enlightenment?" translated by Catherine Porter, in *The Foucault Reader*, edited by Paul Rabinow (New York: Pantheon Books), 49.

30. See Michel Foucault, "The Formation of Enunciative Modalities," in *The Archaeology of Knowledge and The Discourse on Language*, translated by A. M. Sheridan Smith (New York: Pantheon Books, 1972), 50–56. One other work that develops and applies the "enunciative" aspect of Foucault's work on discourse is Linda Hutcheon's *Irony's Edge: The Theory and Politics of Irony* (New York: Routledge, 1994), 90ff.

31. Says Bernauer, "While it might be argued that the conception of man as a unique individual is connected to the social contract model, which confers upon him the status of an abstract juridical figure, Foucault suggests that the view of man as an atom of society owes more to the specific technology of discipline. . . . Individuality is tied to the field of comparison constituted by discipline and within which a differentiation and hierarchy of abilities is established." See his *Michel Foucault's Force of Flight: Toward an Ethics for Thought* (London: Humanities Press International, 1990), 132.

32. "*Entstehung* designates *emergence*, the moment of arising," for Nietzsche, observes Foucault. Drawing from a number of writings, including *The Genealogy of Morals, Beyond Good and Evil,* and *The Dawn,* Foucault traces out the way that Nietzsche understands the difference between the meaning of the "origin" in conventional (metaphysical) histories and in genealogy: "In placing present needs at the origin, the metaphysician would convince us of an obscure purpose that seeks its realization at the moment it arises. Genealogy, however, seeks to reestablish the various systems of subjection: not the anticipatory power of meaning, but the hazardous play of dominations," Foucault, "Nietzsche, Genealogy, History," 148.

33. See Friedrich Nietzsche, *On the Advantage and Disadvantage of History for Life,* translated by Peter Preuss (Indianapolis: Hackett, 1980 [1874]), 14–19; emphasis in the original.

34. The difference between the savage and social man, asserts Rousseau, is "that the savage lives within himself, whereas social man [has] nothing but a deceitful exterior, honor without virtue, reason without wisdom, and pleasure without happiness. It is sufficient that I have proved that this is certainly not the original state of man, and that it is merely the spirit of society, and the inequality which society engenders, that thus change and transform all our natural inclinations," Rousseau, *Discourse on the Origin of Inequality,* 245.

35. *Discourse on the Origin of Inequality,* 254.

36. Foucault, "Nietzsche, Genealogy, History," 160.

37. See Honi Fern Haber, *Beyond Postmodern Politics: Lyotard, Rorty, Foucault* (New York: Routledge, 1994), especially chapter 4, "Evaluating 'Post Philosophies' For Oppositional Politics; Selves, Communities, and the Politics of Difference"; Jana Sawicki, *Disciplining Foucault: Feminism, Power, and the Body* (New York: Routledge, 1991), especially chapter 1, "Foucault and Feminism: Toward a Politics of Difference"; Judith Butler, *Gender Trouble: Feminism and the Subversion of Identity* (New York and London: Routledge, 1990); Luce Irigaray, *An Ethics of Sexual Difference,* translated by Carolyn Burke and Gillian C. Gill (Ithaca, NY: Cornell University Press, 1993 (1984); Charles Taylor, "The Politics of Recognition," and Jürgen Habermas,

"Struggles for Recognition in the Democratic Constitutional State," both in *Multiculturalism: Examining the Politics of Recognition* (Princeton, N.J.: Princeton University Press, 1994); Nancy Fraser, *Justice Interruptus: Re-Thinking Key Concepts of a Post-Socialist Age* (New York: Routledge, 1997); Fažal Rizvi, "The Arts, Education and the Politics of Multiculturalism" in Sneja Gunew and Fažal Rizvi, eds. *Culture, Difference and the Arts* (London: Allen and Unwin, 1994); Bhabha, *The Location of Culture*; and Gayatri Chakravorty Spivak, "Can the Subaltern Speak?" in Cary Nelson and Lawrence Grossberg, *Marxism and the Interpretation of Culture* (London: Macmillan, 1988).

38. Foucault, *Power/Knowledge*, 121.

39. On precisely this point about cutting off the King's head in political theory, Jon Simons accuses Foucault of being "overly schematic" and "reductive." Simons claims that Foucault's analysis is "more appropriate to the French model" than to the American one in which "sovereignty is fragmented" among a plurality of autonomous individuals. See his *Foucault and the Political* (London and New York: Routledge, 1995), 52. But as I shall demonstrate through Foucault, the problems and limitations associated with political theories still uncritically dedicated to issues of sovereignty do not diminish when that sovereignty is dispersed, when we are all "little kings," in other words. On the contrary, those problems are exacerbated, as Simons admits, and as Foucault clearly understands.

Chapter 2: The Subject of Political Discourse

1. Hannah Arendt, *On Revolution*. (New York: Penguin Books, 1963), 45.

2. Michel Foucault, *Discipline and Punish: The Birth of the Prison* (New York: Vintage Books, 1979), 168.

3. See Thomas Merton's Introduction to *The City of God*, xiv. For further discussion of Aristotle's view of the political, see chapter 4.

4. See Hubert L. Dreyfus and Paul Rabinow, "The Methodological Failure of Archaeology," in Dreyfus and Rabinow, *Michel Foucault: Beyond Structuralism and Hermeneutics* (Chicago: University of Chicago Press, 1982), 79–103.

5. See Charles Scott, *The Language of Difference* (Atlantic Highlands: Humanities Press International, 1987), 91–123; and Rudy Visker, *Genealogy as Critique*, translated by Chris Turner. (London: Verso, 1995), 30–73.

6. Foucault, "The Subject and Power," in Dreyfus and Rabinow, *Michel Foucault*, 208.

7. However, as Linda Hutcheon points out, although a Foucauldian (as well as Laconian and deconstructive) view of subjectivity offers "many cogent reasons for abandoning intentionality as the guarantee of meaning," this view need not "deny that intentions exist." See her *Irony's Edge: The Theory and Politics of Irony* (New York: Routledge, 1990), 117. In fact, adding to Hutcheon's point, many of the features traditionally associated with human subjectivity (including, particularly, "Cartesian" aspects of consciousness) need not be entirely abandoned once we recognize their historical contingency, cultural specificity, and other extrasubjectival discursive and non-

discursive elements contributing to their formation and emergence. This point will be especially important later on when we consider processes of subjectivation as well as criticisms about the internal coherency of genealogical views of selfhood.

8. Otto Gierke, *Natural Law and The Theory of Society* (Cambridge: Cambridge University Press, 1958), 40.

9. Jean-Jacques Rousseau, *The Discourse and Foundation of Inequality among Mankind*, in *The Social Contract and Discourse on the Origin and Foundation of Inequality among Mankind*, edited by Lester G. Crocker (New York: Simon and Schuster, 1967), 243; emphasis added.

10. "Political Philosophy," *The Oxford Illustrated History of Western Philosophy*, edited by Anthony Kenny (Oxford: Oxford University Press, 1997), 287.

11. See Quentin Skinner, *The Foundations of Modern Political Thought*, volume 2, *The Age of Reformation* (Cambridge: Cambridge University Press, 1978).

12. Says J. G. A. Pocock, "There is a conventional wisdom, now taught to students, to the effect that political theory became 'liberal' . . . about the time of Hobbes and Locke, and has in America remained so ever since. I find this a serious distortion of history, not because Hobbes and Locke did not take part in a great remodeling of the relation of right to sovereignty, conducted within the premises of the law-centered paradigm, but because to study that paradigm and nothing else leads to a radical misunderstanding of the roles in history played by both liberalism and jurisprudence, as well as of the relations between right and virtue." See his *Virtue, Commerce, and History: Essays on Political Thought and History, Chiefly in the Eighteenth Century* (Cambridge: Cambridge University Press, 1985), 47; see also Pocock's "The Myth of John Locke and the Obsession with Liberalism," in J. G. A. Pocock and Richard Ashcraft, *John Locke* (Los Angeles: Clark Memorial Library, 1980).

13. Pocock himself says, "In Hobbes, we meet the first genuine political *philosopher* encountered in . . . British political *thought*." See his *The Varieties of British Political Thought, 1500–1800* (Cambridge: Cambridge University Press, 1993), 161; emphasis in the original.

14. Thomas Hobbes, *Leviathan* (New York: Penguin Books, 1980), pt. II, ch. 17, 228; emphasis in the original. Hereafter, page numbers will be cited parethetically in the text.

15. We might compare this to Jean Bodin's definition of sovereignty as "that absolute and perpetual power vested in a commonwealth which in Latin is termed *majestas*." See his *Six Books of the Commonwealth* (1576), portions reprinted in *Communism, Fascism, and Democracy* (New York: Random House, 1962); this quote is from page 277.

16. One of the more thoroughgoing examples of this interpretation of Hobbes is Frithiof Brandt's *Thomas Hobbes' Mechanical Conception of Nature* (London: Librairie Hachette, 1928). Brandt's view, in variant form, has been dominant; however, recently the strict mechanistic view of Hobbes has come under fire by a number of critics, including Tracy Strong and Pocock. See, for example, Strong's "How to Write Scripture: Words, Authority, and Politics in Thomas Hobbes," *Critical Theory* 20 (autumn 1993), 128–59, and J.

A. G. Pocock, "Thomas Hobbes: Atheist or Enthusiast? His Place in a Restoration Debate," *History of Political Thought* 11 (winter 1990), 737–68.

17. "The mutual transferring of right, is that which men call CONTRACT." Hobbes, *Leviathan*, I, 14, 192.

18. See Jean Hampton, *Hobbes and the Social Contract Tradition* (Cambridge: Cambridge University Press, 1986).

19. *Two Treatises of Government* was reputedly published as a refutation of the absolutism of both Hobbes and Robert Filmer. But it is believed that Locke actually read very little, if any, of Hobbes's political works: "Indeed it cannot be shown that when he wrote Locke had any recent contact with *Leviathan* or with any other work of Hobbes at first hand. . . . it is a most remarkable fact that it has not been possible to find a single referenced extract from the works of Hobbes in the whole Lockean corpus," Peter Laslett, "Locke and Hobbes," Introduction to *Two Treatises of Government* (Cambridge: Cambridge University Press, 1960), 84, 87.

20. In fact, according to Hampton, the justificational strength and rationality of social contract stems precisely from its hypothetical character. Hampton goes so far as to argue that *"there is no literal contract* in any successful social contract theory," *Hobbes and the Social Contract Tradition*, 4.

21. See C. B. Macpherson, the introduction to Hobbes, *Leviathan*, 25–27.

22. C. B. Macpherson, *The Political Theory of Possessive Individualism* (Oxford: Oxford University Press, 1962), 1.

23. Michel Foucault, *The Archaeology of Knowledge and The Discourse on Language*, translated by A. M. Sheridan Smith (New York: Pantheon Books, 1972), 117; hereafter cited parenthetically as *AK* in the text.

24. Michel Foucault, *The Order of Things: An Archaeology of the Human Sciences* (New York: Vintage Books, 1973), xiv; hereafter cited parenthetically as *OT* in the text.

25. Foucault, *AK*, 118. In every case, "law," "rule," or "principle" refers to a discursive regularity defined with reference to discourse itself in its specificity, and not that which underlies discourse or serves as its ground.

26. For a discussion of the "difference" between *pure* difference, which Foucault defines, appealing to Gilles Deleuze, as "difference that displaces and repeats itself," and categorial differences, whose sense is bound to, and emerges within, "a system of representation, the organizing principles for similarities," see Michel Foucault, "Theatrum Philosophicum," in *Language, Counter-Memory, Practice*, edited by Donald F. Bouchard (Ithaca, N.Y.: Cornell University Press, 1977), 181–87.

27. In distinguishing statements from sentences, propositions, and speech acts, Foucault says, "In all three cases, one realizes that the criteria proposed are too numerous and too heavy, that they limit the extent of the statement, and that although the statement sometimes takes on the forms described and adjusts itself to them exactly, it does not always do so: one finds statements lacking in legitimate propositional structure; one finds statements where one cannot recognize a sentence; one finds more statements than one can isolate

speech acts" (*Archaeology*, 84). Dreyfus and Rabinow have defined statements as "serious speech acts" and in defense of this claim cite Foucault's
own concession to John R. Searle on the identity of speech acts and statements, "I was wrong in saying that statements were not speech acts, but in
doing so I wanted to underline the fact that I saw them under a different
angle than yours" (Foucault's letter to Searle, 15 May 1979). This identity
revolves around the idea that both statements and speech acts have a literal
meaning that is to be taken seriously at face value and that does not presuppose an underlying or hidden meaning. The difference here, say Dreyfus and
Rabinow, is that Searle is concerned with "how the hearer *understands* a
speech act" whereas Foucault is not. This is a crucial difference, I believe,
that Dreyfus and Rabinow tend to minimize. Speech acts presuppose a speaking subject for whom such acts have meaning; statements, on the other hand,
are understood without reference to a speaking subject, and to the extent
they are constitutive of a discursive practice, they provide the space on which
the very idea of speaking subjects can emerge. See Hubert L. Dreyfus and
Paul Rabinow, *Michel Foucault: Beyond Structuralism and Hermeneutics*,
45–48.
28. One might compare this with Heidegger's notion of truth as *Aletheia*, or
"unconcealment." Here truth also refers to an event of sorts, rather than to
an instance of correctness or correspondence. See Martin Heidegger, "On the
Essence of Truth," in his *Basic Writings*, edited by David Farrell Krell (New
York: Harper and Row, 1977), 127–28.
29. Michel Foucault, "Two Lectures," in *Power/Knowledge: Selected Interviews
and Other Writings, 1972–1977*, edited by Colin Gordon (New York: Pantheon Books, 1980), 93.
30. For a discussion of the implicit adherence of contemporary political philosophies to some form of social contract, see William M. Sullivan, *Reconstructing Public Philosophy* (Berkeley and Los Angeles: University of California
Press, 1986), 93ff.
31. See James Wiser, *Political Theory: A Thematic Inquiry* (Chicago: Nelson-
Hall, 1987), 67–105; see also Sullivan, *Reconstructing Public Philosophy*, 93.
32. There is some belief that this notion of political subjectivity actually, in a
sense, "jumped over" the founding fathers. Hannah Arendt, for example,
maintains that the image of political subjectivity on the part of the founding
fathers is more *communal* in nature (closer to the notion of public identity
found in the Greeks) than the private autonomous individualism found in
contemporary liberalism. See Arendt, *On Revolution*, and Joanne Cutting-
Gray, "Franklin's *Autobiography*: Politics of the Public Self," *Prospects: An
Annual of American Cultural Studies* 14 (1989), 31–43.
33. William Bradford, *History of Plymouth Plantation*, quoted in Andrew M.
Scott, ed., *Political Thought in America* (New York: Holt, Rinehart and Winston, 1966), 7.
34. John Wise, *A Vindication of the Government of New England Churches*,
quoted in Scott, ed., *Political Thought in America*, 30–31.
35. Michel Foucault, "What Is Enlightenment?" in *The Foucault Reader*.

Chapter 3: Power and the Political Subject

1. "After 1968, Foucault personally rediscovers the question of new forms of struggle, with GIP (Group for Information about Prison) and the struggle for prison rights, and elaborates the 'microphysics of power' in *Discipline and Punish*," Gilles Deleuze, *Foucault*, translated by Sean Hand (Minneapolis: University of Minnesota Press, 1988), 150, n. 45.

2. Reflecting on these very works, Foucault would later remark, "When I think back now, I ask myself what else it was that I was talking about ... but power." See his "Truth and Power," in *Power/Knowledge: Selected Interviews and Other Writings, 1972–1977*, edited by Colin Gordon (New York: Pantheon Books, 1980), 155. A transitional work might be his inaugural address to the College de France where he comments on several nondiscursive practices attending the circulation of discourse. Among these are the establishment of "fellowships" of discourse, "whose function is to preserve or to reproduce discourse, but in order that it should circulate within a closed community;" the institutionalization of disciplines, such as psychiatry in mental hospitals, which acts to localize and refine the nature of therapeutic practices; the politicization of doctrine as an instrument of adherence "to a class, to a social or racial status, to a nationality or an interest, to a struggle, a revolt, resistance, or acceptance;" and finally, the social appropriation of discourse, through education, for example: "Every educational system is a political means of maintaining or of modifying the appropriation of discourse, with the knowledge and powers it carries with it," *The Archaeology of Knowledge and The Discourse on Language*, 225–27.

3. Michel Foucault, "Two Lectures," in *Power/Knowledge*, p. 93.

4. Ibid., 108.

5. See Ronald Takaki, "The 'Tempest' in the Wilderness: The Racialization of Savagery," chapter 2 of *A Different Mirror: A History of Multicultural America* (Boston: Little. Brown, 1993), 24–50.

6. Richard Hakluyt, *The Portable Hakluyt's Voyages: The Principal Navigations, Voyages, Traffiques and Discoveries of the English Nation Made by Sea or Over-land to the Remote and Farthest Distant Quarters of the Earth at Any Time with the Compasse of these 1600 Yeeres*, edited by Irwin R. Blacker (New York: Viking Portable Library, 1965), 195–96.

7. William Bradford, *Of Plymouth Plantation*, edited by Samuel Eliot Morison (New York: Modern Library, 1967), 25; see also Takaki, "The 'Tempest,' " 31.

8. Says Richard Slotkin, "Of all the anticipated perils, the threat of Indian cannibals evoked the strongest emotion." See his *Regeneration through Violence: The Mythology of the American Frontier, 1600–1860* (Middletown, Conn.: Wesleyan University Press, 1973), 38.

9. See Takaki, "The 'Tempest,' " 34. See also Mortimer J. Adler, ed., *The Annals of America*, vol. 1, *Discovering a New World* (Chicago: University of Chicago Press, 1968), 26.

10. Cotton Mather, *On Witchcraft: Being, The Wonders of the Invisible World* (New York: n.d.; originally published in 1692), 53; emphasis added.

11. See The *Anthology of American Literature*, vol. 1, *Colonial through Romantic*, fifth edition (New York: Macmillan, 1993), 450–51.

12. Michel-Guillaume-Jean de Crèvecoeur, "Distresses of a Frontier Man," quoted in *Anthology of American Literature*, vol. 1, *Colonial through Romantic*, 466; hereafter, page numbers will be cited parenthetically in the text.

13. This perspective arguably reaches its graphic culmination in Charles Deas's painting *A Solitary Indian, Seated on the Edge of a Bold Precipice*, in 1847. Not only is this painting considered perhaps the quintessential artistic rendering of the Noble Savage, it could also be taken to depict the Savage Noble— ruddy individual of rugged physique and decidedly European facial features, the very symbol of autonomous individualism, poised for westward expansion. In fact, it would not be long before American frontier art would revert to depicting the Native American as a heathen threat to that expansion.

14. Slotkin, *Regeneration through Violence*, 233.

15. Thomas Hutchins, quoted by Winthrop D. Jordan, *White Over Black: American Attitudes towards the Negro, 1550–1812* (Baltimore: Penguin Books, 1969), 98; see Slotkin, *Regeneration through Violence*, 234.

16. Slotkin, *Regeneration through Violence*, 233–34. The subsequent popularity of such "Anglo-Indian" figures, says Slotkin, "was partly because of the appeal of the Indian as an exotic but more because of the fashionable notion of the good savage and the natural nobility of man, fostered by Enlightenment philosophy" (234–35).

17. Nancy Hartsock, "Foucault on Power: A Theory for Women?" in *Feminism/Postmodernism*, ed. Linda J. Nicholson (New York and London: Routledge, 1990), 170.

18. "The Subject and Power," 225.

19. Michel Foucault, *Discipline and Punish: The Birth of the Prison*, translated by Alan Sheridan (New York: Vintage Books, 1979), 136; hereafter cited parenthetically as *DP* in the text.

20. Foucault asserts that the subjection of individuals to temporal norms was at first based on the understanding of the body as a "mechanism" which could be manipulated straightforwardly to the temporal demands of any given task. But as these disciplinary techniques became more refined, this mechanistic concept of the body gave way to a more "natural" or "genetic" understanding, as the assignment of individuals to time constraints (of work, education, health) precipitated the adjustment of such constraints to the needs and dictates of the human body.

21. "Is this the birth of the sciences of man?" asks Foucault (*Discipline and Punish*, 191).

22. Michel Foucault, "Two Lectures," in *Power/Knowledge*, 97; hereafter cited parenthetically as *P/K* in the text.

23. Says Clifford Geertz, "To an increasing degree national unity is maintained not by calls to blood and land but by a vague, intermittent, and routine allegiance to a civil state, supplemented to a greater or lesser extent by governmental use of police powers and ideological exhortation." See his "Primor-

dial and Civic Ties," in John Hutchinson and Anthony D. Smith, eds., *Nationalism* (Oxford and New York: Oxford University Press, 1994), 31.

24. We can see that binding individuals to the nation and a national identity need not proceed through a notion of a *private autonomous* individual when we consider, for example, Nazi Germany, which was one of the most disciplined states in modern history, but which organized its nationalism around a central anti-individualistic theme, the idea of the *völkisch*. This rich and polysemic term can be translated, alternately, as "racism," "tribal populism," and "integral nationalism with tribal overtones," observes Joseph Nyomarkay. This concept was an "ideal demagogic tool" used extensively in Nazi propaganda as a symbol of national unity. See Nyomarkay, *Charisma and Factionalism in the Nazi Party* (Minneapolis: University of Minnesota Press, 1967), 55.

25. This *appears* to be the case in all Western societies; whether it is true globally is a matter of debate. I am in agreement with those who think we tend to project national identities onto other countries, when in fact they may not be animated by such a dynamic. This is suggested by, for example, Chantal Mouffe, "For a Politics of Nomadic Identity," in *Traveller's Tales: Narratives of Home and Displacement*, edited by George Robertson, Melinda Mash, Lisa Tickner, Jon Bird, Barry Curtis, and Tim Putman (New York: Routledge, 1994), 110. I would want to add that this *projection* itself is part of our own political subjectivity, informed as it is by a reference to the nation and the discourse of threat.

26. As I have already stated, discourse is not to be understood purely as a mode of speech (which presupposes a founding subject). Rather, discourse provides the space of emergence and determines the possibilities for speech, for speaking subjects.

27. Michel Foucault, *The Archaeology of Knowledge and the Discourse on Language*, translated by A. M. Sheridan Smith (New York: Pantheon Books, 1972), 54; hereafter cited parenthetically as *AK* in the text.

28. Although the status of subjects is determined by the privilege accorded certain subjects to speak certain discourses, this does not mean, of course, that such privilege always corresponds to a privileged (e.g., economic or political) status in society. For example, prisoners, street gangs, religious cult members, and the like, all have their own privileged discourses, which a doctor or prominent politician or even college professor, for instance, would look absurd attempting to speak.

29. The same could be said of the undergraduate who occupies the institutional site of the university. By occupying that site the individual can legitimately partake of the discourse that circulates there; and it is by virtue of his or her participation in the discourse that he or she can be identified as the subject we know as the student.

30. For reasons that should be obvious by now, it is difficult to discuss enunciative modalities apart from relations of power. Suffice it to say that enunciative modalities should be understood as the discursive meanings informing institutionalized practices regarding "real" political subjects. However, although we are assuming the attachment of discursive meanings to real bod-

ies in space, the actual practice of this attachment does not always require a body or bodies present at hand. A discursive practice that puts these enunciative modalities in play can have significant repercussions within the social body (in the form of actual political structures and practices, policy implementations, and social divisions) whether or not we can actually identify bodies to conform to these modalities in every case.

31. Benedict Anderson, *Imagined Communities: Reflections on the Origin and Spread of Nationalism*, (rev. ed.), (New York: Verso, 1991), 6.

32. Walker Connor, "A Nation is a Nation, is a State, is an Ethnic Group, is a . . . ," in Hutchinson and Smith, eds., *Nationalism*, 36.

33. Anderson suggests that even the idea of the nation as having discernible geographical boundaries is, in a sense, an imagined component of its own self-conception: "The nation is imagined as *limited* because even the largest of them, encompassing perhaps a billion living human beings, has finite, if elastic, boundaries, beyond which lie other nations. No nation imagines itself coterminous with mankind." See his *Imagined Communities*, 7.

34. Max Weber, "The Nation," in Hutchinson and Smith, eds., *Nationalism*, 21–25.

35. Connor, "A Nation Is a Nation," 38.

36. Ibid., 37. Slavoj Žižek makes a similar point from a Lacanian point of view; however, he warns against any reductionistic position that views the formation of nationhood as purely the self-reflexive appropriation of a common discursive practice. Says Žižek, "A nation *exists* only as long as its specific *enjoyment* continues to be materialized in a set of social practices and transmitted through national myths that structure these practices. To emphasize in a 'deconstructionist' mode that Nation is not a biological or transhistorical fact but a contingent discursive construction, an overdetermined result of textual practices, is thus misleading; such an emphasis overlooks the remainder of some real, nondiscursive kernel of enjoyment which must be present for Nation *qua* discursive entity-effect to achieve its ontological consistency." See his *Tarrying with the Negative* (Durham, N.C.: Duke University Press, 1993), 213. For a discussion, see David Harvey, *Justice, Nature, and the Geography of Difference* (Oxford: Blackwell, 1996), 98–100.

37. Frederick Jackson Turner, *The Frontier in American History* (New York: Henry Holt, 1920), 22–23.

38. Sacvan Bercovitch, *The Rites of Assent: Transformations in the Symbolic Construction of America* (New York: Routledge, 1993), 51.

39. Observes Richard Slotkin, "Kennedy's use of 'New Frontier' tapped a vein of latent ideological power." See his *Gunfighter Nation: The Myth of the Frontier in Twentieth-Century America* (New York: Harper Perennial, 1993), 2. Of course, the opposition between real and figural frontier is itself problematic. For a critique of the Turner Thesis and its effects on both the American imagination and governmental policy, see Patricia Nelson Limerick, *The Legacy of Conquest: The Unbroken Past of the American West* (New York: W. W. Norton, 1987), esp. chapters 1 and 2. Says Limerick, "There is simply no definition of 'the closing of the frontier' that is anything but arbitrary and

riddled with exceptions and qualifications." For the importance of the frontier motif to immigrant literature, see Wesley Brown and Amy Ling, eds., *Imagining America: Stories from the Promised Land* (New York: Persea Books, 1991).

40. Alex Haley's *Roots* could be viewed as the expression of such an appropriation, as could Dee Brown's *Bury My Heart at Wounded Knee: An Indian History of the American West*, and even arguably Amy Tan's *The Joy Luck Club*. (Of course, I do not want to obviate whatever non-Western ethnic, cultural, or ideological elements these groups brought to this process of assimilation; but I would like to suggest that the American "frontier spirit" has at the least been imposed, perhaps ethnocentrically and anachronistically, upon the experience of minority groups in this country as a framework of interpretation, by the media, popular literature, and even within multicultural histories, however distorting that imposition might be in fact.)

41. Of course, the seminal work on this violent cultural imposition is Frantz Fanon's *The Wretched of the Earth* (Hammondsworth, England: Penguin, 1967 [1961]). For accounts of cultural violence in early America, see Slotkin, *Regeneration through Violence*, esp. chapter 2, "Cannibals and Christians: European vs. American Indian Culture," 25–56, and Takaki, *A Different Mirror*, esp. chapters 2 and 4.

42. Anthony D. Smith, "The Origins of Nations," in Hutchinson and Smith, eds., *Nationalism*, 154.

43. Both Connor and Ernest Barker contend that such self-awareness is crucial to the establishment of a nation. According to Conner, a people constitute a nation precisely to the extent to which nationalist discourse is *self-consciously* appropriated by its inhabitants—and through which their identity as political subjects is both defined and self-imposed. See his "A Nation Is a Nation," 45–46.

44. Jack C. Plano and Milton Greenberg, "Nation," *The American Political Dictionary*, 4th ed. (Hinsdale, Ill.: Dryden Press, 1976), 13; emphasis added.

45. The arbitrary drawing of lines on a map to form nations is no mere metaphor. We have only to consider the effects of Balkanization on Europe and the colonial dissection of the African continent—a history of war, isolationism, and stunted economic growth—to wonder whether these effects stem from a failure by the mapmakers to recognize internal ethnic or tribal antagonisms or, rather, that such antagonisms are fanned into full-blown nationalism by the geopolitical gesture of nation demarcation itself. Asserts Harvey, "Mapping is a discursive activity that incorporates power. The power to map the world in one way rather than another is a crucial tool in political struggles. Power struggles over mapping (again, no matter whether these are maps of so-called 'real' or metaphorical spaces) are therefore fundamental moments in the production of discourses." See his *Justice, Nature, & the Geography of Difference*, 112.

46. Plano and Greenberg, "Nationalism," 399. See also Anderson, who observes that "regardless of the actual inequality and exploitation that may prevail in each, the nation is always conceived as a deep, horizontal comradeship. Ulti-

mately it is this fraternity that makes it possible, over the past two centuries, for so many millions of people, not so much to kill, as willingly to die for such limited imaginings." Anderson, *Imagined Communities*, 7.

Chapter 4: Political Subjectivation and Self-Formation

1. Says Foucault, "[M]y main concern will be to locate the forms of power, the channels it takes, and the discourses it permeates in order to reach the most tenuous and individual modes of behavior, the paths that give it access to the rare or scarcely perceivable forms of desire, how it penetrates and controls everyday pleasure . . . in short, the 'polymorphous techniques of power.'" See his *The History of Sexuality, Volume 1: An Introduction*, translated by Robert Hurley (New York: Vintage Books, 1980), 11 (originally published in France as *La Volenté de savoir* by Editions Gallimard, Paris, 1976).
2. See Foucault, *The History of Sexuality, Volume 1*, 33. The original volumes were to be entitled, respectively: *Flesh and Body, The Children's Crusade, Woman, Mother and Hysteric, Perverts*, and *Population and Races*. See James Bernauer, "Foucault's Ecstatic Thinking," 160.
3. "It is true that when I wrote the first volume of *The History of Sexuality* seven or eight years ago, I absolutely had intended to write historical studies on sexuality starting with the sixteenth century and to analyze the evolution of this knowledge up to the nineteenth century." See "The Return of Morality," interview with Foucault published in *Michel Foucault: Politics, Philosophy, Culture* (New York: Routledge, Chapman and Hall, 1988), 252. This was Foucault's final interview, published originally in *Les Nouvelles*, June 28, 1984, and in English in *Raritan*, summer 1985 as "Final Interview."
4. See Bernauer, "Foucault's Ecstatic Thinking," 161.
5. Ibid., 161.
6. Michel Foucault, "First Preface to The History of Sexuality, Volume 2," in *The Foucault Reader*, edited by Paul Rabinow (New York: Pantheon Books, 1984), 337–38. A transitional essay would be "Omnes et Singulatum," especially where Foucault considers the role of the police.
7. "This word must be allowed the very broad meaning which it had in the sixteenth century. 'Government' did not refer only to political structures or to the management of states; rather it designated the way in which the conduct of individuals or of groups might be directed: the government of children, of souls, of community, of families, of the sick," "The Subject and Power," in Hubert L. Dreyfus and Paul Rabinow, *Michel Foucault: Beyond Structuralism and Hermeneutics* (Chicago: University of Chicago Press, 1982), 221.
8. Michel Foucault, *The Use of Pleasure: Volume 2 of the History of Sexuality*, translated by Robert Hurley (New York: Pantheon Books, 1985), 5. Originally published in France as *L'usage des plaisirs* by Editions Gallimard Paris, 1984. Hereafter cited parenthetically as *UP* in the text.
9. Michel Foucault, "The Concern for Truth" in *Michel Foucault: Politics, Philosophy, Culture*, 259.
10. Michel Foucault, "An Aesthetics of Existence" in *Politics, Philosophy, Culture*, 48.

11. Foucault, *The Use of Pleasure*, 5; see also "Concern for Truth": "Here I set out from the problem that sexual behavior might pose for individuals themselves" (258).

12. See Foucault, "An Aesthetics of Existence," 48; also "First Preface," 339.

13. That is, Foucault considered it important "to address myself to periods when the effect of scientific knowledge and the complexity of normative systems were less, and in order eventually to make out forms of relation to self different from those characterizing the modern experience of sexuality." See "First Preface," 339; see also the introduction to *Use of Pleasure*, 7 (note), where Foucault says that it is important "to examine the difference that keeps us at a remove from a way of thinking in which we recognize the origin of our own, and the proximity that remains in spite of that distance. . . ."

14. For a discussion of why *Les Aveux de la chair*, which focused on early Christian patterns of sexuality, was not published, see Didier Eribon, *Michel Foucault*, translated by Betsy Wing (Cambridge, Mass.: Harvard University Press, 1991), 317–24.

15. Foucault, "The Subject and Power," 208. This reliance on the term "subject" may cause us to object to Foucault, as two interviewers did, that, "your preceding books seemed to ruin the sovereignty of the subject. Is this not a return to an unanswerable question which would be for you the ordeal of an endless toil?" Foucault's reply was that he was not referring to the subject in the substantive sense, as the "condition of possibility of experience." Rather, the subject is the effect of the organization of a domain of experience to which the self relates itself, and through which the self experiences itself as a subject. "It is experience," says Foucault, "which is the rationalization of a process, itself provisional, which results in a subject, or rather, in subjects," Foucault, "The Return of Morality," 252. See also Mark Poster, "Foucault and the Tyranny of Greece," in David Couzens Hoy, ed., *Foucault: A Critical Reader* (Oxford: Basil Blackwell, 1986). "Characteristically Foucault does not spend much time defining his categories of analysis, in this case those of 'self' and 'subject'. It appears from the text that 'self' is a neutral, ahistorical term, almost a synonym for 'individual'. 'Subject' is an active, historical term that refers to a process of interiorization. Foucault, of course, continues to reject philosophies of consciousness by which the individual ontologically constitutes himself or herself through mental activities" (212).

16. See Foucault, *The Use of Pleasure*, 10, and "Final Interview," 10.

17. Michel Foucault, "The Genealogy of Ethics: An Overview of Work in Progress," in Dreyfus and Rabinow, *Michel Foucault*, 237–38. Obviously, in his consideration of the dimension of "ought" in ethical subjectivation, Foucault is not, unlike more traditional moral philosophers, trying to tell us how we "ought" to act in regard to sexuality, but, rather, he is giving us an historical sense, à la Nietzsche, of the modes through which such an "ought" has been constructed.

18. Michel Foucault, "The Ethic of Care for Self as a Practice of Freedom," in Bernauer, ed., *The Final Foucault*, 124.

19. Aristotle, *Politics*, VII, 13, 1132a; see Foucault, *The Use of Pleasure*, 79.

20. Michel Foucault, *The Care of the Self: The History of Sexuality, Volume 3*, translated by Robert Hurley (New York: Pantheon Books, 1986). Foucault characterizes the political transformations of the Greco-Roman world as "the organization of a complex space. Much vaster, much more discontinuous, much less closed than must have been the case for the small city-states. . . . It was a space in which the centers of power were multiple; in which the activities, the tensions, the conflicts were numerous, in which they developed in several dimensions; and in which the equilibria were obtained through a variety of transactions."

21. Foucault more than intimates this in the first volume of the *History of Sexuality*. The relationship between political and sexual subjectivity would become increasingly complex, as the domains of experience peculiar to each gained a measure of autonomy. On the other hand, there are obviously important points of intersection, as are suggested by the political issues of abortion, feminism, contraception, population control, homosexuality, sexual abuse, etc.

22. Foucault, "The Genealogy of Ethics," 250.

23. Michel Foucault "The Ethic of Care for the Self," 122.

24. See Foucault, *UP*, 26–28, and "Genealogy of Ethics," 237–39.

25. John Stuart Mill, *On Liberty*, edited by Elizabeth Rapport (Indianapolis: Hackett Publishing, 1978), 12; hereafter cited parenthetically as *OL* in the text.

26. Isaiah Berlin, "Two Concepts of Liberty," in *Liberalism and its Critics*, edited by Michael Sandel (New York: New York University Press, 1984), 15–16.

27. Ibid., 22–25.

28. See John Stuart Mill, *Considerations on Representative Government* (1861).

29. Berlin, "Two Concepts," 23.

30. "The will of the people practically means the will of the most numerous or the most active *part* of the people—the majority, or those who succeed in making themselves accepted as the majority; the people, consequently, *may* desire to oppress a part of their number, and precautions are as much needed against this as against any other abuse of power." See Mill, *On Liberty*, 4.

31. That is, we think we know what it is to lust after the flesh, or at least we can describe it in positive terms referring to specific acts or feelings. Negative freedom, on the other hand, by definition takes its meaning from that which it is not—namely, the coercive exercise of power.

32. Positive freedom does not necessarily have to appeal to such a political construct, as is evident from the Greeks, who had no such notion of a private autonomous individual.

33. "The acts of an individual may be hurtful to others or wanting in due consideration for their welfare, without going to the length of violating any of their constituted rights. The offender may then be justly punished by opinion, though not by law." See Mill, *On Liberty*, OL, 73. Actually, *On Liberty* offers considerable detail, based on the harm-to-others principle, of what society is authorized to do to an offending individual.

34. For both Smart and Hare, individual liberty can be sacrificed if it would

maximize general happiness. See J. J. C. Smart, "Distributive Justice and Util-itarianism," in *Justice and Economic Distribution*, edited by John Arthur and William H. Shaw (New York: Prentice Hall, 1978), 103–13, and R. M. Hare, "Justice and Equality," also in *Justice and Economic Distribution*, 116–31.

35. The conventional distinction between "right" and "left" derives "from the common practice in European parliaments of seating conservative parties to the right of the presiding officer." See Jack C. Plano and Milton Greenberg "Rightist," in *The American Political Dictionary*, 4th ed. (Hinsdale, Ill.: Dryden Press, 1976), 17.

36. Winston Churchill is reputed to have said, "If you're not a liberal at twenty, you have no heart, and if you're not a conservative at forty, you have no head." Of the 1,274 delegates to a recent Republican National Convention (presumably a bastion of conservatism), 66 percent were men and 92 percent were white. In contrast, only about half of the delegates to the Democratic National Convention (presumably a bastion of liberalism) were men and only 68 percent were white. The average age of the delegates to their respective conventions differed, Churchill's words notwithstanding, by only two years. The question I wish to raise here is not the ideological one of which position is more "correct," or more fair, or more mature. Nor is it primarily a question of the socioeconomic factors that lead people to identify with one political stance rather than another (although such factors are certainly relevant). Rather, the question here is a genealogical one. That is, through what processes of subjectivation, through what modes of self-formation, do individuals identify themselves as liberals or conservatives, as Democrats or Republicans, as fascists or revolutionaries?

37. The political literature of the nineteenth century problematized tolerance, and it has come to be identified with the basic ideology of liberalism. However, I am trying to use the term as neutrally as possible, to characterize activities on both sides of the liberal/conservative continuum.

38. Ronald Dworkin, "Liberalism," in *Liberalism and Its Critics*, 64; hereafter cited parenthetically as Dworkin in the text.

39. T. W. Adorno, Daniel J. Levenson, R. Nevitt Sanford, and Elsa Frenkel-Brunswick, *The Authoritarian Personality* (New York: Harper and Row, 1950), 153; herafter cited parenthetically as Adorno in the text.

40. "To be 'liberal' . . . one must be able actively to criticize existing authority. The criticisms may take various forms, ranging from mild reforms (e.g., extension of government controls over business) to complete overthrow of the status quo." Adorno et al., *The Authoritarian Personality*, 154.

41. In fact, if asked directly, the conservative is likely to resist the theory of equality that Dworkin attributes to her, because it sounds suspiciously like some form of communism.

42. The discussion that follows relies heavily on personal pronouns. While throughout this book I've attempted to alternate gendered pronouns, Jean Bethke Elshtain, who read an earlier draft of the manuscript, commented to me that the conservative position is stereotypically viewed as a "masculine" position, while the liberal position is stereotypically considered "feminine" in

aspect. For this section, I have deliberately chosen pronouns that invert those prejudices.

43. This helps to explain why the conservative tends to value a strong national defense over social programs, and why she strongly supports the individual's right to bear arms—that is, to not only protect personal property, but to preserve a way of life. Both are justified, therefore, by a rigid appeal to the harm-to-others principle.

44. The classic expression of this form of "welfare liberalism" can be found, of course, in T. H. Green, who asserts that the "value of the institutions of civil life" is that "they render it possible for a man to be freely determined by the idea of a possible satisfaction of himself, instead of being driven this way and that by external forces . . . and they enable him to realize his reason, i.e., his idea of self-perfection, by acting as a member of a social organization in which each contributes to the better-being of the rest." See his *Lectures on the Principles of Political Obligation* (Ann Arbor: University of Michigan Press, 1967 [1885]), 34. See also James Wiser, *Political Theory: A Thematic Inquiry* (Chicago: Nelson-Hall, 1986), who notes, "Green effectively established the theoretical foundations for the modern welfare state. From his perspective the state is both to protect its citizens and at the same time create those positive conditions that will advance the general level of their welfare. To the extent that such conditions as poverty or ignorance prevent certain individuals from achieving their own self-protection, the state is obligated to liberate them from the effects of such restraints" (224).

45. "Liberals tend to view social problems as symptoms of the underlying social structure, while conservatives view them as the results of individual incompetence or immorality." Adorno et al., *The Authoritarian Personality*, 155.

46. Needless to say, political subjects can seldom be defined according to such neat designations. Also, although I am using "fascism" in a rather generic sense, I do so fully cognizant of Rey Chow's caution that "'fascism' is a banal term . . . used most often not simply to refer to the historical events that took place in Hitler's Germany and Mussolini's Italy, but also to condemn attitudes or behavior that we consider to be excessively autocratic or domineering." See her *Ethics after Idealism: Theory–Culture–Ethnicity–Reading* (Bloomington: Indiana University Press, 1998), 14. My use of the term is not meant to be so didactic, but to designate as neutrally as possible a mode of political identity found on the political spectrum wherein the individual is considered subordinate to the state; wherein, to quote Alfred Rosenburg, "The nation is the first and *last*, that to which everything else has to be subordinated." See his *The Myth of the Twentieth Century* (1930), quoted in *Communism, Fascism, and Democracy*, ed. Carl Cohen (New York: Random House, 1962). For a discussion of the particularities of anarchism (from a subjectivational more than theoretical standpoint), see Paul Avrich, *Anarchist Voices: An Oral History of Anarchism in America* (Princeton, N.J.: Princeton University Press, 1996), and Emma Goldman, *Anarchism, and Other Essays* (New York: Dover, 1977).

47. Nowhere is this expressed more explicitly than in Rawls. "Political liberal-

ism," says Rawls, "affirm[s] the superiority of certain forms of moral character and encourage[s] certain moral virtues. Thus, justice as fairness includes
an account of certain political virtues—the virtues of fair social cooperation
such as civility and tolerance, of reasonableness and the sense of fairness. . . .
Thus, if a constitutional regime takes certain steps to strengthen the virtues
of toleration and mutual trust . . . it is taking reasonable measures to
strengthen the forms of thought and feeling that sustain fair social cooperation between its citizens regarded as free and equal." See his *Political Liberalism* (New York: Columbia University Press, 1993), 194–95.

48. See Richard Slotkin, *Regeneration through Violence: The Mythology of the
American Frontier, 1600–1860* (Middletown, Conn.: Wesleyan University
Press, 1973), 45. Slotkin observes that the English—Oliver Cromwell in particular as well as other Puritan groups—first attempted to impose the reservation system upon the Irish, who at the time were also viewed as "savages."

49. See Theda Perdue, "Cherokee Women and the Trail of Tears," in *Unequaled
Sisters: A Multicultural Reader in U.S. Women's History*, edited by Vicki L.
Ruiz and Ellen Carol DuBois (New York: Routledge, 1994), 32.

50. See editors' introduction to Perdue, "Cherokee Women," 32. See also Grant
Foreman, *Indian Removal: The Emigration of the Five Civilized Tribes of
Indians* (Norman: Oklahoma University Press, 1932), 229–312.

51. Although I am sympathetic to many aspects of her project, I think Rey Chow
commits something of a false dilemma when she suggests that, when it comes
to identity politics, we must choose between a "new liberal fascism" and an
ethics that no longer "idealizes the other." See her *Ethics after Idealism*, xx,
32. The genealogically informed identity politics I allude to in the following
discussion permits, I believe, an ethical attitude toward the other that steps
cautiously between the horns of this dilemma.

52. See Simone de Beauvoir, *The Second Sex*, translated by H. M. Parshley
(Hammondsworth, England: Pernquin, 1974).

53. The Brownshirts of Nazi Germany, far from lacking a set of moral standards,
had their own mode of subjection as surely as did Andrew Jackson when he
forced a nation of "savages" to march a thousand miles over what became
known as the "Trail of Tears." See, for example, Gregor Zeimer, *Education
for Death: The Making of the Nazi* (Oxford: Oxford University Press, 1941);
Rolf Tell, ed., *Nazi Guide to Nazism* (Washington, D.C.: American Council
on Public Affairs, 1942); R. A. Brady, *The Spirit and Structure of German
Fascism* (New York: Viking Press, 1937).

Chapter 5: Governmentality and the Axes of Political Experience

1. Michel Foucault, "Final Interview," *Raritan* 5, no. 1 (summer 1985), 2.

2. "First Preface to The History of Sexuality, Volume 2 in *The Foucault Reader*,
edited by Paul Rabinow (New York: Pantheon Books, 1984), 336.

3. For example, *Madness and Civilization* can be read, says Foucault, as an
investigation of "first, the formation of a domain of recognitions which constitute themselves as specific knowledge of 'mental illness'; second, the organization of a normative system built on a whole technical, administrative,

juridical, and medical apparatus whose purpose was to isolate and take custody of the insane; and finally, the definition of a relation to oneself and to others as possible subjects of madness," "First Preface," 336. See also "Polemics, Politics, and Problematizations," in Rabinow, ed., *The Foucault Reader*, 383.

4. Foucault, "Polemics, Politics, and Problematizations," 386–87.
5. Michel Foucault, "What Is Enlightenment?" in *The Foucault Reader*, 48.
6. See "Polemics, Politics, and Problematizations," 387; "First Preface," 333–38; and *The Use of Pleasure: Volume 2 of the History of Sexuality* (New York: Pantheon Books, 1985), 11–12.
7. Foucault, "First Preface," 333; emphasis added.
8. Whatever its form, the experience of subjectivity will be constituted by "(1) the formation of sciences (savoirs) that refer to it, (2) the systems of power that regulate its practice, (3) the forms within which individuals are able, are obliged, to recognize themselves as subjects," Foucault, *The Use of Pleasure*, 4. The convergence and interrelation of these factors comprise a dynamic in which emerge certain determined historical figures, i.e., subjects.
9. See "The Repressive Hypothesis," part 2 of *The History of Sexuality, Volume 1* (New York: Vintage Books, 1980), 17–49.
10. "Critical Theory/Intellectual History," in *Politics, Philosophy, Culture*, 37. (This interview was previously published, and is probably better known, as "Structuralism and Post-Structuralism: An Interview with Michel Foucault," *Telos* 55 (spring 1983), 195–211.
11. Michel Foucault, "Two Lectures," in *Power/Knowledge: Selected Interviews and Other Writings, 1972–1977* (New York: Pantheon Books, 1980), 93; hereafter cited parenthetically as *PK* in the text.
12. Says Foucault, "We should not be content to say that power has a need for such-and-such a discourse, such-and-such a form of knowledge, but we should add that the exercise of power itself creates and causes to emerge new objects of knowledge and accumulates new bodies of information," *Power/Knowledge*, 51.
13. Michel Foucault, "History of Systems of Thought," in *Language, Counter-Memory, Practice: Selected Essays and Interviews* (Ithaca, N.Y.: Cornell University Press, 1977), 200.
14. Michel Foucault, "Power and Sex," in *Politics, Philosophy, Culture*, 114.
15. See *Power/Knowledge*, 130–33.
16. "It is not enough to say that the subject is constituted in a symbolic system. . . . It is constituted in real practices—historically analyzable practices. There is a technology of the constitution of the self which cuts across symbolic systems while using them." See Foucault, "The Genealogy of Ethics: An Overview of Work in Progress," in *Michel Foucault: Beyond Structuralism and Hermeneutics* (Chicago: University of Chicago Press, 1982), 250.
17. Foucault, "Critical Theory/Intellectual History," 29.
18. Ibid., 38.
19. Foucault, "Genealogy of Ethics," 250.

20. See Michel Foucault, "Truth and Subjectivity," Howison Lecture, Berkeley (20 October 1980), 7.
21. Ibid., 8; emphasis added.
22. Michel Foucault, "The Subject and Power," in *Beyond Structuralism*, 220–21. See also translator's note, 221.
23. This does not mean, however, that this integration is always smooth. "It is always a difficult, versatile equilibrium with complementarity and conflicts between techniques which assure coercion and processes through which the self is constructed and modified by itself," "Truth and Subjectivity," 8.
24. Since Foucault's work resists systematicity, any attempt to schematize it will be dangerous. Thus the following is at best a heuristic device and at worst a deception, which is to say, both at once.
25. Below I have separated the three "triangles," but I would prefer that the reader refer to the original diagram, to get a sense of the lateral and vertical interplay between the "elements."

Axis of Knowledge
Disciplines/Discipline/Government
Savoir/Pouvoir
Truth

Axis of Power
Discipline/Government/Self-Government
Pouvoir/Conduire
Rules

Axis of Ethics
Government/Self-Government/Self-Formation
Conduire/Rapport àSoi
Ethics

26. "Polemics, Politics, and Problematizations," 388.
27. "It seemed to me there was one element that was capable of describing the history of thought: this was what one could call the element of problems, or more exactly, problematizations," ibid. See also Foucault, *Discourse and Truth: The Problematization of Parrhesia* (Evanston, Ill.: Northwestern University Press, 1985), (a text transcribed by Joseph Pearson from a series of lectures delivered by Foucault at the University of California, Berkeley): "A problematization is always a kind of creation . . . a reply to some concrete and specific aspect of the world,"116.
28. See "First Preface," 336.
29. See "Entretien avec M. Foucault," in *Masques*, 13 (spring 1982), 23.
30. Says Foucault, "The essential role of the theory of right, from medieval times onward, was to fix the legitimacy of power," *Power/Knowledge*, 95.
31. Even if political philosophy appeals to the notion of social contract to explain the emergence of political subjects, this presupposes some mysterious power invested in individuals that likewise has yet to be explained, or is explained only cumbersomely, by reference to "natural law," for example, which is always apologetic, metaphysical, and, more often than not, a poorly concealed appeal to God.

32. John Stuart Mill, *On Liberty*, edited by Elizabeth Rapaport (Indianapolis: Hackett Publishing, 1978), 1.

33. Isaiah Berlin, "Two Concepts of Liberty," in *Liberalism and its Critics*, edited by Michael Sandel (New York: New York University Press, 1984), 28. Coincidentally, Thomas L. Dumm refers to this very passage from Berlin in *Michel Foucault and the Politics of Freedom* (Thousand Oaks, Calif.: Sage, 1996), 54; Dumm focuses particularly on Berlin's phrase "normal human being," and how "by making this move [Berlin] evades an important question concerning how the idea of the normal operates as a form of power."

34. Michel Foucault, *Discipline and Punish: The Birth of the Prison* (New York: Vintage Books, 1979), 169; hereafter cited parenthetically as *DP* in the text.

35. For a discussion of the technology of power that Foucault calls "sovereign power," see "Torture," part 1 of *Discipline and Punish*, 3–69. Like discipline, the object of this power was the body; but its strategy was to control individuals by making the body (of the criminal) serve as an example to others, to discourage acts that failed to respect the authority of the sovereign. Toward this end it employed techniques of torture and public execution. Its apparatuses were the pillory, the scaffold, the gallows: various instruments of torture. It was a technology of power—unlike the subtle mechanisms of discipline—characterized by spectacle and violent intensity. Although it gave the appearance of a power which could be possessed in the traditional sense (so much so that it was the perceived *excess* of power on the side of sovereignty that gave rise to the democratic reforms of the seventeenth and eighteenth centuries), it was still a *relational* power.

36. The list is endless: birth certificates, vaccination reports, school registration and permanent records, social security cards, driver's licenses, W-2 forms, voter's registration cards, coroner's reports—all direct descendants of the original police "rap sheets"?

37. Michel Foucault, *The History of Sexuality: Volume I*, 25.

38. Michel Foucault, "Governmentality," *Ideology and Consciousness* 6 (autumn 1979) 18; hereafter cited parenthetically as *GV* in the text.

39. Foucault has called the power exercised by the state on the individual, and through it the population as a whole, a "bio-power" and "bio-politics" in that it is a power directed toward the body, a power that manipulates habits, diet, sexual relations, health, work, distributions, all of the factors that treat the individual as a biological entity.

40. Perhaps it is a matter of emphasis rather than of genuine disagreement, but I find myself somewhat at odds with Colin Gordon on this issue of how Foucault understands the relationship between liberalism and governmentality. Gordon speaks of the "*liberal* art of government" as if the political rationality of governmentality precisely is a liberal rationality and that the methods and procedures through which government manages a population are precisely those which issue from a liberal agenda; Jeremy Bentham and Adam Smith are cited as archetypical figures in this connection. "What liberalism undertakes," asserts Gordon, "is . . . the construction of a complex domain of governmentality, within which economic and juridical subjectivity can

alike be situated as relative moments, partial aspects of a more englobing element." See his "Governmental Rationality: An Introduction," in *The Foucault Effect: Studies in Governmentality*, edited by Graham Burchell, Colin Gordon, and Peter Miller (Chicago: University of Chicago Press, 1991), 22. I can agree with this characterization up to a point. I think it is the case that liberalism attempts to articulate an economic and juridical subjectivity onto an art of government, and that it is on behalf of such subjectivity that the political and social reforms of Bentham et. al. are offered. These reforms tend to be "governmental" in the way that Foucault understands that term. However, the isomorphism that Gordon (perhaps) wants to assume between liberalism and governmentality really only makes sense at the level of ideology and (to a lesser degree) that of formal state policy. Yet I think liberal ideology is conceptually, if not practically, at odds with the *disciplinary* character of governmentality and all that that entails. Moreover, the liberal notions of power and especially subjectivity in no way resemble either the way that power actually functions in the governmentalized state or the form of subjectivity that it produces as an effect. Bentham thought that he was safeguarding autonomous individuals; he had no way of knowing the degree to which he was actually helping to *fabricate* disciplinized subjects (as opposed to merely disciplining otherwise unruly individuals).

41. Foucault, "The Subject and Power," 215; "Foucault at the College de France 1," *Annuair du College de France* 78 (1977–1978), 445–48, translated by James Bernauer in *Philosophy and Social Criticism* 8 (1981), 235–42. Bernauer sums up Foucault's understanding of pastoral power nicely in his "Michel Foucault's Ecstatic Thinking": "This power is productive, not repressive. Exercising authority over a flock of dispersed individuals rather than a land, the shepherd has the duty to guide his charges to salvation by means of a continuous watch over them and a permanent concern with their well-being as individuals," in *The Final Foucault, Philosophy and Social Criticism* 12 (summer 1987), 162.

42. To the various ways that a nation's identity is propagated beyond its own boundaries we should include today the media of film and television. In fact, these have become such a powerful, if unintended, means of dissemination that many countries have accused the United States, and in particular the Hollywood entertainment industry, of a new form of "cultural imperialism." Film and television dramas from the United States make upwards of 90 percent of what is seen by the indigenous audiences in the countries to which they are exported. This has caused alarm over what is perceived as "a corresponding diminution in the vitality and standing of local languages and traditions, and hence a threat to national identity." See Toby Miller, *The Well-Tempered Self: Citizenship, Culture, and the Postmodern Subject* (Baltimore: Johns Hopkins University Press, 1993), 104.

43. This is true even if the basis of that unity is the free pursuit of disparate individual interests, as is the case, in principle at least, in the United States.

44. A case in point is "the establishment of Jules Ferry's universal primary

schools which entrust history-geography with the task of implanting and inculcating the civic and patriotic spirit." See Michel Foucault, "Questions of Geography," in *Power/Knowledge*, 73.

45. Actually, the role of the police is originally conceived to be much broader than this: "The *police* includes everything. But from an extremely particular point of view. Men and things are envisioned as to their relationships: men's coexistence in a territory; their relationships as to property; what they produce; what is exchanged on the market. It also considers how they live, the diseases and accidents which can befall them. What the police sees to is a live, active, productive man. Turquet employs a remarkable expression: 'the police's true object is man.'" Michel Foucault, "Omnes et Singulatim: Towards a Criticism of 'Political Reason'," *The Tanner Lectures on Human Values 2*, edited by Sterling McMussin (Salt Lake City: University of Utah Press and Cambridge University Press, 1981), 248.

46. "Discipline was never more important or more valorized than at the moment when it became important to manage a population; the managing of a population does not apply only to the collective mass of phenomena, or at the level of its aggregate effects, it also implies the management of the population in its depths and its details." See Foucault, "Governmentality," 19.

47. For example, the 1969 Presidential Commission on Population defined and examined more than 130 aspects of the population, ranging from "Population Stabilization, Migration, and Distribution" to "Adolescent Pregnancy and Children Born out of Wedlock."

48. Foucault, "College de France 2," lectures on liberalism, course summary reproduced by James Bernauer, *Philosophy and Social Criticism* 8 (1981), 349–59.

49. See also Foucault *Discipline and Punish*: "Discipline creates between individuals a 'private' link, which is a relation of constraints entirely different from contractual obligation" (222).

50. Foucault, "The Subject and Power," 214. See also Michel Foucault, "The Political Technology of Individuals," in *Technologies of the Self: A Seminar with Michel Foucault*, edited by Luther H. Martin, Huck Gutman, and Patrick H. Hutton (Amherst: University of Massachusetts Press, 1988), 145–63.

51. Michel Foucault, "The Social Triumph of the Sexual Will: A Conversation with Michel Foucault," trans. Brendan Lemon, in *Christopher Street* no. 4 (1982), 38.

52. "The emergence of social science cannot, as you see, be isolated from the rise of this new political rationality and from this new political technology. . . . If man—if we, as living, speaking, working beings—became an object for several different sciences, the reason has to be sought not in ideology, but in the existence of this political technology which we have formed in our societies." "The Political Technology of Individuals," in Martin, Gutman, and Hutton, eds., *Technologies of the Self*, 162.

53. Ibid., 151–52.

54. Ibid., 152.
55. Ibid., 158.
56. Ibid., 160.
57. Liberalism from the eighteenth century on originates, says Foucault, "in this problem of the positive and negative tasks of the state, in the possibility that the state . . . may have no power of intervention in the behavior of people," ibid., 159–60.
58. An example of such discourse comes from Robert Nozick's *Anarchy, State, and Utopia* (New York: Basic Books, 1974): "The minimal state is the most extensive state that can be justified. Any state more extensive violates people's rights" (49). The entire book is an attempt to support this thesis.
59. Michel Foucault, "La strategie du pourtour," *Le Nouvel Observateur* 759 (28 May 1979), 57.
60. "The essential function of the discourse and techniques of right has been to efface the domination intrinsic to power in order to present the latter at the level of appearance under two aspects: on the one hand, as the legitimate rights of sovereignty, and on the other, as the legal obligation to obey it." See Foucault, *Power/Knowledge*, 95.
61. See Foucault, *Power/Knowledge*, 142.
62. "Power . . . is not in the hands of those who govern." See Michel Foucault, "Intellectuals and Power," in *Language, Counter-Memory, Practice*, 215.
63. Freedom of speech has a long history in Western thought, but it is only fairly recently that it has come to be conceived as a political right. For the Greeks, it was tied to the idea of *parrhesia*, which is literally translated as "free speech," but *parrhesia* referred to a rich complex of political relations and moral qualities. The "parrhesiastic" figure was one who told the truth, but always in a situation where doing so posed a risk to the individual. Parrhesia was a kind of criticism spoken by an individual in a position of inferiority to someone else. A king could not use parrhesia because he risked nothing. Parrhesia also designated a moral quality of an individual, who regarded it as his duty to speak frankly about some problem or situation. Socrates was the quintessential parrhesiastic figure. Something has been retained of parrhesia through history, even in the juridical, rights-based notion of freedom of speech. Says Foucault, "I think that our own moral subjectivity is rooted, at least in part, in these practices." See his *Discourse and Truth: The Problematization of Parrhesia*, passim.
64. Jacques Donzelot describes a situation in which contractual ideology is articulated right onto disciplinary subjugation in the factory system: "The contractual economic relation between worker and employer is coupled with a sort of contractual tutelage of employer over worker, by virtue of the employer's total freedom in determining the code of factory regulations, among which he may include—as is most often the case—a whole series of disciplinary and moral exigencies reaching well outside the sphere of production proper, to exercise control over the habits and attitudes, the social and moral behaviour of the working class outside of the enterprise." Donzelot,

L'invention du social, 144, quoted in Colin Gordon, *The Foucault Effect*, 25–26.

65. Foucault, "The Political Technology of Individuals," 147.

66. Foucault, *Power/Knowledge*, 55.

Chapter 6: "The Most Perfect Freedom"

1. In *Michel Foucault and the Politics of Freedom* (Thousand Oaks, Calif.: Sage, 1996), Thomas L. Dumm offers an insightful study of liberal and Foucauldian notions of freedom, centered on the problematic of "space," that parallels my own. While Dumm discusses the transgressive character of Foucault's view of freedom, he neglects to connect that aspect to counter-memory, without which what I have here called strategic freedom lacks a conceptual grounding.

2. Jean-Jacques Rousseau, *The Social Contract and Discourse on the Origin of Inequality*, 32; hereafter, page numbers will be cited parenthetically in the text.

3. We have to be attentive to the temporal metaphors in Rousseau's anthropological history; he is aware of them as metaphors that permit him to address a present situation of corruption and political subjection. This allowed, we must also observe that these metaphors are grounded on metaphysical presuppositions of the nature of man, that man has a fundamental and essential identity that has been corrupted, but which can be restored.

4. See "Slavery," chapter 5 of Rousseau's *The Social Contract*, 11–16, and Lester G. Crocker's introduction, xxiii.

5. Rousseau, *The Social Contract*, ibid., 40. See also 60, "What, then, is the government? An intermediate body established between the subject and the sovereign for their mutual correspondence, charged with the execution of the laws and with the maintenance of liberty both civil and political."

6. See, for example, chapter 9 of *The Social Contract*, "The Marks of a Good Government," where Rousseau says, "What is the object of political association? It is the preservation and prosperity of its members. And what is the surest sign that they are preserved and prosperous? It is their number and population. . . . All other things being equal, the government under which, without external aids, without naturalizations, and without colonies, the citizens increase and multiply most, is infallibly the best. That under which a people diminishes and decays is the worst. Statisticians, it is now your business; reckon, measure, compare" (87–88).

7. "If there were a nation of gods, it would be governed democratically. So perfect a government is unsuited to men," *The Social Contract*, 71.

8. Citing George Bancroft as an archtype, Sacvan Bercovitch discusses the "myth of continuing revolution" that has been pervasive in the discourse and ideology of America since the Revolutionary War. Bercovitch characterizes this myth as the "vision of a nation conceived in exodus and dedicated to progress—[which] served a crucial mediative function. It posited an organi-

cally conflicted but intrinsically utopian status quo, a millennialism nour-
ished on the persistence through struggle of established social norms.

"It would be hard to overestimate the significance of this concept of revolutionary mediation. . . . [i]n defining America as the battleground for the
future." See his *The Rights of Assent: Transformations in the Symbolic Construction of America* (New York: Routledge, 1992), 183.

9. Nozick claims that he is working with a Lockean rights-based, entitlement theory, and he explicitly rejects utilitarian (or any otherwise teleological) political
theories. Yet he is much closer to Mill than to Locke, not simply historically,
but discursively. In fact, his appropriation of Locke is through nineteenth-century liberalism. This has the effect of distorting Locke, whose rights-based
individualism must be thought in the context of a discursive milieu informed
by the problematization of monarchy and absolute sovereignty.

10. Robert Nozick, *Anarchy, State, and Utopia* (New York: Basic Books, 1974),
171.

11. This shows that the harm-to-others principle need not be based on utilitarian
considerations by any means. Also, the ambiguity of "harm" and "interference" helps to explain the apparent insolubility of liberal/conservative
debates.

12. Nozick, *Anarchy, State, and Utopia*, 32–33.

13. See, for example, Friedrich Hayek, *The Constitution of Liberty* (Chicago:
University of Chicago Press, 1960); James M. Buchanan, *The Limits of Liberty: Between Anarchy and Leviathan* (Chicago: University of Chicago Press,
1975); and Isaiah Berlin, *Four Essays on Liberty* (Oxford: Oxford University
Press, 1969).

14. Michel Foucault, "Politics and Ethics: An Interview," in *The Foucault
Reader*, edited by Paul Rabinow (New York: Pantheon Books, 1984), 374.
This statement is reminiscent of Nietzsche's remarks, in *Thus Spoke
Zarathustra*, that one must struggle "step by step with the giant, 'Accident.'"
For Foucault, freedom involves the same sort of struggle with a similar sort
of giant, as well as with Nietzsche's "ascetic priest," an entrenched part of
our lineage from which we will not easily free ourselves.

15. Michel Foucault and Catherine Baker, "Interview de Michel Foucault," *Actes*
45–46 (June 1984), 5.

16. Michel Foucault, "Power and Strategies," in *Power/Knowledge: Selected
Interviews and Other Writings, 1972–1977* (New York: Pantheon Books,
1980), 142.

17. Ibid.

18. Says Foucault, "One of the first things that has to be understood is that
power isn't localized in the State apparatus and that nothing in society will
be changed if the mechanisms of power that function outside, below and
alongside the State apparatuses, on a much more minute and everyday level,
are not also changed." See his *Power/Knowledge*, 60.

19. Observes Priscilla Wald, "National narratives actually shape personal narratives by delineating the cultural practices through which personhood is
defined. The role of married women or the rights of indigenous peoples are

examples of how a culture, through its institutions and its conventions, defines individuals' existence—defines, that is, how they will experience and understand themselves as people and as part of a people." See her *Constituting Americans: Cultural Anxiety and Narrative Form* (Durham, N.C.: Duke University Press, 1995), 4.

20. Friedrich Nietzsche, "The Genealogy of Morals: An Attack," in *The Birth of Tragedy and The Genealogy of Morals*, translated by Francis Golffing (New York: Doubleday, 1956), 192–93.

21. See Nietzsche, "'Guilt,' 'Bad Conscience,' and Related Matters," ibid., 189ff. Unfortunately, Golffing translates *Vergesslichkeit* in this passage as "oblivion," which is not incorrect, but I think that "forgetfulness" is more concrete and less ambiguous—or at least serves my purposes better. See also Jacques Derrida, "The Ends of Man," in *Margins of Philosophy*, translated by Alan Bass (Chicago: University of Chicago Press, 1982), 136.

22. See Michel Foucault, "Intellectuals and Power," in *Language, Counter-Memory, Practice: Selected Essays and Interviews*, edited by Donald F. Bouchard (Ithaca, N.Y.: Cornell University Press, 1977), 209.

23. The freedom alluded to here is similar to that anticipated by Nietzsche in *The Gay Science*: "At last the horizon appears free again to us, even granted that it is not bright; at last our ships may venture out again, venture out to face any danger; all the daring of the lover of knowledge is permitted again; the sea, *our* sea, lies open again; perhaps there has never yet been such an 'open sea.'" In *The Portable Nietzsche*, edited and translated by Walter Kaufmann (New York: Penguin, 1976), 448.

24. For a more general discussion of Foucault's understanding of transgression, see Michael Clifford, "Crossing (Out) the Boundary: Foucault and Derrida on Transgressing Transgression," *Philosophy Today* 31 (1987), 223–33.

25. Michel Foucault, "Nietzsche, Genealogy, History," in Bouchard, ed., *Language, Counter-Memory, Practice*, 161–62.

26. Ibid., 145–46.

27. Ibid., 142.

28. Michel Foucault, "What Is Enlightenment?" in *The Foucault Reader*, edited by Paul Rabinow (New York: Pantheon Books, 1984), 46.

29. Michel Foucault, *The Use of Pleasure: Volume 2 of the History of Sexuality* (New York: Pantheon Books, 1985), 8.

30. See Foucault, "What Is Enlightenment?" 50.

31. Michel Foucault, "Critical Theory/Intellectual History," in *Michel Foucault: Politics, Philosophy, Culture*, edited by Lawrence D. Kritzman (New York: Routledge, Chapman and Hall, 1988), 36; emphasis added.

32. Dennis Altman, *Homosexual Oppression and Liberation* (New York and London: New York University Press, 1971), 241. Interestingly, at the time that Altman wrote the book, he had not read Foucault, but, in the afterword to the 1993 reprinting, Altman admits that his ideas were similar to Foucault's in that he understands sexual identity as "a particular historical construction" (253). This point is confirmed by Jeffrey Weeks, who in the new introduction to the book suggests that Altman anticipates Foucault in his

view of "the category of homosexual [as] a historical and social invention, formed in specific historical conditions, and likely to disappear as conditions changed" (8). Of course, Foucault has had an enormous influence, both positive and negative, on the development of Queer Theory and Queer Politics. See, for example, David M. Halperin, *Saint Foucault: Towards a Gay Hagiography* (Oxford: Oxford University Press, 1995).

33. By "recalcitrant" I do not mean rights-based or inviolable. I mean simply to express an analytical connection. That is, if there is no possibility of transformation, then there is no freedom.

34. Michel Foucault, "An Interview: Sex, Power, and the Politics of Identity," *The Advocate* 400 (August, 1984), 28.

35. Ibid., 28.

36. See, for example, Charles Taylor, "Foucault on Freedom and Truth," in *Foucault: A Critical Reader*, edited by David Couzens Hoy (Oxford: Basil Blackwell, 1986), 69–102.

37. "Where the determining factors saturate the whole there is no relationship of power; slavery is not a power relationship when a man is in chains. (In this case it is a question of a physical relationship of constraint)," Michel Foucault, "The Subject and Power," in Hubert L. Dreyfus and Paul Rabinow, *Michel Foucault: Beyond Structuralism and Hermeneutics* (Chicago: University of Chicago Press, 1982), 221.

38. Michel Foucault, "The Ethic of Care for the Self as a Practice of Freedom," in *The Final Foucault: Studies on Michel Foucault's Last Works*, edited by James Bernauer; special issue, *Philosophy and Social Criticism* 12 (summer 1987), 123.

39. Foucault, "The Subject and Power," 221.

40. Foucault, "The Ethic of Care for the Self as a Practice of Freedom," 123.

41. Ibid., 121.

42. Ibid., 123.

43. Foucault, "The Subject and Power," 222.

44. Michel Foucault, "Power and Sex," in Kritzman, ed., *Michel Foucault*, 122.

45. Foucault, "The Subject and Power," 225.

46. Foucault, "An Interview," 29.

47. Michel Foucault, "Revolutionary Action: 'Until Now'," in Bouchard, ed., *Language, Counter-Memory, Practice*, 227.

48. Foucault, "The Subject and Power," 212.

49. Ibid.

50. Foucault says we seem to have "no solid recourse available to us today" against disciplinary mechanisms other than "the return to a theory of right organized around Sovereignty. . . . But I believe that we find ourselves in a kind of blind alley: it is not through recourse to sovereignty against discipline that the effects of disciplinary power can be limited, because sovereignty and disciplinary mechanisms are two absolutely integral constituents of the general mechanisms of power in society." See his *Power/Knowledge*, 108.

51. Foucault, "An Interview," 29.

52. Foucault himself is not above using such a strategy. See "Face aux gouvern-

ments, les droits de l'homme," *Actes* 54 (1986), 22. This is the published version of Foucault's address at Geneva (June 1981) to the International Committee on the problem of the boat people, in which he defends the rights of individuals against political oppression. However, the "rights" that Foucault defends here are not the passive and metaphysically empty rights of traditional ideology. He appeals, rather, to a "droit nouveau" that consists of permitting individuals to intervene effectively in the order of politics and "strategies internationales."

53. Foucault, "The Subject and Power," 216.
54. "The important question here . . . is not whether a culture without restraints is possible or even desirable, but whether the system of constraints in which society functions leaves individuals the liberty to transform the system." See Michel Foucault, "Sexual Choice, Sexual Act: An Interview with Michel Foucault," *Salmagundi* 58–59 (winter 1982), 16.
55. Michel-Guillaume-Jean de Crèvecoeur, "Distresses of a Frontier Man," in *The Anthology of American Literature*, vol. 1, *Colonial through Romantic*, 469.
56. Ibid., 471.
57. Jean-Paul Sartre, "Existentialism Is a Humanism," (1949), reprinted in *Existentialism*, edited by Robert C. Solomon (New York: Random House, 1974), 205.
58. Simone de Beauvoir, *The Ethics of Ambiguity* (1948), translated by Bernard Frechtman (Carol Publishing Group, 1994), 23–24.
59. De Beauvoir characterizes her ethics of freedom as "individualistic" in that "it accords to the individual an absolute value and that it recognizes in him alone the power of laying the foundations of his own existence. It is individualism in the sense in which the wisdom of the ancients, the Christian ethics of salvation, and the Kantian ideal of virtue also merit this name; it is opposed to the totalitarian doctrines which raise up beyond man the mirage of Mankind," ibid., 156.
60. Michel Foucault, "The Genealogy of Ethics: An Overview of Work in Progress," In Dreyfus and Rabinow, *Michel Foucault*, 237.
61. Foucault, "An Interview," 27.
62. This is a generalization of Altman's characterization of the gay liberation movement in his *Homosexual Oppression and Liberation*. See chapter 4, "Oppression: The Denial of Identity," 50–79.
63. A case in point would be the signing of the Declaration of Rights and Sentiments at Seneca Falls, the 150th anniversary of which was recently celebrated with much fanfare, including an appearance by Hillary Clinton. Says Foucault, "I've always been a little distrustful of the general theme of liberation . . . there is the danger that it will refer back to the idea that there does exist a nature or a human foundation which, as a result of a certain number of historical, social or economic processes, found itself concealed, alienated, or imprisoned in and by some repressive mechanism." See his "The Ethic of Care for the Self as a Practice of Freedom," 113. Of course, one might object that even popular political movements are not merely liberationist and that

movements for equal justice may have nothing at all to do with movements for the liberation of repressed identities or desires. My point here is that issues of justice and of identity cannot be so easily separated; on the contrary, the latter has a direct formative bearing on the degree and manner of the former (and no doubt vice versa). I believe this to be one of the central messages of such authors as Judith Butler, bell hooks, Minnie Bruce Pratt, Altman, Weeks, Halperin, and others.

64. Seyla Benhabib, *Situating the Self: Gender, Community and Postmodernism in Contemporary Ethics* (New York: Routledge, 1992), 5.

Chapter 7: Genealogy and Other-Politics

1. Michel Foucault, "Genealogy of Ethics: An Overview of Work in Progress," in Hubert L. Dreyfus and Paul Rabinow, *Michel Foucault: Beyond Structuralism and Hermeneutics* (Chicago: University of Chicago Press, 1982), 234.

2. Michel Foucault, "Nietzsche, Genealogy, History," in *Language, Counter-Memory, Practice: Selected Essays and Interviews*, edited by Donald F. Bouchard (Ithaca, N.Y.: Cornell University Press, 1977), 150.

3. Ibid., 140.

4. Michel Foucault, "Is It Useless to Revolt?" trans. James Bernauer, in *Philosophy and Social Criticism* 8, no. 1 (spring 1981), 8.

5. John Rawls, in a footnote to a section entitled, "The Political Conception of the Person," in his *Political Liberalism* (New York: Columbia University Press, 1993), 29; emphasis added.

6. Seyla Benhabib, *Situating the Self: Gender, Community and Post-modernism in Contemporary Ethics* (New York: Routledge, 1992), 7.

7. See Jürgen Habermas, "Taking Aim at the Heart of the Present," in *Foucault: A Critical Reader*, edited by David Couzens Hoy (Oxford; Basil Blackwell, 1986), 108. A similar objection comes from Nancy Fraser: "Why is struggle preferable to submission? Why ought dominations to be resisted? Only with the introduction of normative notions could [Foucault] begin to tell us what is wrong with the modern power/knowledge regime and why we ought to oppose it," "Foucault on Modern Power: Empirical Insights and Normative Confusions," *Praxis International*, vol 1 (1981), 238. See also Habermas, *Der philosophische Diskurs der Moderne: Zwolf Vorlesungen* (Frankfurt: Suhrkamp, 1985), chapters 9 and 10; and David Couzens Hoy, introduction to *Foucault: A Critical Reader*, 8.

8. Says Haber, "Michael Walzer argues that Foucault gives us no reason to believe the new codes and descriptions that will be produced will be any better than the ones we live with. But this misses the point. . . . Fraser, Rorty, et al., all criticize Foucault because they take him to be doing something he is not. They are trying to force him to conform to their notion of what a concerned social critic must be—but he does not want to fit that mold." See Honi Fern Haber, *Beyond Postmodern Politics: Lyotard, Rorty, Foucault* (New York: Routledge, 1994), 91–92.

9. Says Nietzsche, "Judgments, judgments of value, concerning life, for it or

against it, can in the end, never be true. They have value only as symptoms."
See his *Twilight of the Idols*, trans. R. J. Hollingdale (New York: Penguin,
1968), 30.

10. Someone may object that there is, in fact, some fixed, objective standard that
would tell one what one "ought" to do here: namely, avoidance of pain. But
suppose that holding one's hand above the flame is part of some religious cer-
emony or some tribal rite of passage—then both the normative standard and
the "ought" it prescribes would be very different, and dependent upon the
context. My point is that it is *experience* that tells one what one's options
are. Experience is equivalent to a form of knowledge. Similarly, genealogy
provides us with a form of knowledge by rendering a given historically contingent experience—such as that pertaining to the instantiation of disciplinary coercions—visible to us. In fact, the success of such coercions to a large
extent stems from their ability to function silently and without being noticed
as such. It is precisely the effect, if not the aim, of genealogy to expose those
coercions in such a way that new possibilities—minimally, the possibility that
things might be *otherwise*—are revealed.

11. "What the intellectual can do is to provide instruments of analysis . . . that
makes it possible to locate lines of weakness, strong points, positions where
the instances of power have secured and implanted themselves. . . . That is
the intellectual's role. But as for saying, Here is what you must do!, certainly
not," Michel Foucault, "Body/Power," in *Power/Knowledge: Selected Interviews and Other Writings, 1972–1977*, edited by Colin Gordon (New York:
Pantheon Books, 1980), 62.

12. Foucault, "The Genealogy of Ethics," 232–32.

13. Michel Foucault, "The Ethic of Care for the Self as a Practice of Freedom,"
in *The Final Foucault: Studies on Michel Foucault's Last Works*, edited by
James Bernauer; special issue of *Philosophy and Social Criticism* 12 (summer
1987), 129.

14. "Genealogy of Ethics," 232.

15. See James Bernauer, *Michel Foucault's Force of Flight*, 180–184.

16. For example, John Rajchman asserts, "For Foucault, freedom was thus not a
state one achieves once and for all, but a condition of an "undefined work"
of thought, action, and self-invention. As such he tried to introduce it into
politics and ethics. To be free, he argued, we must be able to question the
ways our own history defines us." See his *Truth and Eros: Foucault, Lacan,
and the Question of Ethics* (New York: Routledge, 1991), 111. See also John
Rajchman, *Michel Foucault: The Freedom of Philosophy* (New York: Columbia University Press, 1985), *passim*, and Thomas L. Dumm, *Foucault and the
Politics of Freedom* (Thousand Oaks, Calif.: Sage, 1996), 137–44. On the
other hand, Charles Scott has argued that Foucault's thought "does not constitute or lead to ethics." See his *The Question of Ethics: Nietzsche, Foucault, Heidegger* (Bloomington: Indiana University Press, 1990), 58. This
does not refer to a flaw or omission in Foucault's thought; rather, it refers to
the idea that in Foucault's thought the very possibility of ethics is put into
question.

17. Alasdair MacIntyre, *Three Rival Versions of Moral Enquiry: Encyclopaedia, Genealogy, and Tradition* (Notre Dame, Ind.: University of Notre Dame Press, 1990), 50, 55.

18. Ibid., 54.

19. "By 'self-consuming' I mean that the concept in question requires as a condition of its intelligibility (or even its possibility) the very contrast it wishes to set aside or would have us set aside," Bernd Magnus, "Self-Consuming Concepts," *International Studies in Philosophy* 11, no. 2 (summer 1989), 64.

20. "Alas, what are you after all, my written and painted thoughts! It was not long ago that you were still so colorful, young and malicious, full of thorns and secret spices—you made me sneeze and laugh—and now? You have already taken off your novelty, and some of you are ready, I fear, to become truths! They already look so immortal, so pathetically decent, so dull! And has it ever been different? What things do we copy, writing and painting, we mandarins with Chinese brushes, we immortalizers of things that *can* be written. . . . Alas, always only birds that grew weary of flying and flew astray and now can be caught by hand—by our hand! We immortalize what cannot live and fly much longer—only weary and mellow things!" Friedrich Nietzsche, *Beyond Good and Evil*, translated by Walter Kaufmann (New York: Vintage Books, 1966), 236–37.

21. Jacques Derrida, "Différance," in *Margins of Philosophy*, translated by Alan Bass (Chicago: University of Chicago Press, 1982), 7, 26.

22. Scott, *The Question of Ethics*, 58–59.

23. MacIntyre, *Three Rival Versions*, 54.

24. Ibid., 209.

25. Ibid., 210.

26. Michel Foucault, "The Masked Philosopher," in *Michel Foucault: Politics, Philosophy, Culture*, edited Lawrence D. Kritzman (New York: Routledge, Chapman and Hall, 1988), 322–23.

27. "Practicing Criticism," in *Michel Foucault: Politics, Philosophy, Culture*, 154.

28. Michel Foucault, "Power and Sex," in Kritzman, ed., *Michel Foucault*, 120–21.

29. Foucault, *Power/Knowledge*, 121.

30. Luce Irigaray, *This Sex Which Is Not One* (Ithaca, N.Y.: Cornell University Press, 1985), 26.

31. Of course, political theory must be wary of engaging in what Chow calls "facile idealist and idealistic projections" of identity onto the victimized Other. Nevertheless, to point out the intimacy between identification and victimization is not, *pace* Chow, "to relate to alterity through mythification; to imagine 'the other,' no matter how prosaic or impoverished, as essentially different, good, kind, enveloped in a halo, and beyond the contradictions that constitute our own historical place." See Rey Chow, *Ethics after Idealism: Theory—Culture—Ethnicity—Reading* (Bloomington: Indiana University Press, 1988), xx–xxi.

32. Irigaray, *This Sex Which Is Not One*, 76.

33. Ibid.

34. I cannot here begin to do justice to the complexity of the political strategem to which Irigaray refers. The thrust of what she is describing, I think, has been toward what is called the politics of the "performative." For a discussion, see Judith Butler, *Excitable Speech: A Politics of the Performative* (New York: Routledge, 1997).

35. And also in different forms by Judith Butler, Honi Fern Haber, Jana Sawicki, and Iris Marion Young. Haber distinguishes hers from a strictly 'postmodern' orientation, which she claims tends to valorize difference itself in the way that traditional political philosophies valorize identity. By contrast, she characterizes her own version of a politics of difference as an "oppositional politics" in that "it pays attention to difference" while at the same time promoting the possibility of a political community comprised of "oppositional identities." See her *Beyond Postmodern Politics: Lyotard, Rorty, Foucault,* 2–3, 134. See also Laura Kipnis, *Bound and Gagged: Pornography and the Politics of Fantasy in America* (New York: Grove Press, 1996), Linda Williams, *Hard Core; Power, Pleasure, and the Frenzy of the Visible* (Berkeley: University of California Press, 1989); and M. G. Lord, "Pornutopia: How Feminist Scholars Learned to Love Dirty Pictures," *Lingua Franca* (April/May 1997), 40–48.

36. See Charles Taylor, "The Politics of Recognition," and Michael Walzer's reply, both in *Multiculturalism: Examining the Politics of Recognition,* edited by Amy Gutman (Princeton, N.J.: Princeton University Press, 1984), 25–73, 99–103. See also Michael Walzer, "Multiculturalism and Individualism," *Dissent* (spring 1994), 185–91. Actually, I think that both Chow and Rizvi would view the Taylor and Walzer versions of multiculturalism as themselves species of that "politics of assimilation concerned with domesticating egalitarian demands. By invoking the universalist ideal of a society governed by a set of social principles for a common humanity, in which we can all participate happily without reference to class, ethnicity, race, or gender, [this version of] multiculturalism . . . can only deal with differences by making them marginal; by being tokenistic," Fažal Rivzi, "The Arts, Education, and the Politics of Multiculturalism," quoted in Chow, *Ethics,* 12.

37. The literature here is enormous and growing almost daily. See, for example, Gloria Anzaldúa, *Borderlands/La Frontera* (San Fransisco: Spinsters/Aunt Lute, 1987); Iris Marion Young, *Justice and the Politics of Difference* (Princeton, N.J.: Princeton University Press, 1990); Minnie Bruce Pratt, "Identity: Skin, Blood, Heart," in *Yours in Struggle: Three Feminist Perspectives on Anti-Semitism and Racism* (New York: Firebrand Books, 1992); Ronald Takaki, *A Different Mirror: A History of Multicultural America* (Boston: Little, Brown, 1993); Edward Said, "The Politics of Knowledge," in *Race, Identity and Representation in Education,* edited by Cameron McCarthy and Warren Crichlow (New York: Routledge, 1993); Lawrence Foster and Patricia Herzog, *Defending Diversity: Contemporary Philosophical Perspectives on Pluralism and Multiculturalism* (Amherst: University of Massachusetts Press, 1994); Gabriella Ibieta and Miles Orvell, eds., *Invent-

ing America: Readings in Identity and Culture; Nancy Fraser, *Justice Interruptus: Re-Thinking Key Concepts of a Post-Socialist Age* (New York: Routledge, 1997).

38. Nicholas Thomas, *Colonialism's Culture: Anthropology, Travel, and Government* (Princeton, N.J.: Princeton University Press, 1994), 3.

39. Homi K. Bhabha, *The Location of Culture* (New York: Routledge, 1994), 58.

40. Ibid., 37.

41. Gayatri Chakravorty Spivak, "Can the Subaltern Speak?" in *Marxism and the Interpretation of Culture*, edited by Cary Nelson and Lawrence Grossberg (London: MacMillan Press, 1988), 307.

42. Frantz Fanon, *The Wretched of the Earth* (Penguin Books, 1969), 30, 33.

43. "The group rape," says Spivak, "perpetrated by the conquerors is a metonymic celebration of territorial acquisition." See her "Can the Subaltern Speak?" 303.

44. Jean-Paul Sartre, preface to Fanon, *The Wretched of the Earth*, 7.

45. Bhabha, *The Location of Culture*, 39.

46. Frederick Jackson Turner, *The Frontier in America History* (New York: Henry Holt, 1920), 3.

Bibliography

Adler, Mortimer J., ed. *The Annals of America*, vol. 1, *Discovering a New World.* Chicago: University of Chicago Press, 1968.

Adorno, T. W., Daniel J. Levinson, R. Nevitt Sanford, Else Frenkel-Brunswick. *The Authoritarian Personality.* New York: Harper and Row, 1950.

Altman, Dennis. *Homosexual Oppression and Liberation.* New York: New York University Press, 1971.

Anderson, Benedict. *Imagined Communities: Reflections on the Origin and Spread of Nationalism,* Revised Edition. New York: Verso, 1991.

Anzaldúa, Gloria. *Borderlands/La Frontera.* San Francisco: Spinsters/Aunt Lute, 1987.

Arendt, Hannah. *On Revolution.* New York: Penguin Books, 1963.

Aristotle. *The Politics.* Revised Edition. Trans. T. A. Sinclair. New York: Penguin, 1983.

Auzias, Jean-Marie. *Michel Foucault: qui suis-je?* Lyon: La Manufacture, 1986.

Avrich, Paul. *Anarchist Voices: An Oral History of Anarchism in America.* Princeton, N.J.: Princeton University Press, 1996.

Beauvoir, Simone de. *The Ethics of Ambiguity.* (1948) Trans. Bernard Frechtman. New York: Carol Publishing Group, 1994.

———. *The Second Sex,* Trans. H. M. Parshley. Hammondsworth, England: Penguin, 1974.

Benhabib, Seyla. *Situating the Self: Gender, Community and Postmodernism in Contemporary Ethics.* New York: Routledge, 1992.

Bercovitch, Sacvan. *The Rites of Assent: Transformations in the Symbolic Construction of America.* New York: Routledge, 1993.

Berlin, Isaiah. *Four Essays on Liberty.* Oxford: Oxford UniversityPress, 1969.

———. "Two Concepts of Liberty." In *Liberalism and Its Critics.* Ed. Michael Sandel. New York: New York University Press, 1984.

Bernauer, James. *Michel Foucault's Force of Flight: Toward an Ethics for Thought.* London: Humanities Press International, 1990.

———. "Foucault's Ecstatic Thinking." In *The Final Foucault: Studies on Michel Foucault's Last Works.* Ed. James Bernauer. Special issue of *Philosophy and Social Criticism* 12 (summer 1987), 156–93.

Bhabha, Homi K. *The Location of Culture.* New York: Routledge, 1994.

Bird, Alexander. "Squaring the Circle: Hobbes on Philosophy and Geometry." *Journal of the History of Ideas*, April 1996. 217–31.

Bove, Paul. "The Foucault Phenomenon." Foreword to *Foucault*, by Gilles Deleuze. Trans. Sean Hand. Minneapolis: University of Minnesota Press, 1988.

Bradford, William. *Of Plymouth Plantation*. Ed. Samuel Eliot Morrison. New York: Modern Library, 1967.

Brady, Robert A. *The Spirit and Structure of German Fascism*. New York: The Viking Press, 1937.

Brandt, Frithiof. *Thomas Hobbes' Mechanical Conception of Nature*. London: Librairie Hachette, 1928.

Brown, Wesley, and Amy Ling, eds. *Imagining America: Stories from the Promised Land*. New York: Persea Books, 1991.

Buchanan, James M. *The Limits of Liberty: Between Anarchy and Leviathan*. Chicago: University of Chicago Press, 1975.

Burchell, Graham, Colin Gordon, and Peter Miller, eds. *The Foucault Effect: Studies in Governmentality*. Chicago: University of Chicago Press, 1991.

Butler, Judith. *Excitable Speech: A Politics of the Performative*. New York: Routledge, 1997.

———. *Gender Trouble: Feminism and the Subversion of Identity*. New York: Routledge, 1990.

Chow, Rey. *Ethics after Idealism: Theory–Culture–Ethnicity–Reading*. Bloomington: Indiana University Press, 1998.

Clifford, Michael. "Crossing (Out) the Boundary: Foucault and Derrida on Transgressing Transgression," *Philosophy Today* 31 (1987), 223–33.

Croce, Benedetto. *History as the Story of Liberty*. Trans. Sylvia Sprigge. New York: W. W. Norton, 1941.

Crocker, Lester G. Introduction to Jean-Jacques Rousseau, *The Social Contract and Discourse on the Origin of Inequality*. New York: Simon and Schuster, 1967.

Cutting-Gray, Joanne. "Franklin's *Autobiography*: Politics of the Public Self." *Prospects: An Annual of American Cultural Studies*, 14 (1989), 31–43.

Davidson, Arnold I. "Archeology, Genealogy, Ethics." In *Foucault: A Critical Reader*. Ed. David Couzens Hoy. Oxford: Basil Blackwell, 1986.

Deleuze, Gilles. *Foucault*. Trans. Sean Hand. Minneapolis: University of Minnesota Press, 1988.

Derrida, Jacques. *Margins of Philosophy*. Trans. Alan Bass. Chicago: University of Chicago Press, 1982.

Devigne, Robert. *Recasting Conservatism: Oakshott, Strauss, and the Response to Postmodernism*. New Haven, Conn.: Yale University Press, 1994.

Dreyfus, Hubert L., and Paul Rabinow. *Michel Foucault: Beyond Structuralism and Hermeneutics*. Second Edition. Chicago: University of Chicago Press, 1982.

Dumm, Thomas L. *Michel Foucault and the Politics of Freedom*. Thousand Oaks, Calif.: Sage, 1996.

Dworkin, Ronald. "Liberalism." In *Liberalism and Its Critics*. Ed. Michael Sandel. New York: New York University Press, 1984.

Eribon, Didier. *Michel Foucault*, Trans. Betsy Wing. Cambridge: Harvard University Press, 1991

Fanon, Frantz. *The Wretched of the Earth*. Hammondsworth, England: Penguin, 1967 (1961).

Foreman, Grant. *Indian Removal: The Emigration of the Five Civilized Tribes of Indians*. Norman: University of Oklahoma Press, 1932.

Foster, Lawrence, and Patricia Herzog. *Defending Diversity: Contemporary Philosophical Perspectives on Pluralism and Multiculturalism*. Amherst: University of Massachusetts Press, 1994.

Foucault, Michel. "An Aesthetics of Existence." Interview by Alessandro Fontana. In *Michel Foucault: Politics, Philosophy, Culture*. Ed. Lawrence D. Kritzman. New York: Routledge, Chapman and Hall, 1988.

———. *The Archeology of Knowledge and The Discourse on Language*. Trans. A. M. Sheridan Smith. New York: Pantheon Books, 1972.

———. *The Care of the Self: History of Sexuality, Volume 3*. Trans. Robert Hurley. New York: Pantheon Books, 1986.

———. "The Concern for Truth." Interview by François Ewald. In *Michel Foucault: Politics, Philosophy, Culture*. Ed. Lawrence D. Kritzman. New York: Routledge, Chapman and Hall, 1988.

———. "Critical Theory/Intellectual History." Interview by Gérard Raulet. In *Michel Foucault: Politics, Philosophy, Culture*. Ed. Lawrence D. Kritzman. Trans. Alan Sheridan et al. New York: Routledge, Chapman and Hall, 1988.

———. *Discipline and Punish: The Birth of the Prison*. Trans. Alan Sheridan. New York: Vintage Books, 1979.

———. *Discourse and Truth: The Problematization of Parrhesia*. Text compiled and transcribed by Joseph Pearson from a series of lectures delivered by Foucault at the University of California, Berkeley, fall 1983. Evanston, Ill.: Northwestern University Press, 1985.

———. "Entretien avec M. Foucault," *Masques* 13 (spring 1982), 15–24.

———. "The Ethic of Care for the Self as a Practice of Freedom." In *The Final Foucault: Studies on Michel Foucault's Last Works*. Ed. James Bernauer. Special issue of *Philosophy and Social Criticism* 12 (summer 1987), 112–31.

———. "Face aux gouvernements, les droits de l'homme." *Actes* 54 (1986), 22.

———. "Final Interview." Trans. Thomas Levin and Isabelle Lorenz. *Raritan* 5, no. 1 (summer 1985), 1–13.

———. "First Preface to The History of Sexuality, Volume 2." In *The Foucault Reader*. Ed. Paul Rabinow. New York: Pantheon Books, 1984.

———. "Foucault at the College de France 1: A Course Summary." Trans. James Bernauer. *Philosophy and Social Criticism* 8, no. 2 (summer 1981), 235–42. A summary of the course given at the College de France in 1978. Originally published as "Histoire des systemes de pensée." *Annuaire du College de France* 78 (1978), 445–49.

———. "Foucault at the College de France 2: A Course Summary." Trans. James Bernauer. *Philosophy and Social Criticism* 8, no. 3 (fall 1981), 349–59.

A summary of the course given at the College de France in 1979. Originally published as "Histoire des systemes de pensée." *Annuaire du College de France* 79 (1979), 367–72.

———. "The Genealogy of Ethics: An Overview of Work in Progress." In Hubert L. Dreyfus and Paul Rabinow, *Michel Foucault: Beyond Structuralism and Hermeneutics*. Second Edition. Chicago: University of Chicago Press, 1982.

———. "Governmentality." Trans. Rosi Braidotti. *Ideology and Consciousness* 6 (autumn 1979), 5–21.

———. *The History of Sexuality: Volume I*. Trans. Robert Hurley. New York: Vintage Books, 1980.

———. "History of Systems of Thought." In *Language, Counter-Memory, Practice: Selected Essays and Interviews*. Ed. Donald F. Bouchard. Trans. Donald F. Bouchard and Sherry Simon. Ithaca, N.Y.: Cornell University Press, 1977.

———. "Intellectuals and Power." Conversation with Gilles Deleuze. In *Language, Counter-Memory, Practice: Selected Essays and Interviews*. Ed. Donald F. Bouchard. Trans. Donald F. Bouchard and Sherry Simon. Ithaca, N.Y.: Cornell University Press, 1977.

———. "Is it Useless to Revolt?" Trans. James Bernauer. In *Philosophy and Social Criticism* 8, no. 1 (spring 1981), 1–9.

———. *Language, Counter-Memory, Practice: Selected Essays and Interviews*. Ed. Donald F. Bouchard. Trans. Donald F. Bouchard and Sherry Simon. Ithaca, N.Y.: Cornell University Press, 1977.

———. *Madness and Civilization: A History of Insanity in the Age of Reason*. Trans. Richard Howard. New York: Vintage Books, 1973.

———. "The Masked Philosopher." Interview by Christian Delacampagne. In *Michel Foucault: Politics, Philosophy, Culture*. Ed. Lawrence D. Kritzman. Trans. Alan Sheridan et al. New York: Routledge, Chapman and Hall, 1988.

———. "Michel Foucault, An Interview: Sex, Power, and the Politics of Identity." Interview by Bob Gallagher and Alexander Wilson, June 1982. *The Advocate* 400 (August 1984), 26–30, 58.

———. "Nietzsche, Genealogy, History." In *Language, Counter-Memory, Practice*. Ed. Donald F. Bouchard. Trans. Donald F. Bouchard and Sherry Simon. Ithaca, N.Y.: Cornell University Press, 1977.

———. "Omnes et Singulatim: Towards a Criticism of 'Political Reason'." Lectures delivered at Stanford University, October 10 and 16, 1979. In *The Tanner Lectures on Human Values 2*. Ed. Sterling McMussin. Salt Lake City: University of Utah Press and Cambridge University Press, 1981.

———. *The Order of Things: An Archaeology of the Human Sciences*. New York: Vintage Books, 1973.

———. "Polemics, Politics, and Problematizations." In *The Foucault Reader*. Ed. Paul Rabinow. New York: Pantheon Books, 1984.

———. "The Political Technology of Individuals." In *Technologies of the Self: A Seminar with Michel Foucault*. Ed. Luther H. Martin, Huck Guckman, and Patrick H. Hutton. Amherst: University of Massachusetts Press, 1988.

———. "Politics and Ethics: An Interview." In *The Foucault Reader*. Ed. Paul Rabinow. New York: Pantheon Books, 1984.

———. *Power/Knowledge: Selected Interviews and Other Writings, 1972–1977.* Ed. Colin Gordon. Trans. Colin Gordon, et al. New York: Pantheon Books, 1980.

———. "Power and Sex." Discussion with Bernard-Henri Levy. Trans. David J. Parent. In *Michel Foucault: Politics, Philosophy, Culture. Interviews and Other Writings 1977–1984.* Ed. Lawrence D. Kritzman. Trans. Alan Sheridan et al. New York: Routledge, Chapman and Hall, 1988.

———. "Practicing Criticism." Interview with Didier Eribon. In *Michel Foucault: Politics, Philosophy, Culture.* Ed. Lawrence D. Kritzman. Trans. Alan Sheridan et al. New York, Routledge, Chapman and Hall, 1988.

———. "Questions of Geography." In *Power/Knowledge: Selected Interviews and Other Writings, 1972–1977.* Ed. Colin Gordon. Trans. Colin Gordon et al. New York: Pantheon Books, 1980.

———. "The Return of Morality." Interview by Gilles Barbadette and Andre Scala, June 1984. In *Michel Foucault: Politics, Philosophy, Culture.* Ed. Lawrence D. Kritzman. Trans. Alan Sheridan et al. New York: Routledge, Chapman and Hall, 1988.

———. "Revolutionary Action: 'Until Now'." In *Language, Counter-Memory, Practice.* Ed. Donald F Bouchard. Trans. Donald F. Bouchard and Sherry Simon. Ithaca, N.Y.: Cornell University Press, 1977.

———. "Sexual Choice, Sexual Act: An Interview with Michel Foucault." Interview by James O'Higgins, March 1982. *Salmagundi* 58–59 (winter 1982), 10–24.

———. "The Social Triumph of the Sexual Will: A Conversation with Michel Foucault." Trans. Brendan Lemon. *Christopher Street* 64 (1982), 36–41.

———. "La strategie du pourtour." *Le Nouvel Observateur* 759 (28 May 1979), 57.

———. "Structuralism and Post-Structuralism: An Interview with Michel Foucault." Interview by Gerard Raulet. Trans. Jeremy Harding. *Telos* 55 (spring 1983), 195–211.

———. "The Subject and Power." In Hubert L. Dreyfus and Paul Rabinow. *Michel Foucault: Beyond Structuralism and Hermeneutics.* Second edition. Chicago: University of Chicago Press, 1982.

———. "Theatrum Philosophicum." In *Language, Counter-Memory, Practice.* Ed. Donald F. Bouchard. Trans. Donald F. Bouchard and Sherry Simon. Ithaca, N.Y.: Cornell University Press, 1977.

———. "Truth and Power." In *Power/Knowledge: Selected Interviews and Other Writings, 1972–1977.* Ed. Colin Gordon. New York: Pantheon Books, 1980.

———. "Truth and Subjectivity." Howison Lecture. Presented at University of California-Berkeley, October 20, 1980.

———. "Truth, Power, Self: An Interview with Michel Foucault." In *Technologies of the Self: A Seminar with Michel Foucault.* Ed. Luther H. Martin, Huck Guckman, and Patrick H. Hutton. Amherst: University of Massachusetts Press, 1988.

———. *The Use of Pleasure: Volume 2 of the History of Sexuality.* Trans. Robert Hurley. New York: Pantheon Books, 1985.

———. "What Is Enlightment?" Trans. Catherine Porter. In *The Foucault Reader*. Ed. Paul Rabinow. New York: Pantheon Books, 1984.

Foucault, Michel, and Catherine Baker. "Interview de Michel Foucault." *Actes* 45–46 (June 1984), 3–6.

Fraser, Nancy. "Foucault on Modern Power: Empirical Insights and Normative Confusions." *Praxis International* 1 (1981), 272–87.

———. *Justice Interruptus: Re-Thinking Key Concepts of a Post-Socialist Age.* New York: Routledge, 1997.

Gierke, Otto. *Natural Law and the Theory of Society.* Cambridge: Cambridge University Press, 1958.

Gillan, Garth. "Foucault's Philosophy." *Philosophy and Social Criticism* 12 (1987), 145–55.

Goldman, Emma. *Anarchism, and Other Essays.* New York: Dover, 1977.

Green, T. H. *Lectures on the Principles of Political Obligation.* Ann Arbor: University of Michigan Press, 1967.

Haber, Honi Fern. *Beyond Postmodern Politics: Lyotard, Rorty, Foucault.* New York: Routledge, 1994.

Habermas, Jürgen. "Struggles for Recognition in the Democratic Constitutional State." In *Multiculturalism: Examining the Politics of Recognition.* Princeton, N.J.: Princeton University Press, 1994.

———. "Taking Aim at the Heart of the Present." In *Foucault: A Critical Reader*. Ed. David Couzens Hoy. New York: Basil Blackwell, 1986.

———. *Der philosophische Diskurs der Moderne: Zwolf Vorlesungen.* Frankfurt: Suhrkamp, 1985.

Hakluyt, Richard. *The Portable Hakluyt's Voyages: The Principal Navigations Voyages Traffiques & Discoveries of the English Nation Made by Sea or Over-land to the Remote and Farthest Distant Quarters of the Earth at Any Time with the Compasse of these 1600 Yeeres.* Ed. Irwin R. Blacker. New York: Viking Portable Library, 1965.

Halperin, David M. *Saint Foucault: Towards a Gay Hagiography.* Oxford: Oxford University Press, 1995.

Hampton, Jean. *Hobbes and the Social Contract Tradition.* Cambridge: Cambridge University Press, 1986.

Hare, R. M. "Justice and Equality." In *Justice and Economic Distribution*. Ed. John Arthur and William H. Shaw. New York: Prentice Hall, 1978.

Hartsock, Nancy. "Foucault on Power: A Theory for Women?" In *Feminism/Postmodernism*. Ed. Linda J. Nicholson. New York: Routledge, 1990.

Harvey, David. *Justice, Nature, & the Geography of Difference.* Oxford: Blackwell, 1996.

Hayek, Friedrich. *The Constitution of Liberty.* Chicago: University of Chicago Press, 1960.

Heidegger, Martin. "On the Essence of Truth." In *Basic Writings*. Ed. David Farrell Krell. New York: Harper and Row, 1977.

———. *Being and Time.* Trans. John Macquarrie and Edward Robinson. New York: Harper and Row, 1962.

Hobbes, Thomas. *Leviathan.* Ed. C. B. Macpherson. New York: Penguin, 1980.

Hoy, David Couzens, ed. *Foucault: A Critical Reader*. New York: Basil Blackwell, 1986.

Hutcheon, Linda. *Irony's Edge: The Theory and Politics of Irony*. New York: Routledge, 1994.

Hutchinson, John, and Anthony D. Smith, eds. *Nationalism*. Oxford: Oxford University Press, 1994.

Ibieta, Gabriella, and Miles Orvell, eds. *Inventing America: Readings in Identity and Culture*. New York: St. Martin's Press, 1996.

Irigaray, Luce. *An Ethics of Sexual Difference*. Trans. Carolyn Burke and Gillian C. Gill. Ithaca, N.Y.: Cornell University Press, 1993 (1984).

———. *This Sex Which Is Not One*. Trans. Catherine Porter. Ithaca, N.Y.: Cornell University Press, 1985 (1977).

Jefferson, Thomas. *Notes on the State of Virgina* (1785), "Query VI," reprinted in *The Heath Anthology of American Literature*, Volume 1. Second edition. Ed. Paul Lauter. Boston: D.C. Heath and Company, 1994.

Jordan, Winthrop D. *White Over Black: American Attitudes towards the Negro, 1550–1812*. Baltimore: Penguin, 1969.

Kenny, Anthony, ed. *The Oxford Illustrated History of Western Philosophy*. Oxford: Oxford University Press, 1997.

Kipnis, Laura. *Bound and Gagged: Pornography and the Politics of Fantasy in America*. New York: Grove Press, 1996.

Kritzman, Lawrence D., ed. *Michel Foucault: Politics, Philosophy, Culture. Interviews and Other Writings 1977–1984*. Trans. Alan Sheridan et al. New York: Routledge, Chapman and Hall, 1988.

Laslett, Peter. "Locke and Hobbes." Introduction to *Two Treatises of Government*. Revised edition. Cambridge: Cambridge University Press, 1960.

Limerick, Patricia Nelson. *The Legacy of Conquest: The Unbroken Past of the American West*. New York: W. W. Norton, 1987.

Locke, John. *Two Treatises of Government*. Ed. Peter Laslett. Cambridge: Cambridge University Press, 1960.

Lord, M. G. "Pornutopia: How Feminist Scholars Learned to Love Dirty Pictures." *Lingua Franca* (April/May 1997), 40–48.

Lukes, Steven. *Individualism*. Oxford: Basil Blackwell, 1973.

MacIntyre, Alasdair. *Three Rival Versions of Moral Enquiry: Encyclopaedia, Genealogy, and Tradition*. Notre Dame, Ind.: University of Notre Dame Press, 1990.

Macpherson, C. B. Introduction to Thomas Hobbes, *Leviathan*. New York: Penguin, 1980.

———. *The Political Theory of Possessive Individualism*. Oxford University Press, 1962.

Magnus, Bernd. "Self-Consuming Concepts." *International Studies in Philosophy* 11, no. 2 (1989), 63–72.

Mather, Cotton. *On Witchcraft: Being, The Wonders of the Invisible World*. New York: n.d.; originally published in 1692.

Mill, John Stuart. *Considerations on Representative Government* (1861). Portions reprinted in *Communism, Fascism, and Democracy*. Ed. Carl Cohen. Chicago: University of Chicago Press, 1962.

———. *On Liberty*. Ed. Elizabeth Rapaport. Indianapolis: Hackett, 1978.

Miller, Toby. *The Well-Tempered Self: Citizenship, Culture, and the Postmodern Subject*. Baltimore: Johns Hopkins University Press, 1993.

Mouffe, Chantal. "For a Politics of Nomadic Identity." In *Travellers' Tales: Narratives of Home and Displacement*. Ed. George Robertson, Melinda Mash, Lisa Tickner, Jon Bird, Barry Curtis, and Tim Putman. New York: Routledge, 1994.

Nietzsche, Friedrich. *The Birth of Tragedy and the Genealogy of Morals*. Trans. Francis Golffing. New York: Doubleday and Co., 1956.

———. *Beyond Good and Evil*. Trans. Walter Kaufmann. New York: Vintage Books, 1966.

———. *Twilight of the Idols*. Trans. R. J. Hollingdale. New York: Penguin, 1984.

———. *The Portable Nietzsche*. Ed. and trans. Walter Kaufmann. New York: Penguin, 1976.

———. *On the Advantage and Disadvantage of History for Life*. Trans. Peter Preuss. Indianapolis: Hackett, 1980.

Nozick, Robert. *Anarchy, State, and Utopia*. New York: Basic Books, 1974.

Nyomarkay, Joseph. *Charisma and Factionalism in the Nazi Party*. Minneapolis: University of Minnesota Press, 1967.

O'Farrell, Clare. *Foucault: Historian or Philosopher?* London: Macmillan, 1990.

Perdue, Theda. "Cherokee Women and the Trail of Tears," in *Unequaled Sisters: A Multicultural Reader in U.S. Women's History*. Ed. Vicki Ruiz and Ellen Carol DuBois. New York: Routledge, 1994.

Plano, Jack C., and Milton Greenberg. *The American Political Dictionary*. Fourth edition. Hinsdale, Ill.: Dryden Press, 1976.

Pocock, J. G. A. "The History of Political Thought: A Methodological Enquiry," in *Philosophy, Politics and Society*. Second series. Ed. P. Laslett and W. Runciman. Oxford: Oxford University Press, 1972.

———. "The Myth of John Locke and the Obsession with Liberalism," in J. G. A. Pocock and Richard Ashcraft, *John Locke*. Los Angeles: Clark Memorial Library, 1980.

———. *Virtue, Commerce, and History: Essays on Political Thought and History, Chiefly in the Eighteenth Century*. Cambridge: Cambridge University Press, 1985.

———. "Thomas Hobbes: Atheist or Enthusiast? His Place in a Restoration Debate," *History of Political Thought* 11 (winter 1990), 737–68.

———. *The Varieties of British Political Thought, 1500–1800*. Cambridge: Cambridge University Press, 1993.

Poster, Mark. "Foucault and the Tyranny of Greece," in *Foucault: A Critical Reader*. Ed. David Couzens Hoy. Oxford: Basil Blackwell, 1986.

Pratt, Minnie Bruce. "Identity: Skin, Blood, Heart." *Yours in Struggle: Three Feminist Perspectives on Anit-Semitism and Racism*. Ed. Elly Bulkin, Barbara Smith, and Minnie Bruce-Pratt. New York: Firebrand, 1992.

Rabinow, Paul, ed. *The Foucault Reader*. New York: Pantheon Books, 1984.

Rajchman, John. *Truth and Eros: Foucault, Lacan, and the Question of Ethics.* New York: Routledge, 1991.

———. *Michel Foucault: The Freedom of Philosophy.* New York: Columbia University Press, 1985.

Rawls, John. *Political Liberalism.* New York: Columbia University Press, 1993.

Rizvi, Fažal. "The Arts, Education and the Politics of Multiculturalism." In *Culture, Difference and the Arts.* Ed. Sneja Gunew and Fazal Rizvi. London: Allen and Unwin, 1994.

Rosenburg, Alfred. *The Myth of the Twentieth Century* (1930). In *Communism, Fascism, and Democracy.* Ed. Carl Cohen. New York: Random House, 1962.

Rousseau, Jean-Jacques. *The Social Contract and Discourse on the Origin of Inequality.* Ed. Lester G. Crocker. New York: Simon and Schuster, 1967.

———. *Basic Political Writings.* Ed. Peter Gay. Indianapolis: Hackett, 1987.

Said, Edward. "The Politics of Knowledge." In *Race, Identity and Representation in Education.* Ed. Cameron McCarthy and Warren Crichlow. New York: Routledge, 1993.

Saint Augustine. *The City of God.* Trans. Marcus Dods. New York: The Modern Library, 1993.

Sartre, Jean-Paul. "Existentialism Is a Humanism." (1949) Reprinted in *Existentialism.* Ed. Robert C. Solomon. New York: Random House, 1974.

Sawicki, Jana. *Disciplining Foucault: Feminism, Power, and the Body.* New York: Routledge, 1991.

Scott, Andrew M., ed. *Political Thought in America.* New York: Holt, Rinehart and Winston, 1966.

Scott, Charles E. *The Question of Ethics: Nietzsche, Foucault, Heidegger.* Bloomington: Indiana Unversity Press, 1990.

———. *The Language of Difference.* Atlantic Highlands, N.J.: Humanities Press, 1987.

———. "Foucault's Practice of Thinking." *Research in Phenomenology* 14 (1985), 75–85.

Simons, Jon. *Foucault and the Political.* New York: Routledge, 1995.

Skinner, Quentin. *The Foundations of Modern Political Thought.* Volume 1. Cambridge: Cambridge University Press, 1978.

———. "Hobbes's *Leviathan.*" *Historical Journal* 7 (1964), 322–333.

Slotkin, Richard. *Gunfighter Nation: The Myth of the Frontier in Twentieth-Century America.* New York: Harper Perennial, 1993.

———. *Regeneration through Violence: The Mythology of the American Frontier, 1600–1860.* Middletown, Conn.: Wesleyan University Press, 1973.

Smart, J. J. C. "Distributive Justice and Utilitarianism." In *Justice and Economic Distribution.* Eds. John Arthur and William H. Shaw. New York: Prentice Hall, 1978.

Spivak, Gayatri Chakravorty. "Can the Subaltern Speak?" In *Marxism and the Interpretation of Culture.* Ed. Cary Nelson and Lawrence Grossberg. London: MacMillan Press, 1988.

Strong, Tracy. "How to Write Scripture: Words, Authority, and Politics in Thomas Hobbes." *Critical Theory* 20 (autumn 1993), 128–59.

Sullivan, William M. *Reconstructing Public Philosophy*. Berkeley and Los Angeles: University of California Press, 1986.

Takaki, Ronald. *A Different Mirror: A History of Multicultural America*. Boston: Little, Brown, 1993.

Taylor, Charles. "The Politics of Recognition." *Multiculturalism: Examining the Politics of Recognition*. Ed. Amy Gutman. Princeton, N.J.: Princeton University Press, 1994, 25–74.

Tell, Rolf, ed. *Nazi Guide to Nazism*. Washington, D.C.: American Council on Public Affairs, 1941.

Thomas, Nicholas. *Colonialism's Culture: Anthropology, Travel, and Government*. Princeton, N.J.: Princeton University Press, 1994.

Turner, Frederick Jackson. *The Frontier in American History*. New York: Henry Holt, 1920.

Visker, Rudy. *Genealogy as Critique*. Trans. Chris Turner. London: Verso, 1995.

Wald, Priscilla. *Constituting Americans: Cultural Anxiety and Narrative Form*. Durham, N.C.: Duke University Press, 1995.

Walzer, Michael. "Multiculturalism and Individualism." *Dissent* (spring 1994), 185–91.

———. "The Communitarian Critique of Liberalism." *Political Theory* 18, no. 1 (February 1990), 6–23.

White, Hayden. *Tropics of Discourse*. Baltimore: Johns Hopkins University Press, 1978.

Williams, Linda. *Hard Core; Power, Pleasure, and the Frenzy of the Visible*. Berkeley and Los Angeles: University of California Press, 1989.

Wiser, James. *Political Theory: A Thematic Inquiry*. Chicago: Nelson-Hall, 1986.

Young, Iris Marion. *Justice and the Politics of Difference*. Princeton, N.J.: Princeton University Press, 1990.

Zeimer, Gregor. *Education for Death: The Making of the Nazi*. Oxford: Oxford University Press, 1941.

Zizek, Slavoj. *Tarrying with the Negative*. Durham, N.C.: Duke University Press, 1993.

Index